B52

Insects and Flowers

FRIEDRICH G. BARTH

Insects and Flowers

The Biology of a Partnership

Translated by M. A. Biederman-Thorson

Princeton University Press • Princeton, New Jersey

For Ortrun, Natalie, and Raphael

Library of Congress Cataloging-in-Publication Data

Barth, Friedrich G., 1940–
  [Biologie einer Begegnung. English]
  Insects and flowers : the biology of a partnership / Friedrich G. Barth ; translated
by M. A. Biederman-Thorson.
      p.   cm.—(Princeton science library)
  Translation of: Biologie einer Begegnung.
  Includes bibliographical references and index.
  ISBN 0–691–02523–1
  1. Insect-plant relationships. 2. Pollination by insects. 3. Flowers. 4. Angiosperms.
5. Coevolution. I. Title.
II. Series.
QL496.B3613   1991
574.5'24—dc20   90–28975

First printed in German as *Biologie einer Begegnung: Die Partnerschaft der Insekten und
Blumen* © 1982 by Deutsche Verlags-Anstalt GmbH, Stuttgart

First English language printing © 1985 by Princeton University Press

This book has been composed in Linotron Galliard
Princeton University Press books are printed on acid-free paper, and meet the guide-
lines for permanence and durability of the Committee on Production Guidelines for
Book Longevity of the Council on Library Resources

Printed in the United States of America by Princeton University Press, Princeton,
New Jersey

10 9 8 7 6 5 4 3 2 1
(Pbk.)

Contents

The Senses and Behavior

Coevolution

Preface

Flowers are conspicuous things, too colorful and appealing to be overlooked. One need not be an experienced naturalist to appreciate their aura of poetry. They are among the small miracles we all occasionally discover. But the flowers are not there for us; their beauty is not for our pleasure. What we see has a much more serious biological function. Beneath the charming surface lies a sober business—survival itself is at stake. In evolution, the better is the implacable enemy of the good. Looking beyond what appeals so strongly to our human sensations, we find masterpieces of biological adaptation.

We cannot really understand flowers unless we know something about the insects that visit them. What is happening between them is a trade: food in exchange for pollination. The kaleidoscope of flower shapes, the rainbow of brilliant colors, the bouquet of scents—all these evolved because it was advantageous to give some guidance to insects searching for nectar and pollen. Moreover, each species was helped to survive by developing its own identifying characteristics, features that made it distinguishable from all the other occupants of the same habitat. Flowering plants pollinated by insects reveal more of their genetic diversity in their blossoms than in their other organs. This display enables the pollinators to decide among the plants they encounter—an important decision, because they must carry the right pollen to the right pistil.

The fascinating panorama of interactions between flowers and insects that we see today is the result of long coevolution. The colorful field of flowers is an insect environment that reflects the insects themselves. Conversely, this intimate partnership, at least a hundred million years old, has altered the insects, too, in many ways. It has affected not only the structure and function of their collecting organs, but also their sensory faculties, their behavior, and even such complex abilities as learning.

My book is meant as an introduction to this world. It emphasizes the zoological aspects, with particular attention to the capabilities of the various insect senses. I have done this not only because zoology is my field; it also seems an important emphasis because so many of the other general works on the subject have been written from the botanical viewpoint, pollination ecology having traditionally been the domain of the botanists. Modern zoologists, focusing on some of the central issues, have brought a rather different approach to bear. By asking new questions and successfully applying new techniques, they have gone far beyond the level of descriptive cataloging—important as that is—and provided insights into mechanisms that in some cases were mysteries only a few years ago, and that even now are understood only by a small circle of specialists. This is the "new" biology of plant–animal relations. It is, and must be, based upon the classical work as a house rests on its foundation. Despite the emphasis on zoology, therefore, it is essential to provide at least a modest botanical background. Many of the masterly works of earlier times have remained significant to the present day, and I hope that I have done justice to them in the appropriate contexts. Furthermore, it not uncommonly happens that a problem becomes particularly transparent when the light shed by the historical development of the question falls upon it.

This book is by no means an encyclopedia; it makes no claim to completeness, and although objective considerations determined the problems to be treated, the choice was ultimately subjective. I have written it because I believe that what modern biology has to say about this theme is too interesting to be left to the curiosity of a few scientists.

Modern biology is an experimental science. In several places I have described the actual experimental procedure rather extensively, with two aims: to show precisely the logical sequence of thought, and to give the reader a direct glimpse into the workshop of the biologist. We must have our eyes wide open if we want to go beyond the stage of mere marvelling. The real wonder of many a natural phenomenon resides in its details, so I hope the reader will forgive me for what may occasionally seem overenthusiasm about the fine points. To experience the pleasure of discerning harmonious interrelations, and to know something of the joy that comes from fitting diverse observations into an orderly pattern, one must take some pains with the details. If we do not look beyond the poetic and aesthetic attributes that first attracted us, we shall see only the dim, blurred reflection of something much more deserving of our attention. It may be that biologists took the Copernican—and, later, the Darwinian—revolution more to heart than many of their contemporaries; for biologists, in any case, man is not always the center of the universe. Because of this attitude, it seems to me, they are often more willing to leave natural things in their original state, to grant them their individuality, to refrain from measuring them on the human scale and thereby obscuring them.

The illustrations are designed to bridge the gap between the direct personal experience from which every idea springs and the rigid formalism research imposes on this experience. The pictures made with the scanning electron microscope provide a glimpse into the magic realm of small dimensions, where natural objects—quite unlike the works of human hands—lose none of their fineness.

A reference list is provided for those interested in further details.

"If prudence depends upon experience of affairs, to whom does the honor of this attribute belong? To the wise man, who, by reason partly of modesty and partly of faint-heartedness, will attempt no action? Or to the fool, who is not deterred from any enterprise by modesty, of which he is innocent, or by peril, which he never pauses to weigh?" (Erasmus of Rotterdam, 1508, in *The Praise of Folly*.) In the end I send forth this book as does a father his grown-up child—both determined and hesitant.

I am greatly obliged to my friend of many years, R. Loftus, S.J., for permission to reproduce twelve color photos. They awaken vivid memories of the time we spent together in Munich, when they were taken. I thank K.-E. Kaissling for the picture of the silkmoth antenna, and M. Mühlenberg for one and U. Maschwitz for two color photos in Plate 11. S. Peters kindly identified some tropical bees (Pls. 9 and 35). Finally, I am grateful to J. Müller-Rabe and H. Hahn, and in particular to G. Tambour, who performed the graphic work with much expertise and patience. A. Heidt skilfully carried out important darkroom work, and U. Ginsberg and my wife devoted much time and effort to typing a large part of the manuscript. M. Andersen of the Vikingeskibshallen in Roskilde and G. Krüger of the Flugschule in Bremen provided me with valuable information about the sun stone of the Vikings and the aeronautical sky compass, respectively. I am obliged to the Deutsche Verlags-Anstalt for their helpful collaboration. Finally, I extend hearty thanks to my colleagues W. Kaiser and U. Maschwitz for critical reading of major parts of the text, to T. Butterfass for some valuable comments, and to M. A. Biederman-Thorson for her careful and competent translation from the German and for helpful discussion.

The most profound gratitude, however, is owed to my wife, whose generous understanding of the peculiarities of a writing husband underlies each line, as does the considerable time that I should have spent with her and the children.

Insects and Flowers

1 Sycamore Figs in Egyptian Royal Tombs

> Among the large, hundred-year-old fig trees, their gray trunks
> entwined in the chilly shade like opulent thighs beneath a skirt,
> the night was dozing still; and the broad leaves—with which
> Adam and Eve once arrayed themselves—guarded a treasure, a
> fine tissue of small pearls of dew, which lent their soft green a
> paler hue.
>
> *Juan Ramón Jiménez, "Platero y Yo," 1965*

Again and again, archaeologists excavating royal tombs in Egypt
found that under all the splendor of thousand-year-old treasures
were the preserved remains of fruits of the sycamore fig tree (*Ficus
sycomorus*). Five thousand years ago the Egyptians treasured this
tree because of its fruit and its valuable hard wood, from which
they carved household items as well as temple statues and coffins
for mummies. Because the sycamore is a particularly large tree
with a spreading crown, they probably also connected it with the
idea of protection and shade. For them it was a holy tree.

J. Galil, professor of botany at the University of Tel Aviv, took
a closer look at these old funerary figs in 1967.[1] Some of them
were found in a small basket from the time of the Twentieth Dynasty (1186–1085 B.C.). They were large specimens, with conspicuous holes at one end. In figs from other graves Galil found
the special object of his search—small fig wasps, which had crept
into the figs thousands of years ago and died there. The dryness
of the climate had preserved them perfectly to the present day.
Death in a fig has always been part of the normal life cycle of this
species of wasp.

Like Pliny the Elder (A.D. 23–79) in his monumental *Naturalis
Historiae*, the generations that followed—until late in our century—knew little or nothing about the life of the fig wasps. But

since antiquity the fig tree has been economically important in the Mediterranean region, and figs have always been as much a part of daily life there as wine. People knew what to do to make sure that the "true fig" (*Ficus carica*) would set fruit. To increase the harvest one had to plant so-called caprifigs, related trees that do not bear edible fruit, among fruiting forms of the true fig, or simply to hang blooming caprifig branches in their crowns. But they did this without knowing why it worked, and the facts remained hidden until our own time.

Now we know many of the details. Figs are an old group of plants, known to have existed in the Cretaceous Period. The ancestors of the fig wasps (Chalcidoidea) lived as early as the Jurassic.[5] In over a hundred million years a relationship developed that is one of the most complicated symbioses between animal and plant. The reciprocal adaptations are so fundamental and diverse that neither partner can exist without the other (at least, not unless humans interfere).

We begin the book with this story, for it offers a most impressive example of the biology of insect–flower interactions and illustrates vividly the power of evolution in the creation of intimate, finely adjusted partnerships.

Figs and Fig Wasps

The fig trees belong to a group (family Moraceae) found chiefly in the tropics, which includes the mulberries. Most of its members are woody plants; some produce a milky sap that is used to make rubber. (The rubber trees so popular as house plants are but a pale shadow of the giant wild trees of tropical Asia.) The leaves of the Chinese white mulberry are the food of silkworms. The genus *Ficus*, which includes the fig trees, is one of the largest of all plant genera, with more than seven hundred species. Some of them are truly giant trees. Of these, some germinate not on the ground but on the trunk or branches of other trees. These "strangler figs" send their roots down to the ground, eventually wrapping them around the trunk of the host tree so tightly that they prevent it from growing thicker and actually choke it to death.

All *Ficus* species form goblet-shaped inflorescences, within which hundreds of flowers are hidden (Fig. 1). There is only one opening to the outside. These inflorescences become the figs. All wild *Ficus* species require fig wasps for pollination, and these insects have adapted in a special way to the structure enclosing the flowers they seek.

The fig wasps (family Agaonidae) are small creatures, only a few millimeters in length. All of the more than thirty species live quite differently from the wasps familiar to everyone as an annoyance at picnics. Their life is so intimately interwoven with that of the figs that I shall present their structure and biology, so perfectly adapted to this peculiar situation, together with those of the fig. The species we consider, the sycamore fig tree (not related to the American sycamore—a plane tree—or the English sycamore—a maple), has been particularly well studied and illustrates the general scheme quite clearly. Its original homeland is Abyssinia, but it can now be found from Palestine to eastern Africa. Its name appears often in the Bible; Luther erroneously translated it as "mulberry tree."

Ceratosolen arabicus and the Sycamore

What do the fig wasps do in the inflorescences of the sycamore? The answer to this question comes mainly from studies carried out by J. Galil and D. Eisikowitch in the 1970s, on plants in Israel and in their natural habitat in eastern Africa, in Magadi, not far from Nairobi. Figure 2 summarizes the results.[2,3]

Let us begin with the winged female. Chemically attracted by "her" particular fig species, she pushes her way into the young fig. She must overcome considerable mechanical resistance, for the entrance to the inflorescence is small and barred by scales (Fig. 1). Morphological adaptations such as the laterally flattened head are of some help, but eventually she loses her wings in the struggle, and often parts of the antennae break off. Not all attempts to enter

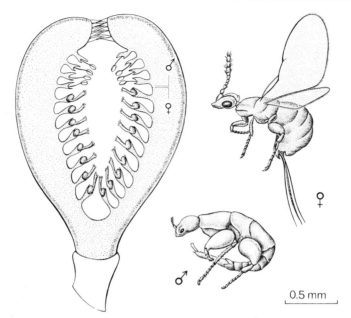

Fig. 1:
Figs and fig wasps. *Left*: The inflorescence of a fig in longitudinal section, with male flowers near the top and female flowers below them.
Right: male and female of the fig wasp *Blastophaga quadraticeps*.

succeed, but some females do get in. Often whole bundles of torn-off wings are stuck around the opening of a young fig. In the darkness of the interior, at the time when the wasp chooses a fig, the female flowers are mature and ready for pollination, whereas the male flowers are still small and immature. *Ceratosolen arabicus*, as the wasp species associated with the eastern African sycamore is called, then lays several hundred eggs. She bores her long ovipositor deep into the tissue of the style (Fig. 3). As a result galls form, masses of plant tissue that offer the young wasps—gall wasps—protection and food during their development. Does this mean the end of the fig?

No, because there are two kinds of female flowers, some with long styles and some with short styles. The stigmas of the two

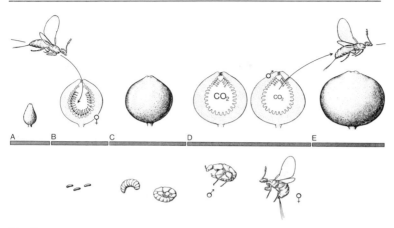

Fig. 2:
Stages in the developmental cycle of the fig and its wasp.

types are so close to one another that they form a continuous surface. The female fig wasp crawls about on them to lay her eggs, probing all the styles with her ovipositor; but she can lay successfully only in the flowers with short styles. Only there can she reach down to the ovary (Fig. 3). The ovaries of the long-styled flowers are undamaged and develop seeds.

Then there is a period of gall maturation and larval development. The females that entered the fig die after laying their eggs. But a few weeks later something remarkable happens. The larvae have pupated, and finally the new generation of wasps emerges. First come the males, which look quite different from the females and have no wings (Fig. 2). They creep about excitedly in the fig, seeking out galls containing females, which have not yet hatched. Having found one, a male drills through the wall of the gall and copulates with the female through this small opening. What follows is even more remarkable. The males burrow holes through the wall of the fig to the outside. A little later the females enlarge the copulatory openings made in their galls and emerge; they leave the fig, within which the male flowers have now matured, by way of the tunnel made by the male wasps, and look for another fig

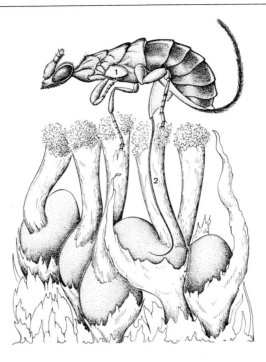

Fig. 3:
The female of the fig wasp *Ceratosolen arabicus* laying eggs. The forelegs are reaching into the pocket (1) at the side of the thorax to take out the pollen she carries. The long ovipositor (2) can reach the ovary of the flower only if the style is of the short type.

still in the female stage. After tunneling through the fig wall the male wasps fall to the ground or die in the same fig in which they were born. The cycle has been closed.

But we have not yet touched upon a number of questions. How does pollination occur? Why do the male wasps tunnel through the fig after copulation? How does the newly emerged female find a new fig? And many more.

Pollen Containers and Active Pollination

In 1969 Galil and Eisikowitch described an intriguing structure, which earlier researchers on fig wasps had seen but could not interpret. The female of *Ceratosolen arabicus* has pollen pockets about

0.2 mm long, one on either side of the thorax; each is covered by a movable lid and has a slit on the underside (Fig. 3). After hatching from the galls, the wasps fill these pollen containers before they leave the fig. At this time the male flowers have just become mature. The wasps tap the open anthers with the tips of their forelegs, which they then bring under the thorax so that the pollen can be scraped off into the pocket with a comb of stiff bristles at the base of the foreleg.[3] When the female wasp later forces herself into a new fig, unprotected pollen sticking to the surface of the body would be mostly rubbed off and become useless for pollination. Carried in the pocket, the pollen is available to be dusted over the stigmas whenever the wasp lays an egg. She pulls it out, a few grains at a time, with the tips of the forelegs and either strokes the stigma surface directly with them or rubs them together over it. Rationed in this way, the pollen supply suffices for the many female flowers in the fig. This is most intriguing. It looks as though this behavior were intentional—as though the wasp were thinking two generations ahead, knowing that her species depends on survival of the species *Ficus sycomorus* even though pollination is of no direct benefit either to herself or to the larvae that will develop from her eggs. Of course, no one claims that the wasp really knows what she is doing. Evolution has selected those genetic variants with behavior better programmed for the maintenance of their own species. William Ramirez,[7] of the University of Costa Rica, discovered pollen pockets at the same time as Galil and Eisikowitch, in his case on both sides of the midthorax of New World fig wasps. Some of these species also have pollen baskets on the upper part of the forelegs, depressions in the exoskeleton surrounded by bristles to keep the pollen in. But not all species of fig wasps have a pollen pocket.[8] Even *Blastophaga psenes*, upon which the true edible fig of the Mediterranean (*Ficus carica*) depends for pollination, lacks both the pockets and the associated comb of bristles on the forelegs.

Carbon Dioxide as a Timing Signal

We know now the origin of the holes in the figs from the Egyptian tomb of the Twentieth Dynasty—the male wasps drilled them, to allow not themselves but the females to escape from the fig. The behavior of the males must proceed in a strict sequence: hatching, copulating with the female through the gall wall, and then biting a hole in the fig. The females thereupon hatch, load themselves with pollen, and leave the fig. Not only are the developmental cycles of male and female fig wasps synchronized closely with one another; so, too, are those of the fig and the wasps. If the fig were to ripen too soon and fall to the ground, the larvae in it could not develop fully and would die. If the wasps hatched when the fig was still immature, it would be too hard for them to burrow through. They would be trapped in a deadly prison.

This synchronization of plant and animal involves carbon dioxide (CO_2). The fig's content of this gas rises to 10 percent in Stage C (Fig. 2), as it begins to ripen.[4] This high concentration inhibits hatching of the females. This can easily be seen by observing the behavior of the animals in a closed chamber with known CO_2 content. At high CO_2 concentrations the males behave entirely normally; they are adapted to the interior of the ripening fig. But the females do not leave their galls as long as the CO_2 concentration is above 2 percent. When it becomes lower, they emerge. The males behave in just the opposite way. They are inactive in low CO_2 concentration and do not mate with the females, which therefore free themselves from their galls unmated—that is, too soon. Galil and his colleagues measured the composition of the gas within the fig at brief intervals. It turned out that the CO_2 concentration rises about two days before the male flowers become mature—a state that lasts only a few hours. Not until the male wasps have copulated with the females and are working together to bite a tunnel through the fig wall does the CO_2 concentration fall again, as it equilibrates with the outside air. Now the females can emerge from the gall and from the fig, passing the male flowers just when the pollen is ripe for collecting. And not until this happens does the fig ripen completely; in two or three days it becomes soft and dark. If the CO_2 concentration is artificially kept high, the fig stays green.

These fascinating observations on the control of Phase D were made with the pipal tree (*Ficus religiosa*) and its fig wasp *Blasto-*

phaga quadraticeps. About the same thing happens in the sycamore and the true figs. The special departures from the general scheme need not concern us here.[4] But what is the point of the ancient custom of hanging "blooming" caprifig branches in the crowns of the edible fig? The edible fig of the Mediterranean has been propagated from cuttings for millennia and as a result two kinds of trees now exist, those with only fertile female flowers having long pistils, and those in which the only functional flowers are male, the female flowers having short pistils and never developing seeds (gall flowers). These male trees were called *caprificus* ("goat fig") by the Romans, because of their unpalatable fruit. It is in these inflorescences that the fig wasp larvae develop and the pollen is formed. The pollen-bearing wasps that leave the caprifigs can pollinate edible figs, if they have access to them. Hence the practice of hanging ripe caprifigs in the branches of the edible fig trees, as the Romans themselves used to do.

"A remarkable fact about the fig is that this alone among all the fruits hastens to ripen with a rapidity due to the skill of nature. There is a wild variety of fig called the goat-fig which never ripens, but bestows on another tree what it has not got itself, since it is a natural sequence of causation. . . . Consequently this fig engenders gnats which, being cheated out of nutriment in their mother tree, fly away . . . to the kindred tree, and by repeatedly nibbling at the figs . . . they open their orifices and so make a way into them, bringing with them the sun into the fruit for the first time and introducing the fertilizing air through the passages thus opened."[6] For us today, what Pliny the Elder had to say about the fig almost two thousand years ago is an interesting mixture of correct observations, errors, and ignorance.

But even today many questions remain open. For example, it would be interesting to know how the CO_2 (and the simultaneously changing amounts of oxygen and ethylene) in the fig acts on the nervous system of the wasp, why the effects on males and females are so different, what sense organs show the male in the fig the way to the female in her gall, and how the emerging females find their way to figs in which to lay their eggs.

The example of the fig and the fig wasp shows us that insects and flowers can be linked to one another so extensively to mutual advantage that hardly any aspect of their lives can be understood apart from this relationship. The fig wasps demonstrate the way the evolution of an insect responds to the hidden position of the flowers—a distinctive characteristic of the figs. It is a comprehensive response, affecting the entire life cycle, the shape of the wasp, its behavior, and the performance of its sense organs. It has produced differences in the structure and habits of the sexes, and adjustments to life inside an inflorescence, with its special microclimate.

These are extreme adaptations, and even small departures from the genetically preprogrammed path are fatal. The complexities of fig–wasp development and the precise timing required leave very little room for error.

In this book the story of the encounter between insects and flowers is told in separate parts, to make it easier to understand. It will become apparent that these separate aspects, when examined closely, are themselves quite complicated. Although we are considering the encounter particularly from the viewpoint of the insects, the plants are just as intricately involved. Some basic botanical facts will give us a framework for the rest of the tale.

2   What Is the Flower for?

> But when the pollen has come onto the stigma, it does not
> burrow in itself, for it is far too bulky; it sends fine fertilizing
> beings which it contains through the stigma and into the interior
> of the ovary. . . .
>
> *Christian Konrad Sprengel, "Das entdeckte Geheimnis der Natur,"*
> *1793*

"I hope that the contents of this book will also be of some interest
to those persons who find pleasure in contemplating the works of
Nature, but who have lacked the time or the opportunity to ac-
quire scientific knowledge of natural phenomena in general and
the plants in particular. With no notion of the elements of the
flowers, they would have difficulty understanding the book: Thus
I have thought it my duty to provide the following brief instruc-
tion. . . ." Almost two hundred years ago Christian Konrad Sprengel
wrote this introduction to his now classic book, which marked the
beginning of pollination ecology. Any present-day author who tries
to bring alive the encounter between flowers and insects for the
nonspecialist public, to lure such people into this enchanted garden of forms, colors, fragrances, fascinating sensory achievements,
and behavior, faces the same problem. Without a few basic facts,
it can't be done. So what is a flower, actually, and what is it good
for?

The botanist tells us that the flower is a shoot termination serv-
ing for sexual reproduction. Within a flower male and female sex
cells (gametes) are produced. When they fuse a seed is formed,
containing the embryo, and the fruit develops. The female gametes correspond to the ova of animals, and the male gametes, to
the animal sperm. But sperm as highly motile as those of animals
are found only in phylogenetically old plants such as the ferns and
mosses. The male reproductive cells of the flowering plants, with

which we are most concerned, are greatly modified and incapable
of locomotion.

The Two Generations of Ferns

If we first take a close look at the ferns, we shall be better able to
understand the peculiarities of the flowering plants. Figure 4 is a
schematic illustration of the reproductive events in a common European fern, *Dryopteris filix-mas*. The first thing to note is that the
life cycle is composed of two generations quite different in appearance. This situation is called heteromorphic alternation of
generations. One of the two generations reproduces itself sexually,
by means of gametes, and the other reproduces asexually, by means
of spores. The familiar leaflike fronds belong to the asexually reproducing generation, the sporophyte. At certain times little brown
dots or rings can be seen, even without a microscope, on the underside of the fronds. These are ingenious containers for a multitude of microscopically small spores, with a special mechanism to
catapult the spores into the open. It is worthwhile considering this
mechanism in detail, because the anthers of the flowering plants
open in a very similar way. The spore capsules, or sporangia, include a ring of cells with elastically thickened side and back walls
(called the annulus, from the Latin for "ring"). At maturation they
die, and their water-rich contents begin to evaporate. As a result,
the walls bend toward one another and the structure becomes in-
dented on the outer surface, producing tension along the ring
parallel to the surface. Under this force the capsule eventually tears
open at a preformed weak spot. But the spores are not thrown
out until the wall tension has become greater than the forces of
cohesion and adhesion of the water in the annulus cells. Then the
outside wall springs away from the water within the cell, and the
annulus snaps back into the original position.

Having been cast onto the ground, the spores germinate, forming a threadlike structure that ultimately becomes the sexual plant,
the prothallus. The prothallus measures at most a few centimeters

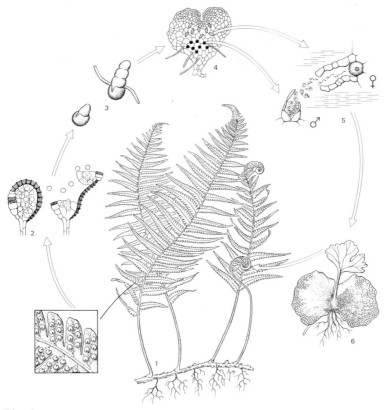

Fig. 4:
The developmental cycle of a fern. The frond (1) forms spore containers
(2) on its underside. Catapulted out of these sporangia, the spores (3)
germinate, giving rise to the prothallus (4) with the reproductive organs
(5). Male and female gametes join, and from them grows the new fronded
fern (6).

and is easily overlooked next to the large fern—especially since it
lies close to the ground and has a relatively limited life span.
Nevertheless, important things happen here. On its underside, next
to the damp soil, male and female reproductive organs develop.
The botanist calls them archegonia and antheridia. Within them
the ova and sperm ripen. The prothallus, then, is the second, sexually reproducing generation of the fern. The sperm cell has many

flagella, so that it can swim actively to the ovum in the moist milieu of the prothallus undersurface, and finally fuse with it. This sperm cell is thus entirely comparable with that of an animal.

It is interesting that the female reproductive organ hangs out a sign for the sperm, so to speak; it secretes traces of malic acid. The sperm cells detect this and move in the direction of increasing concentration, until they reach the ovum. In the mosses glucose plays a similar role, and in *Lycopodium* it is citric acid.

The product of fusion of the male and female gametes on the prothallus gives rise to a new frond-bearing fern. The complex alternation of generations is thereby completed and can begin anew.

The Hidden Generation

The plants that flower and produce seed have an alternation of generations phylogenetically related to that of the ferns. However, the sexually reproducing generation in this case is not externally visible at all. What we see as a flower in a meadow is the spore-producing generation, the sporophyte, corresponding to the fern frond. But have we not just been discussing flowers as agents of sexual reproduction?

We can resolve the apparent contradiction by finding the part of a flowering plant that corresponds to the prothallus of the fern. Wilhelm Hofmeister, in 1851, realized what Christian Konrad Sprengel did not yet know—that the gamete-producing generation, the gametophyte, is hidden within the flower, in an extremely regressed form. To understand this ourselves, we must first examine the parts of the flower and their arrangement more closely. The basic flower structures are diagrammed in Figure 5. The outermost parts are the petals and sepals of the flower, ordinarily the most visually conspicuous structures. Think, for example, of the red petals of a poppy and the yellow petals of the marsh marigold (Pl 5. 1, 2, 26). Inside these are the stamens, filaments with swollen ends (the anthers) that contain many tiny grains of pollen. The center of the flower, finally, is occupied by the pistil;

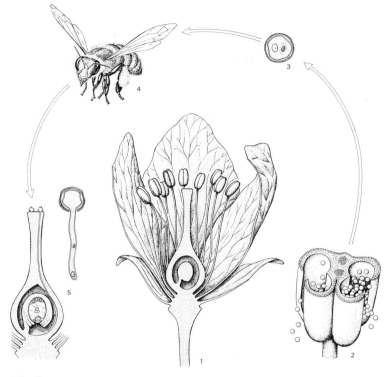

Fig. 5:
The route taken by the pollen and the role of pollinating insects. (1) The flower with its pistil, stamens, and visually striking petals and sepals. The ripe anther (2, in cross-section) releases the pollen (3). An insect (4) transports it to the stigma of another flower of the same species. Having arrived on the correct stigma (5), the pollen grain germinates; the pollen tube grows down to the ovary, where the ovum is produced and fertilized.

this consists of a swollen ovary at the base, a flattened stigma at the top, and a style connecting the two.

All these parts of the flower are "sporophyte" structures. The flower is more complicated than the fern shown in Figure 4 in that it produces two different kinds of "spores." The anthers and the ovary are homologous to the spore capsules of the ferns; the "spores" they produce are the pollen grains and a clump of cells within the ovary, respectively.

The gamete-producing generation of the flower never sees the light of day. The female gametophyte develops entirely within the ovary, producing an egg cell. The male gametophyte is enclosed within the pollen grain until the pollen grain lands on a stigma. Then the pollen begins to germinate, in a process very similar to germination of a fern spore; each grain produces a pollen tube, which makes its way through the tissue of the style to the ovary. And now, hidden away in the style, cell division within the pollen tube produces two sperm cells. The male gametes drift down the pollen tube, and eventually one of them reaches an egg cell and fuses with it. The seed, a resting plant embryo produced by the joining of the two gametes, starts to develop.

We can now understand what the botanist means by saying that a flower serves for sexual reproduction, and we see the important role played by the "hidden generation."

Not all flowers are of the hermaphrodite or "perfect" type, with both stamens and pistil. There are plants in which some of the flowers have only stamens and the rest, only pistils. In fact, there are even so-called dioecious species, in which all the flowers on each individual are of a single type, some individuals having only staminate flowers and others only pistillate flowers.

3 The Kaleidoscope of Flower Forms

If someone loves a flower . . . he can say to himself:
"Somewhere, my flower is there. . . ." But if the sheep eats the
flower, in one moment all his stars will be darkened. . . .

Antoine de Saint-Exupery, "The Little Prince," 1943

Anyone who has strolled with open eyes through a summer meadow
will have been fascinated by the variety of flower forms. Let us try
to bring a little order into the colorful bouquet of summer blossoms, for only then can we really appreciate its diversity.

Basic Flower Shapes

Things can be put in order according to different aspects. In this
case, one method is to prepare floral diagrams in which the principles of symmetry and the relative positions of the individual parts
of the flower are expressed, very much as in drawing the floor
plan of a house.

Figure 6 gives an example. The outermost structures are the
perianth—the sepals of the calyx encircling the petals of the corolla; within this are the stamens and, at the center, the pistil. It
is obvious at first glance that the patterns of symmetry are different in the wall-pepper, bleeding heart, and dead nettle. Therefore
we can assign these flowers, in that order, to the following categories: radially symmetrical flowers (with several axes of symmetry—that is, treating the flower as a cylinder we can vary the angle
of the longitudinal section and so cut it into several sets of mirror-
image halves), bilaterally symmetrical flowers (the right half is the
mirror image of the left), and dorsiventral flowers (in which, in
addition, the upper part is constructed quite differently from the
lower part). So far, so good.

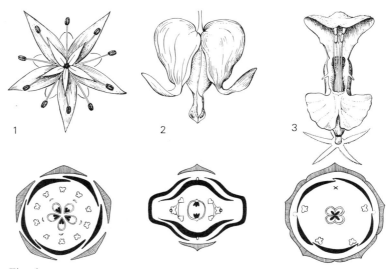

Fig. 6:
Types of flower symmetry, with the floral diagram drawn below each
type. (1) Wall-pepper (*Sedum*), (2) bleeding heart (*Dicentra*), (3) dead
nettle (*Lamium*).

A floor plan, however, gives very incomplete information about
the three-dimensional structure. The examples from the figwort
family (Scrophulariaceae) show this quite clearly. Although the
floral diagrams of flowers of the mullein, the common toadflax,
and the foxglove would be very similar—indeed, almost identical—the shapes of the flowers are very different (Fig. 7).

Ecological Criteria

For the systematist the basic plan of a flower, as seen in cross
section, is an important clue to its relationships. But the pollination ecologist regarding the flower in the context of its insect visitors pays less attention to its basic plan. He sees special features
of its shape—bell forms, funnels, disks, good landing sites, and so
on. Hans Kugler, a well-known German pollination ecologist, cat-

Fig. 7:
Different shapes of flowers in the same family (Scrophulariaceae). (1)
Mullein (*Verbascum nigrum*), (2) common toadflax (*Linaria vulgaris*), (3)
foxglove (*Digitalis purpurea*).

egorizes flowers as disk flowers, funnel flowers, bell flowers, stalked-
plate flowers, lip flowers, butterfly flowers, head or basket flowers,
clublike flowers, brush flowers, and insect-trap flowers.[3] Typical
members of these groups appear in Plates 3 to 7. Let us take a
closer look at them.

   The rock-rose *Helianthemum nummularium*, found in sunny,
grassy habitats in southern Germany, is one of the disk flowers,
for its yellow petals are spread out in a flat circle. Insects seeking
food have no trouble landing there, and the food—pollen and
nectar—is easily accessible. Accordingly, the number of visitors is
large. They include not only bees and bumblebees but also beetles,
flies, and butterflies. Disk flowers are common. The corn poppy
(*Papaver rhoeas*, Pl. 2), the yellow adonis (*Adonis vernalis*, Pl. 12),
the marsh marigold (*Caltha palustris*, Pl. 26), the rose (e.g., *Rosa
arvensis*, Pl. 3), and many others belong to the group.

Next comes the stemless gentian (*Gentiana clusii*, Pl. 4), one of the most beautiful flowers in wet Alpine meadows. Funnel flower in the key term here. Nectar-seeking insects must find their way to the bottom of the funnel. Among the familiar members of this category are some other gentians, the meadow saffron, the crocus, and many smaller flowers such as those of the mint and tunic flower.

It is not difficult to see why the alpine snowbell (*Soldanella alpina*, Pl. 4) is categorized as a bell flower. To put it simply, bell flowers are inverted funnels, bells with the opening pointing down. Naturally, the group includes many of the plants assigned by systematists to the bellflower family (Campanulaceae), but it also contains representatives of other families, such as the heather, the snowdrop, the columbine (Fig. 22), the Turk's-cap lily (Pl. 19), and the cyclamen.

The stalked-plate flowers have a disk-shaped, flattened part set on a tubular stalk. The cowslip is a familiar example, as are the bird's-eye primrose (Pl. 27) and the spring gentian. Another member of the gentian family is the common centaury (*Erythraea centaurium*). Like the alpine snowbell, a kind of primrose, it shows that the plant families of systematic botany by no means coincide with the categories of pollination ecology. When the corolla tube is as slender as in the centaury, only insects with a long, thin proboscis can reach the nectar at its base. Here we are right to expect butterflies.

The monkey flower (*Mimulus guttatus*, Pl. 5) is a good example of the dorsiventral structure of the lip flowers. It is always possible to identify an upper lip and a lower lip. In the typical case the corolla tube of the lip flowers is narrow, broadening at the end as it merges with the lips. If other tubes are present the flower is of the "gullet" type. To flying pollinators a lip flower offers a good landing platform—the lower lip, on which the insect can stand to dip its proboscis into the corolla tube, or from which it can push its head or whole body into the "gullet." Meadow clary, butterwort (*Pinguicula*, Pl. 5), touch-me-not, monkshood (*Aconitum*,

Fig. 22), and many orchids (species of *Ophrys* and *Orchis*, Pl. 28, 38, 39) are flowers of the same type.

The name "butterfly flower" is also derived directly from the flowers' shape, and does not imply that only butterflies visit them. The large petal of the meadow pea (*Lathyrus pratensis*, Pl. 6) that stands up in the plane of the color photo is called the "standard" by morphologists, and the two petals in front of it are the "wings." They cover the so-called "keel," within which the stamens and pistil are hidden. Butterfly flowers are visited especially often by bees and bumblebees. They frequently possess ingenious devices for pushing out or exposing the pollen as soon as an insect lands on the wings or the keel.

This nearly ends the list. We shall mention further only the very familiar head or basket flowers and the insect-trap flowers, which are uncommon in temperate latitudes.

The head or basket type is represented by the brown-rayed knapweed (*Centaurea jacea*, Pl. 6). What looks to the uninitiated like a single flower is in fact an inflorescence—an assemblage of many flowers. The illusion is particularly convincing when the florets around the edge, as in the example illustrated, are specifically for the purpose of display (they are sterile), encircling all the other flowers. In thistles a corresponding function is served by bracts, which form a conspicuous halo around the center (Pl. 28). And the "showy" part of the daisy is the circlet of white tongue-shaped florets around the differently colored central florets. For an insect a visit to a basket flower is rewarding, because the food containers are densely packed. But often the dense packing means that the flowers are tall thin tubes, so that a long proboscis is required to reach the food.

Finally, the insect-trap flowers are exemplified by the lady's slipper (*Cypripedium calceolus*, Pl. 7) and the cuckoopint (*Arum maculatum*). As the name of this category suggests, the insects fall for some kind of trick. In the case of the lady's slipper that often literally happens; in trying to crawl into the large, bulging, yellow slipper the insects lose their footing and fall to the bottom. Because the surface is so steep and smooth, it is very difficult for them to get out again. The flower uses this trick to ensure its being pollinated; the details are described in Chapter 23.

The Metamorphosis of the Leaf

In his famous work on an *Attempt to Explain the Metamorphosis of Plants* (1790), Johann Wolfgang von Goethe begins with the statement, "Anyone who pays even a little attention to plant growth will soon notice that certain external parts of the plants sometimes change, taking on the shape of the adjacent parts either entirely or to a certain degree. For example, a single flower usually changes into a double one when in the place of the stamens petals develop, which may be identical to the other petals of the corolla in color and shape or may still bear visible signs of their origin." And a little later in the same book Goethe writes, "The secret relationship of the various external plant parts—the leaves, the calyx, the corolla, the stamens—which develop in sequence and, as it were, from one another, has long been recognized by researchers in general and even been a special object of study, and the process by which one and the same organ appears in diverse modifications has been called the metamorphosis of plants."

All parts of a flower are modifications of the leaf; they are often linked to one another by transitional forms. From the bud scale and the green leaves of the plant, at their varying levels of complexity, there are all kinds of transitions to the sepal, petal, and stamen. The leaf, then, is an extraordinarily flexible organ, in morphogenetic terms. This is one of the major causes of the astonishing diversity of flower forms—manifest not only in the basic plan of the flower and its general shape but even in its individual parts (Fig. 7).

4 Self-Pollination and Cross-Pollination

> How different it is in the organic world! Above the level of the molecule identity no longer exists, at least not in diploid, sexually reproducing individuals.
>
> *Ernst Mayr, "Grundgedanken der Evolutionsbiologie," 1969*

It is not irrelevant where pollen comes from. Pollination is usually most successful when the pollen comes from the flowers of another individual of the same species, and not from the flower that contains the stigma or even from another flower on the same plant. Self-pollination and pollination by neighboring flowers are inferior, as a rule, to pollination from afar.

In dioecious plants, species in which each individual bears either only male or only female flowers, the pollen must clearly be transferred from one individual to another. That even in monoecious species interindividual pollination is the only possible, or at least the most likely, method is less obvious—particularly since the stamens are so often immediately adjacent to the pistil.

Why should reproduction without a partner be prevented in such cases? The advantages of cross-pollination are genetic in nature and must be viewed in relation to evolution, which is treated separately in Chapter 30. Advantage Number One: the mixing and recombination of the different hereditary material of two plants introduces variability among the progeny, increasing the range of variation in the population. This is a prerequisite for evolution. Advantage Number Two: cross-pollination increases the probability that unfavorable hereditary features that are recessive (i.e., with no effect as long as they are present only singly in the double set of genes) will be ineffective, for the genetic complement of the partners is likely to be different.

There are several mechanisms by which plants enforce cross-pollination. One of these is self-sterility, which may have a number of different causes. For example, the pollen of self-sterile plants may not germinate on stigmas of the same plant, whereas on those of other individuals it grows down into the style quite normally. In these cases the stigma and the style are a kind of ontogenetic filter. Mechanisms of this sort are found, for example, in primroses, in the white lily, in the Turk's-cap lily (Pl. 19), in many members of the peaflower family, in asters, in the poppy, in the buttercup, in many orchids, and in many plants of the apple and plum families. In many other self-sterile plants the pollen does germinate but does not effect fertilization. In quite a few cases the genetic basis of self-sterility is known, and involves so-called self-sterility genes. The pollen germinates normally only when the self-sterility genes of pollen and stigma do not match. One possible molecular mechanism may have something to do with immune responses.

The flowers of the primrose are the often-cited prime examples of another mechanism that favors cross-pollination. Here the length of the style varies in the flowers on different plants; there are long-styled flowers with short stamens, so that the anthers are deep in the corolla, and short-styled flowers with anthers raised above the stigma. Cross-pollination occurs because a particular insect has a proboscis of constant length, so that it always operates at the same level. Therefore an animal with a long proboscis, such as a butterfly, will carry the pollen of a flower with a long style to a stigma on a short style. On the other hand, the shorter proboscis of a bee does not reach so deep into the flower. Therefore bees pollinate stigmas on long styles with the pollen from short-styled flowers. In the last century Darwin devoted considerable thought to these questions, and in experiments lasting for years he manually dusted stigmas with the pollen from various kinds of flowers. He found that the seed set best when pollen fell on a stigma at the same level as the anther from which it came. Only then does the size of the pollen grain match that of the stigma papillae. Darwin went a step further by taking the plants produced by "illegitimate" pollination and pollinating them "legitimately." Some of them failed to produce a single seed during the four years of his study.

Heterostyly, as this second mechanism is called, is common. It also occurs in the lungwort, sorrels, the bog bean, bedstraws, and many other plants. Darwin experimented extensively with the cowslip, and in 1862 he published a long report of his findings in the *Journal of the Proceedings of the Linnean Society*. He also devoted a long time to the purple loosestrife (*Lythrum salicaria*), for a good reason: in this plant the principle of heterostyly has reached a peak. The flowers have not only short and long styles but also styles of intermediate length. Similarly, the anthers are not at two, but at three different levels. Each individual flower has twelve anthers, arranged in two "stories." But examination of many flowers shows that there are three types, with stamens of three lengths arranged in different combinations of two. Viable seeds are produced when pollen from one of the three stories encounters a stigma at the same level. So the situation is the same as in the primrose, except that in the loosestrife there are three successful combinations, each flower providing the pollen for two of them. The complicated business of pollinating these flowers is accomplished by a number of butterflies. It may be that the different coloration of the two types of anther in a given flower is an important feature for identification.

A third mechanism to prevent self-pollination is simpler: the anthers and stigma mature at different times (dichogamy). In some cases the stigmas are quicker, and in others the pollen ripens first. The botanists refer to this as proterogyny and protandry, respectively. Protandry is widespread among the Compositae, bellflowers, Umbelliferae, and other plant groups, to which the grass of Parnassus (Pl. 20) and the yellow adonis (Pl. 12) belong. Proterogyny is much less common; an example is the pasqueflower (Pl. 12).

Mechanism Number Four again involves the spatial arrangement of anthers and stigmas. The iris (Pl. 19) exemplifies the principle. Outermost are the large outer segments of the perianth, with their brownish stripes. The almost pure yellow inner perianth segments are inside these and alternate with them. Spread like a roof over the inner surfaces of the outer segments are the large, petal-like style arms. Next to the shaft of each of these styles lies an anther, opening downward. The stigma is quite inconspicuous—there is a small lobe at the end of the style arm on its underside, and the upper surface of this is the actual structure capable of receiving pollen, the stigma. Because the stigma is above the anther, gravity alone would never bring the pollen to the stigma. But when an insect pushes into the flower, it bends the stigma lobe over, dusting it on the correct side with the foreign pollen it carries. When the insect crawls out, on the other hand, laden with pollen from this flower, it must press the stigma surface of the lobe upward against the style arm—thereby preventing self-pollination.

The negative consequences of self-pollination are that the advantages of pollination by another plant are missed; there is less chance of a new combination of the genes and therefore a smaller range of variation of individuals in the population. Nevertheless, there are plants that regularly self-pollinate with no apparent disadvantage. When the pollinating insects are rare or do not visit reliably enough because of prolonged inclement conditions such as rain, cold, drought, and the like, self-pollination may even be the method of choice (*Ophrys apifera*, Chapter 24 and Pl. 28). And it may also prevail when individuals, or a few pioneers, are at the edges of a population, colonizing new, hostile habitats or regions only briefly habitable. Then full seed set even in the absence of pollinators, with large numbers of genetically similar offspring as a consequence of self-pollination, may well be an advantage.

5 Transport Problems, Darwin, and "The Secret of Nature Revealed"

> Order is not something formal, but rather means that the hierarchy, the relationships, and the subdivisions that make visible what is being formed manifest themselves as an element in the existence of the beautiful.
>
> *Ernesto Grassi, "Die Theorie des Schönen in der Antike," 1962*

When most plants prevent self-pollination or allow it only as an occasional substitute, a severe problem is created. Who transports the pollen to the appropriate stigma? After all, even in hermaphrodite flowers—despite the name—it does not suffice for the pollen simply to fall down onto the stigma.

In our brief excursion into botany we have already seen that the male gametes of the phylogenetically older plants, the ferns and mosses, bear flagella. They swim actively, through a film of water, to the female sex organ. It is no accident that ferns and mosses are most common in very damp regions.

The great majority of the higher terrestrial plants have taken a quite different direction. They inhabit even dry regions, and tower above the moist ground. Therefore their gametes must be protected from drying out—the male gametes, in particular, because it is they that must travel to another plant, whereas the female gametes need not leave the shelter of the ovary. The solution to the problem: the male gametes remain within the pollen grain (which corresponds to the microspore of ferns), making their dangerous journey within the protection of its resistant wall. But this rules out the possibility of active movement to the female organ. It is understandable, then, that the pollen—incapable of moving by its own power—must be transported from plant to plant.

The means of transport available to the pollen are the moving air, in rare cases flowing water, and especially—of course—motile animals. Here we are concerned only with the animals, and among the animals only with the insects, because especially in temperate latitudes they are by far the most important vehicles for pollen transport.

A large proportion of the flowering plants, then, depend on the transport services of the insects for survival. Conversely, many animals are equally dependent on the food supplied by the plants. Over millions of years of evolution the plants and animals have developed intimate relations that are among the most enthralling subjects in biology. The reciprocal adaptations involve not only the morphology and anatomy; physiology and behavior have been modified as well. One is constantly impressed anew by their perfection and specialization. Again and again they confront us with the remarkable fact that mutation and selection, the driving forces for evolution, have directed various organisms—utterly different in form of organization—toward simultaneous adjustments of mutual benefit, toward coadaptation (Chapter 30).

A School Principal in Spandau and Charles Robert Darwin

The principal of a school in the Prussian city of Spandau was the first to realize the basic features of the web of interactions linking flowers and insects and to describe them with admirable meticulousness, as far as the knowledge of his time permitted. Christian Konrad Sprengel's (1750-1816) book on *The Secret of Nature Revealed in the Structure and Pollination of Flowers* was printed for the first time in 1793.[2] It contains twenty-five copperplate prints with hundreds of individual drawings (Fig. 8). Today Sprengel's book is recognized as the first publication in the field of scientific pollination ecology, but it was not always so. For a long time no one understood the depth of its perceptiveness, and perhaps Sprengel's contemporaries cannot be blamed for this. Few had the leisure to

Fig. 8:
A page from Christian Konrad Sprengel's classic (1793) work, *Das ent-deckte Geheimnis der Natur im Bau und in der Befruchtung der Blumen*.

admire flowers and cogitate upon insects. In the stormy years of the French Revolution there were other things to worry about; Prussia was at war with France.

Not until Charles Darwin (1809-1882) spelled out the evolutionary significance of the relationship between insects and flowers did the value of Sprengel's work begin to be understood. In Chapter 4 of Darwin's book *The Origin of Species by Means of Natural Selection or the Preservation of Favoured Races in the Struggle for Life*,[1] which was published in 1859 and has hardly an equal in its impact on the intellectual world, he wrote: "Now, let us suppose that the juice or nectar was excreted from the inside of the flowers of a certain number of plants of any species. Insects in seeking the nectar would get dusted with pollen, and would often transport it from one flower to another. The flowers of two distinct individuals of the same species would thus get crossed; and the act of crossing, as can be fully proved, gives rise to vigorous seedlings which consequently would have the best chance of flourishing and surviving. The plants which produced flowers with the largest glands or nectaries, excreting most nectar, would oftenest be visited by insects, and would oftenest be crossed; and so in the long-run would gain the upper hand and form a local variety. The flowers, also, which had their stamens and pistils placed, in relation to the size and habits of the particular insects which visited them, so as to favour in any degree the transportal of the pollen, would likewise be favoured."

On the basis of his assumptions, then, Darwin presents just the same arguments as Sprengel with regard to the pollen, and concludes that regular visits by insects, for which he presents much evidence, can be advantageous to the plants because pollination is accomplished even if the visitor should eat nine-tenths of the pollen. A little later, in the same chapter about insects, one can read: "Let us now turn to the nectar-feeding insects; we may suppose the plant, of which we have been slowly increasing the nectar by continued selection, to be a common plant; and that certain insects depended in main part on its nectar for food. I could give many facts showing how anxious bees are to save time: for instance, their habit of cutting holes and sucking the nectar at the bases of certain flowers, which, with a very little more trouble, they can enter by the mouth. Bearing such facts in mind, it may be believed that under certain circumstances individual differences in the curvature or length of the proboscis, &c., too slight to be appreciated by us, might profit a bee or other insect, so that certain individuals would be able to obtain their food more quickly than others; and thus the communities to which they belonged would flourish and throw off many swarms inheriting the same peculiarities."

Darwin's concluding words are crystal-clear. "Thus I can understand how a flower and a bee might slowly become, either simultaneously or one after the other, modified and adapted to each other in the most perfect manner, by the continued preservation of all the individuals which presented slight deviations of structure mutually favourable to each other." Darwin did not hesitate to draw the most wide-ranging conclusions from his observations. Even though considerable ignorance prevailed in the biology of his time (for example, nothing was known about the mechanism of gamete fertilization or about heredity), he stated unequivocally how the adaptations of insects and flowers can become progressively better matched in the course of evolution. All that is required is that genetic survival—reproduction—always be more likely for those individuals that are better equipped than others of the same species for receiving the visits of insects and providing them with food. In the final chapter of this book we shall return to these important questions.

6 The Flowers' Guests

Whether fully aware of it or not, we human beings are immersed in a world of insects.

T. Eisner and E. O. Wilson, "The Insects," 1977

It is worth taking an hour or so to sit quietly in a sunny, flowery meadow just to see what the flowers attract. The insects that come represent many different systematic groups. This is especially obvious if we pay attention to the flowers of the open type, in which the nectar and pollen are exposed and accessible even to unspecialized visitors. They are all looking for food, after all, and not working to pollinate the flowers on purely altruistic grounds.

But this bewilderingly varied crowd can be assigned to a few orders of the insect class, if we neglect the species that come only occasionally or play an insignificant role in pollination for other reasons. The chief pollinators all belong to four orders; the bees and wasps (Hymenoptera) are most numerous, then the flies (Diptera), the butterflies and moths (Lepidoptera), and finally the least important group, the beetles (Coleoptera). As early as 1898 Paul Knuth, in his *Handbook of Flower Biology*,[4] noted that among the insects visiting Central European flowers, these four orders were present in the following proportions: 47 percent were hymenopterans, 26 percent were flies, 10 percent were lepidopterans, and 15 percent were beetles. Only 2 percent was left for the vast remainder of the insect class.

The Hymenoptera—Honeybees and Bumblebees

Let us look at these groups more closely. Without doubt the Hymenoptera are the most important. Chief among them are the bumblebees and honeybees; indeed, the latter is the most important insect pollinator of all, and therefore deserves consideration.

The significance of the honeybees (*Apis mellifera*) in pollination ecology is related to several circumstances. For one thing, there are vast numbers of honeybees; a single colony can consist of more than 50,000 individuals. The great majority of them belong to the worker caste, which is responsible for the pollination activities outside the hive and for bringing in food. The honeybees live together as "social insects," in highly organized groups. They take great care of their brood—an arduous task, which begins as the weather warms up. In the spring the queen bee (a bee colony is a matriarchy) lays as many as 2,000 eggs per day, one every forty-three seconds! Her daily production approximately equals her own body weight.

After only three days the elongated egg opens and the larva hatches out. It looks like a fly maggot, and is an enormously voracious creature. Bee larvae are first fed by the internal staff of the hive, the nurses, with nothing but pure "bee milk" for three days. During this time their weight increases a hundredfold. It is as though a seven-pound human baby were to grow to the size of a young bullock by the third day after its birth. The fuel for this development—the bee milk—is produced by the worker bees in paired glands on the head, from the protein-rich pollen. After the first three larval days honey and pollen that has not been specially processed are added to the menu. After only five and a half days the larvae are ready to pupate.

All the forms of food originate in materials brought to the hive by the forager bees. No wonder they appear so industrious on their collecting flights. Karl von Frisch, the world-famous bee researcher, cited a few impressive numbers in his book *Aus dem Leben der Bienen*:[2] ". . . and our collector must fly to something like a thousand to fifteen hundred single clover blossoms to fill its stomach once. When many a bee colony nevertheless manages, under favorable conditions, to store more than a kilogram of honey in a day, it becomes clear how busily they are working." Taking the weight of a single stomach filling as 50 milligrams, we arrive at no less than about 20 million flower visits for this one kilogram of honey!

Of course, the worker bees do not collect so assiduously all their life long. Each in turn graduates through a sequence of main jobs.[7] They begin as cleaners, preparing the empty cells of the comb for the queen to lay her eggs, and also treating them with an antibacterial secretion. After three days of this labor the worker moves on to something quite different. Now it is a nurse bee, taking care of the brood. Accordingly, at this time its nurse glands are especially well developed. But this job is also soon over; the wax glands on the underside of the abdomen develop, equipping the bee for building activity. This occupies it from about the tenth to the sixteenth day of its life. After that the bee tamps down pollen for storage in the hive and receives the nectar from the returning collectors. After a few days spent guarding the hive entrance the period of interior service, covering three weeks, is completed. Only then does the worker bee leave the hive to collect nectar and pollen from the flowers. This occupies the last eight to fourteen days of the life of a summer bee. By following the life of an individual marked worker bee day after day, as Martin Lindauer[7] did with remarkable perseverance—177 hours at a time, for example, in the case of Bee No. 107—one learns that the times of the different activities overlap, so that a bee always has sidelines in addition to its main responsibility of the moment. That is, the individual activities by no means occur in a fully automatic, rigidly preprogrammed sequence. It came as a particular surprise that apparent idleness and patrolling the interior of the hive take up far more time than any other activity.

Are the bees lazy, then? Of the 177 hours during which Bee No. 107 was observed, 69 hours and 53 minutes were spent in idleness. The biological significance of this surprising result was expressed concisely by Lindauer as follows.

1. During the extensive patrols each bee acquires its own information as to what needs to be done in the hive.

2. The periods of inactivity are of crucial significance, because unoccupied bees constitute a reserve force, available to pitch in wherever needed and able to respond quickly to sudden danger—overheating of the hive, for instance, or an invasion by predators.

Brood care, from early spring (in March) on into October, is not the only incentive for the bees to visit flowers. An animal flying around so busily is itself in need of fuel. A foraging bee supplies the food for its own metabolism. And there is another important factor: a honeybee colony, unlike the related societies of bumblebees, wasps, and hornets, lives throughout the winter. In winter no temperate-zone plants are in bloom, and there is no source of food. The bees are not able to endure starvation like the few young bumblebee females that survive the winter hidden, dormant, in a secluded corner and in spring found a new colony; rather, the bees lay up supplies for themselves. A glance at a brood comb in a beehive shows us their arrangements. In the middle is the nursery, and around it are cells filled with pollen or honey. A bee colony with 20,000 individuals needs about fifteen kilograms of honey to sustain it over the winter. If a beekeeper takes away the food gathered with such effort during the summer, he must provide a substitute. Otherwise all his bees would not only go hungry but freeze to death. The food, especially the carbohydrate-rich honey, is also fuel for the bees' winter heating system. The bees' metabolism is a form of combustion, and therefore it produces heat. Each bee running around in the hive is a small furnace, fueled with flower materials. Many small furnaces in a restricted area can achieve appreciable heating. In the winter the bees cluster in a densely packed mass, within which the temperature can reach 30°C even on a day of sharp frost.

To produce heat the carbohydrates are burned in the flight musculature, especially, with the bee not actually flying (in neutral gear, as it were). From the standpoint of the foraging worker bee, these winter bees are well off. When they hatch in the fall the hive is well stocked and there is no more brood to be tended, for the queen has stopped laying eggs. The winter bees live for some months, becoming considerably older than the bees of the warm season, which have a life expectancy rarely exceeding four to five weeks.

Later we shall see how important is the bees' excellent capacity for learning (enabling them, for instance, to visit the same species of flower again and again), and how fundamentally their elaborate array of effective sense organs influences their visits to the flowers.

Bees, Stone Age Humans, and the Song of Solomon

Let us turn briefly to something quite different. Certainly no other insect has had such a continuous intimate relationship to human cultural history as the bee. There is convincing evidence from the Stone Age that the honeybee has provided food for man over at least ten thousand years. In the Cuevas de Araña, caves near Valencia in southern Spain, an artist in the dim past captured an exciting scene. Drawn in red on the rock wall, the picture was presumably meant to conjure success in the hunt. A broad-hipped Stone Age woman is courageously clinging to one of three ropes of a ladder, by grasping it with one leg. With her arm she is reaching into a hole in the rock where wild bees have their nest, and around her is a flurry of the bees, apparently eager to attack. Or is she smoking the nest out with a torch? In her left hand she holds a container for the combs she steals.[9] Our Figure 9 shows similar documentation from a cave in the Matopo Hills in Zim-

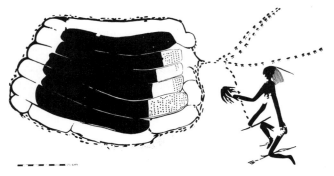

Fig. 9:
A Stone Age honey thief smokes out a beehive. Rock painting from the Matopo Hills in Zimbabwe.

babwe. Here the bees' nest is certainly being smoked out. Kneeling, the Stone Age honey thief holds his torch up to an oversized comb drawn in curiously twisted perspective. The streams of insects flying out confirm his success.

The bee accompanies all subsequent epochs of human history, and its status depends not only on its economic value. It appears repeatedly as a symbolic figure of deep mystical and religious significance. In the Egypt of the Pharaohs representations of bees are exceedingly common, not only as witnesses of the highly developed beekeeping industry (the ancient Egyptians used special clay pipes stacked in layers, and there were special officials for the acquisition and storing of honey). The bee was also a symbol of upper Egypt—ruler over bee and reeds, ruler over Upper and Lower Egypt. From a papyrus over 3,000 years old we learn that the bees arise from the tears of the sun god Ra as they fall to earth.

In ancient Greece and Rome, too, the bee was more than just a provider of food. Among the Greeks it became a symbol of fertility. Coins stamped with bees were used in Ephesus, site of the fabulous Ionic temple described by Pliny, one of the seven wonders of the ancient world, from the sixth century B.C. onward (Fig. 10). Bees were associated with the virginal Artemis, the protector of women in childbirth, mother goddess, and ruler of the animals. This relationship appears in its most intimate form in the remarkable figures with the bodies of bee and woman combined, as in the gold relief from Rhodes shown in Figure 10.

Aristotle (384–322 B.C.), in his *Historia animalium*, gives a lively mixture of true and false reports about the honeybee. The Mayan beekeepers had two holy festivals—Tzec and Mol, in the fifth and eighth months of their calendar—which no doubt became quite high-spirited when the wine they brewed from honey and tree bark had been flowing freely. In the Middle Ages honey was still the only sweetener available, and beeswax was indispensable for making candles. Until the present day the honeybee has retained its great practical and cultural significance. It appears on the coronation regalia of Napoleon and is emblazoned on many coats of arms. Its honey, now as ever, is prized as health-giving, and its

Fig. 10:
Above: Bee on a Greek coin from Ephesus,
380 B.C. *Below*: Bee-Artemis from
Rhodes, gold relief.

sweetness remains a symbol of the pleasant and erotic. Even today
our popular songs occasionally drip "honey." And this is nothing
new. In the fourth chapter of the Song of Solomon we read, "Your
lips distil nectar, my bride; honey and milk are under your tongue;
the scent of your garments is like the scent of Lebanon."

Other Hymenoptera

The other large hymenopteran groups have yet to be considered.
The wasplike "sawflies" (Symphyta) and the stingless, usually parasitic wasps (Terebrantes) are of so little importance as pollinators
of flowers that we need not discuss them here. Among the Hymenoptera with stings (Aculeata), we might think that, in addition to the bees (Apidae), the ants (Formicidae) and hornets (Vespa)
would be significant pollinators, for both groups live in large societies and have a well-known preference for sweet food. But we

Plate 1   41

The fern is not showy in any way that would attract insects. Visually, it tends to vanish into the green background. But the flowering plants pollinated by insects surround the hidden sexual generation with the colorful display of the flowers. The blossoms of the large yellow foxglove (*Digitalis grandiflora*) stand out strikingly from the background. Of course, to the bees (as to other insects) these surroundings look quite different than they do to us. Bees cannot distinguish yellow very well from pure green, but the complex background that looks green to us here is usually "beegray" to them, so that the effective contrast with the yellow flowers is perceptible to them as well.

The corn poppy (*Papaver rhoeas*) is a typical pollen flower. It produces no nectar. Its pure red is extremely rare in temperate-zone flowers, a fact associated with the red blindness of insects. To bees and many other insects, the red that looks so magnificent to us would appear black, if it were not for the ultraviolet radiation reflected by the petals. Insects can see ultraviolet. To them, the poppy flower has a color unimaginable to us.

◊

Above: The field rose (*Rosa arvensis*).
Below: The rock-rose (*Helianthemum nummularium*). From an ecological standpoint these two flowers are "disk flowers," particularly easily accessible to insects. The rock-rose is a "bee-purple" flower, which reflects ultraviolet in addition to the yellow we can see.

Plate 3   43

Above: The alpine snowbell (*Soldanella alpina*), a "bell flower" related to the primrose. It is pollinated especially by bumblebees and butterflies. As soon as such insects settle inside the flower the dry pollen rains down upon them, for it is shaken out of the anthers by the slightest touch.
Below: The stemless gentian (*Gentiana clusii*), a bee-blue "funnel flower." Its nectar is produced at the bottom of the funnel. As in many comparable cases, deep in the funnel its wall is brightly translucent. Because many insects avoid darkness but willingly run toward the light, this feature represents an adaptation of the flower to its pollinators.

Two "lip flowers." *Above*: The common butterwort (*Pinguicula vulgaris*). Stable hairs on the lower lip press the insect (bee or fly) against the reproductive organs located above them. The insect finds the nectar in a spur about half as long as the corolla. The butterwort is a meat-eating plant, a specialization that allows it to exist in boggy habitats lacking in nitrogen. Its prey is trapped and digested in the light green leaf rosettes, the greasy look of which has given the plant its name.

Below: The monkey flower (*Mimulus guttatus*) is a lip flower with a "gullet." The visiting insect uses the broad lower lip as a landing platform and perch. The entrance into the corolla is closed except for a narrow slit.

Plate 7   47

The lady's slipper (*Cypripedium calceolus*), a temperate-zone orchid that rivals its tropical relatives in shape and color, is an "insect-trap" flower. The yellow bowl into which the insects fall is the enlarged, curled lip of the flower. The only way the insect can get out of the trap is to pass by the greasy pollen mass and by the stigma.

◊

Above: The meadow pea (*Lathyrus pratensis*), a "butterfly flower." Stamens and pistil are in the lower part of the flower, the keel. The weight of the landing insect presses the keel downward, exposing the stigma and pollen. The flaglike petal towering over it at the back is appropriately called the standard. Two lateral petals enclose the keel, the so-called wings.
Below: The brown-rayed knapweed (*Centaurea jacea*), a "head flower." It consists of many individual tubular flowers, or florets. The florets around the periphery are only for show; they are especially large, but sterile. A special feature of the fertile inner florets is the mechanically stimulatable pollen threads. Touched by an insect, they shorten by about one-third in a few seconds. As a result, the closed anther tube is pulled downward, and the style, growing in the middle of it, acts like the piston of a pump to push the pollen up and out, toward the insect. Not until the entire mass of pollen has been picked up does the style grow out of the anther tube. This knapweed, then, is an example of a protandrous flower.

A bumblebee about to land on a wild rose. It has already
extended its proboscis.

Plate 9 49

Above: Small stingless bee of the species *Trigona (Oxytrigona) jaty*, photographed in the central highlands of Guatemala at the entrance to its nest. *Below*: The "pantaloon" (pollen basket) on the hindleg of a European bumblebee.

The hawkmoth *Pergesa* at a white campion (*Melandryum album*). Like other hawkmoths, *Pergesa* is a twilight flyer that hovers in front of the flower while sucking nectar. In contrast in many other flowers, but as would be expected from the habits of its pollinator, the white campion flowers are open in the evening.

◊

Flower visitors.
Top: On the left an especially pretty representative of the long-horned beetles, the musky-smelling musk beetle (*Aromia moschata*); on the right *Hoplia farinosa*, a frequent flower visitor, which is related to the cock-chafer and can easily be identified by its green scales.
Middle: On the left a hover fly (*Syrphus ribesii*) and on the right a bee fly (*Bombylius medius*).
Bottom: It is not always peaceful on the flowers, for predatory insects and spiders have also discovered this niche. Left, the checkered beetle *Trichodes alvearius*, the larvae of which feed on the larvae and pupae of solitary bees and of the honeybee. The adult beetle lies in wait for small insects on flowers. Right, a honeybee meets its end in the clutches of a crab spider (*Misumena*), a diurnal hunter that does not build a web but rather sits motionless in flowers, waiting for a victim. Some of these crab spiders can match their coloration to that of the flower, changing from white through butter yellow to green. But this camouflage is probably meant to hide them from their own enemies, the birds, rather than from their prey.

Plate 11

51

Plate 12

would be wrong. Ants are among the classical "nectar thieves"; their small bodies can reach the nectar of most flowers without touching the anthers at all. Moreover, they are not very hairy and so, unlike the honeybee, are not morphologically suited for pollen transport. The hornets produce large broods but feed them predominantly with animal material. The nectar the adult hornets draw from flowers is eaten by themselves. There is an exception to the rule: the Masaridae, close relatives of the Vespidae, show us that the use of pollen instead of animal food (the phylogenetically earlier method) to nourish the larvae has evolved twice in the hymenopteran group. But masarids are rare. The only species native to Germany uses specialized hairs on the front of the head to gather the pollen (Fig. 16).

The situation is quite different in the case of bumblebees (*Bombus*), among the closest relatives of the honeybee. They are regular and important pollinators which, like the honeybee, live entirely on nectar and pollen and feed their brood with them. The bumblebee proboscis is longer than that of the honeybee (see Chapter 11), and can reach the nectar in many flowers too "deep" for the honeybee. Moreover, bumblebees are ordinarily heavier and stronger than honeybees, so that they can often push themselves into flowers with tightly closed corolla tubes (for example, the snapdragon) that are a barrier to the honeybee. Nevertheless, they contribute less to pollination. Their season of activity is considerably shorter; at least in the temperate zone, bumblebee populations do not sur-

◊

Two typical pollen flowers from the buttercup family. *Above*: The pasqueflower (*Pulsatilla patens*), a very early-blooming flower which, like the yellow adonis, is rare in Central Europe. The pasqueflower is proterogynous; its many papillose stigmas are ready to receive pollen long before its own pollen becomes available. In addition to the pollen, the insects find nectar at the base of the flower.
Below: The yellow adonis (*Adonis vernalis*) offers no nectar, but its pollen is freely and abundantly available; accordingly, it receives a diverse crowd of visitors (bees, beetles, flies). The flowers are protandrous, and later in the season can pollinate themselves. The yellow adonis is very sensitive to shade; its flowers open fully only in bright sunshine. Its actual home is in the steppes of Asia and southeastern Europe.

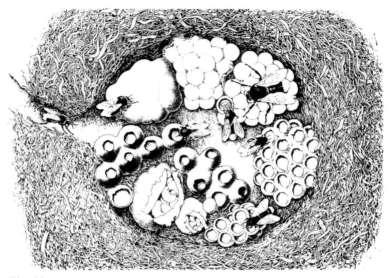

Fig. 11:
A colony of bumblebees (*Bombus lapidarius*) in an abandoned mouse nest.
The large queen is at the upper right, sitting on cells containing pupae; at
the lower left are opened communal cells with larvae; in the middle are
honey pots and at the lower right, empty pupal cells being used as pollen
pots.

vive the winter, so they need not collect winter stores. And bumblebee populations are smaller. In midsummer a bumblebee nest
contains only a few hundred individuals (Fig. 11).

Contrary to popular belief, by the way, bumblebees have a sting
and know very well how to use it, despite their innocuous woolly
appearance.

The Flies

Of the army of flies and midges (Diptera) that inhabits temperate
regions, dozens of species can sometimes be seen to arrive at open
flowers, especially those of the umbel type, in a short period of
observation. But the regular flower visitors, which feed entirely or

predominantly on flowers as adults, belong to few families; here we consider only two of the most common of these.

First the hover flies (Syrphidae), of which there are over 300 species in Germany. Whereas the larvae parasitize the eggs and young stages of other insects, the adult animals live entirely on nectar and pollen. The hover flies can easily be identified by their characteristic flight pattern: trembling briefly at one position in midair and then suddenly plunging forward to a new position. But most people take hover flies to be bees, wasps, or bumblebees (and therefore, erroneously, armed with a sting), because of their coloration. Humans so deceived are, as we shall see, in the best company. Bright coloration—yellow, light brown, black—is typical of these flies, and the conspicuous pattern usually consists of yellow crosswise spots or bands on a dark ground. The hover flies thus resemble honeybees, wasps, and bumblebees so closely that the mistake is easy to make, at least as long as the hover fly is perched on a flower (Pl. 11). The good company mentioned above includes birds and toads. They learn to avoid the stinging hymenopterans after a few unpleasant experiences, not only because of the danger of being stung but also because the poison evidently has a repulsive taste. The mimicry practiced by the hover flies— their assumption of a false identity—increases their chance of being avoided by predators that confuse them with unpalatable insects. The ancient idea that bee swarms originate in rotting cattle cadavers may be a similar case of mistaken identity. The larvae of *Eristalis*, a common hover fly, live in oxygen-poor pits of liquid manure, in mud puddles, and probably also in the fluid that accumulates in a rotting cadaver.

With their long proboscises (*Eristalis* 4-8 mm, *Rhingia rostrata* 11-12 mm; see Chapter 11) hover flies can suck nectar even from deep tubular flowers. They scoop up pollen with their labella, flattened lobes at the end of the proboscis which we shall examine more closely later in another fly.

The bee flies (Bombyliidae) feed similarly. Many of them are very hairy and in this respect, as well as in their coloration, resemble bumblebees (Pl. 11)—another case of mimicry. Like the hover flies, bee flies are expert fliers, practically unexcelled in speed and agility in the air. They can also hover in one spot and then fly away in a flash, to one side or even backward. While sucking nectar with their proboscises, which in some cases are very long (*Bombylius discolor* 10-12 mm), many of them hover over the flower. Unsuitable for pollen-collecting, the proboscis sticks out in front of the fly and cannot be folded or retracted. It can easily be seen when the fly is maneuvering it into the flower and out again, by hovering a little closer or further away with fine precision.

Central Europe is the home of at least a hundred species of bee flies. Their larvae live as parasites on other insects or their eggs and larvae. To ensure that the larvae have access to food, many bee fly females have invented a method of depositing their eggs from the air, with such good aim that the eggs land in the immediate vicinity of the intended host—grasshopper eggs, for example, or the entrance to the underground nest of a solitary bee or wasp.

Soldier flies (Stratiomyidae), dance flies (Empidae), true flies (Muscidae), blowflies (Calliphoridae)—all these families include some members that can be found on flowers, and the list is by no means complete. Here we shall limit ourselves to one concluding remark.

All these flies exploit different kinds of food sources. None of them exhibit brood care at all comparable with that of the bees. They visit flowers irregularly and their importance in pollination is limited in general, as compared with that of the honeybee or bumblebee—especially since they have little or no tendency to restrict themselves to one kind of flower.

The Beetles

Like the flies, the beetles (Coleoptera) contribute relatively little to pollination. Beetles are a phylogenetically old group of insects, with old-fashioned biting–chewing mouthparts. As a rule, the only way these can be used to feed on nectar is by licking it up from exposed surfaces (for exceptions see Chapter 11), but they are very suitable for chewing pollen. Often they are real pollen crushers (see Chapter 9). The majority of the flower-visiting beetles presumably damage the flowers more than they help them. Too often they destroy their host, even eating its petals until they have cleared a path to the delicacies. But there are some beetles that feed on pollen and nectar and visit the flowers regularly to the benefit of both parties. Among these are certain longhorn beetles (Cerambycidae), some of which are magnificent specimens. To see these outdoors it is best to watch umbelliferous flowers. Like the other longhorn beetles, they can be recognized by their slender shape and the long antennae for which they are named (Pl. 11). Further examples of useful beetles are found in the families of the soldier beetles (Cantharidae, Malacodermata), checkered beetles (Cleridae), and metallic wood-borers (Buprestidae).

The gloriously iridescent green rose chafer (*Cetonia aurata*) and *Hoplia farinosa* (Pl. 11), with its light-green silvery scales, are both regular flower visitors. They, like *Scarabaeus*, the holy pill-rolling beetle of the ancient Egyptians, are lamellicorn beetles (Lamellicornia). But both of them are the kind of visitor likely to damage the flowers.

. . . and the Butterflies and Moths

Now we turn to the last insect order of importance in pollination, the Lepidoptera. Many of its members, both butterflies and moths, visit flowers regularly. The butterflies (Rhopalocera) are the bright beauties we see fluttering on a sunny summer day—the swallowtail (*Papilio machaon*), the peacock (*Vanessa io*), the blues (*Lycaena bellargus* and others), the fritillaries (*Argynnis* species), and so on and on. The prosaic zoologist recognizes the butterflies by a characteristic feature, the wedge- or button-like thickening at the end of the antenna.

The moths (Heterocera) are far more numerous than the butterflies. But because they tend to be active in the evening and at

night they are much less noticeable. Anyone who takes the trouble
to go outdoors on a mild summer night and to set up a lamp, if
possible with ultraviolet in its light, in front of a white cloth, may
well find streams of them flying by. A collection made under these
conditions reveals the amazing abundance of life in the still of the
night. A common representative of the hawkmoths or sphinxes
(Sphingidae), *Pergesa elpenor*, is shown in Plate 10. Another, the
hummingbird hawkmoth (*Macroglossum stellatarum*), with a striking fanlike structure at the end of the abdomen, is atypical in that
it flies by day in full sunshine. Other day-active moths include the
burnets (Zygaenidae). The family with the largest number of species is the owlet moths (Noctuidae). With training, one can identify owlets by a pattern on the forewing consisting of three spots
(cone-, kidney-, and ring-shaped). Moths of the family Geometridae as caterpillars are called inchworms, because in locomotion
they look as though they were measuring the route.

Lepidopterans feed on flowers only as adults. They collect just
for themselves, not for their offspring, and they use only the nectar, sucking it up with the proboscis (see Chapter 11). The often
enormous length of this appendage gives them access to the nectar
in flowers with long, narrow corolla tubes, which most other insects cannot reach. But there is an exception to every rule! The
phylogenetically ancient Micropterygidae have chewing mouthparts rather than the typical proboscis, and they use them to eat
pollen. Butterflies usually perch on the flower while feeding. The
hawkmoths, however, hover above the flower; typical hawkmoth
flowers offer no place to land. Noctuids and geometrids usually
do both at the same time, holding on with the legs while the
wings are beating. Transport of the pollen is an incidental event;
it is carried to the next flower on the proboscis or the body, wherever it happens to stick while the insect is feeding.

Hemimetabolous Insects

Certain groups of insects are practically never seen visiting flowers.
Among them are the dragonflies and damselflies (Odonata), the

Orthoptera (a group of straight-winged insects including the cock-roaches, grasshoppers, and crickets), the stoneflies (Plecoptera), and the mayflies (Ephemeridae). All these insects belong to the category Hemimetabola (a name that implies "incomplete meta-morphosis"). Their larval stages resemble the adult, and a pupal stage (during which the insect, enclosed in a chrysalis, becomes transformed) is entirely lacking. All the really important flower visitors—the Hymenoptera (honeybees, bumblebees, and wasps), the Lepidoptera (butterflies and moths), the Coleoptera (beetles), and the Diptera (flies)—belong to the other large group of insects, the Holometabola, which undergo a "complete metamorphosis." Holometabolous larvae are quite unlike the adults, and the trans-formation occurs during a pupal stage. No one looking at a but-terfly caterpillar or a fly maggot, or even the pupae they form, would arrive spontaneously at the idea that it would eventually become a butterfly or fly—animals vastly different from these ear-lier stages, not only in external appearance but also in behavior. Among the holometabolous insects a single species makes use of various food sources at different stages, and can be at home in completely different ecological niches. The caterpillar crawls and grazes on plant leaves and, accordingly, has pincerlike chewing mouthparts. But the adult butterfly flutters from flower to flower, unrolling its long elastic proboscis to suck up the nectar. It is hardly possible to imagine a greater contrast during the develop-ment of an individual animal.

Holometabolism is also of interest in that all insects have a rigid exoskeleton, which cannot simply expand as the animal grows. Therefore the insects (like other arthropods) change their armor from time to time by molting, slipping out of the old, tight shell. Having emerged, they are one size larger. Certainly holometabo-lism can be regarded as a virtue made by evolution out of the special necessity of an exoskeleton. If one cannot avoid molting, one can take advantage of the opportunity to remodel.

Phylogenetically, holometabolism is more recent than hemime-tabolism.

7   Sociobiology and the Selfish Gene in the Bee Society

The genes are master programmers, and they are programming for their lives.

Richard Dawkins, "The Selfish Gene," 1976

How mistaken it is to associate with the word "bee" only the familiar honeybee! There are furry bees and shiny bees, bees with stings and bees without, mining and mason and carpenter bees, bees that line their nests with petals, leaves, cotton, or resin, bees that nest in empty snail shells, and even "cuckoo" bees, which leave their eggs in the nests of others. Zoologists have identified about 20,000 species of bees in the present-day world. The specialist considers them all as members of the superfamily Apoidea. The Apoidea have all departed from the original wasp habit of feeding the brood on other insects and spiders; they have changed over to nectar and pollen, the latter being collected either together with the nectar in the crop or on the body surface, by hairs on the abdomen or by the legs. Depending on the method of pollen transport, then, they are called crop, abdominal, or leg collectors.

In Central Europe the bees (in this broad sense) are a sizable crowd of about 560 species. Most of them are solitary; a single female builds a nest for herself alone. She constructs a cell, fills it with a supply of nectar-pollen mixture sufficient for the needs of a larva, lays an egg on it, closes the cell, and then proceeds to build and supply a number of additional cells. The females of many species are dead before their young have emerged from the nest. Figure 12 shows one of the typical nesting sites of such individualistic bees: small holes in the ground, cracks in walls, decaying

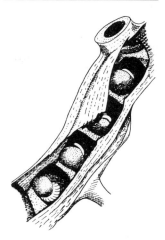

Fig. 12:
The nest of a wood-burrowing bee (*Xylocopa violacea*) in a dead branch. In three of the four cells an egg lies on the ball of food, and in the lowest cell is a larva.

wood. The solitary bees that are parasites require no food from flowers, and have no collecting apparatus.

There are all kinds of intermediates between the solitary bees and the social bees. The culmination is reached with the eusocial (truly social) species. Their special characteristics, in brief, are as follows. Several individuals cooperate in caring for the brood; there are special castes for reproduction, and more or less sterile worker individuals. The generations overlap, so that young animals coexist with their parents for at least part of their lives. The best example is the honeybee. The curious thing about the bees (Apoidea) is that they have evolved true social behavior at least eight times.[4] Surveying the Hymenoptera in general, we find that the situation is not much different among the wasps and ants. Correction, then: the strong tendency toward social behavior is a peculiarity of the hymenopterans as a whole. The only other insects that exhibit anything like it are the termites.

Because the social life style of the honeybees in particular (though also of the bumblebees and stingless bees) is so closely linked to our subject, it is worth pausing briefly to consider an exciting new interpretation of the way it developed.

Here we encounter a particularly interesting question. The central dogma of Darwin's theory of evolution is natural selection. The most diligent and best suited will prosper—"survival of the fittest." The measure of fitness is ultimately the number of progeny and hence the amount of hereditary material successfully passed on to the next generation. How, then, can childlessness have persisted throughout evolution? What can have caused the development of infertile worker castes, individuals that raise their siblings rather than reproducing themselves?

We shall soon see that the altruistic behavior of these animals is not at all as selfless as at first appears.

One answer to our questions is offered by sociobiology, a field of biology that has sprung up very recently, is widely discussed, and has caused some controversy. Its subject is the biological basis of social behavior.

First we must express more precisely the postulate of Darwin cited above. The organism is ultimately only a vehicle for the reproduction of the genes. The hereditary material, deoxyribonucleic acid, is used by the organism for reproducing itself. *The Selfish Gene*, title of a book by Richard Dawkins, captures this situation succinctly. Once again: the egg makes itself into a chicken so that the chicken can produce another egg.

All mechanisms that cause more of certain genes to be passed on to the next generation, owing to natural selection, will become established as characteristics of the species. Social behavior is to be regarded as one such mechanism. The genetic theory of the origin of social behavior can be traced back to William D. Hamilton, a British researcher, who published a long paper on the subject in 1964.[1] In highly simplified terms, Hamilton's message was that "selfless" social behavior can develop only by the selection of genes of identical origin regardless of the individuals that house them. The technical term for this notion is "kin selection." The more closely individuals are related, the more likely it is that several copies of the same gene will be present in the group. Highly social, altruistic behavior can thus become established only in family groups. Only there is it fairly certain that renunciation of one's own reproduction (e.g., by worker bees) will be worthwhile, in that genetic material identical to one's own will be protected by an increase in the fitness of the conspecifics and in their reproductive ability. In no other case can altruism be transmitted down the generations.

Now, a bee colony is in fact a family, consisting of a queen (the mother) and her daughters (workers) and sons (drones). In the Hymenoptera sex is determined as follows: unfertilized eggs give rise to males, and fertilized eggs, to females. On her nuptial flight the queen bee acquires a store of male semen; later it is up to her whether to fertilize the eggs she lays with it or not. At any time she can control the production of workers or drones. A result of this kind of reproduction is that the male animals are fatherless and will themselves never have sons.

Because of this genetic difference between the sexes, it follows (Fig. 13) that mothers are less closely related to their own daughters—that they have fewer genes in common with them—than are sisters to one another. This consequence brings us to the heart of the question posed at the outset. If we consider the overall fitness

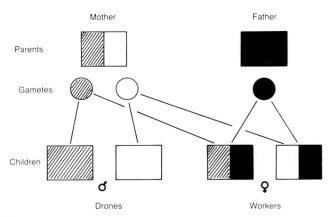

Fig. 13:
In the bees and bumblebees the females (workers) grow from fertilized eggs and the males (drones), from unfertilized eggs. Therefore only the females have two parents. The males have no father, nor can they have sons.

of the population and the contribution of all the genes of identical origin, regardless of individual, an infertile female caste (e.g., worker bees) can be advantageous from a genetic viewpoint if it has taken over the job of caring for and raising its sisters. The worker bee confers a greater advantage on her own genetic complement in tending her sisters than if she were to devote her energies to producing offspring of her own. This is the most distinctive characteristic of insect societies—the subject of this chapter.

By the way, this same line of reasoning sheds light on quite a number of other details. The male hymenopterans—honeybee drones, for instance—do not engage in brood care; the females tolerate them only for the purpose of reproduction. Here, again, the theory fits excellently. The males are on average less closely related to the females than the latter to one another (Table 1). Knowledge of the genetic relations, then, would allow us to predict the organization of social behavior in this case as well.

Table 1. Degree of genetic relationship among honeybees

| | Degree of relatedness of the | |
	Female	Male
To: Mother	0.5	1.0
Father	0.5	0
Sister	0.75	0.5
Brother	0.25	0.5
Daughter	0.5	1.0
Son	0.5	0

It would surely be a mistake to regard the degree of relatedness as the only factor determining social behavior. The genetic theory of social behavior has by no means solved all the problems. But it caused a great stir when it appeared on the scene, and in the long term its main value may lie in the fact that it allows the formulation of hypotheses that can be tested; it makes a multitude of phenomena of social behavior accessible, for the first time, to the only reliable form of proof—experimentation. No other theory embedded in the general theory of evolution has accomplished this.

The old concept of fitness must be extended in the sense of the stimulating findings of the sociobiologists. The fit individual is not only the one that survives and produces offspring of its own, but also the one that increases the chance of close relatives to survive and have descendants. It goes without saying that the sociobiologists apply their theories to vertebrates as well and include mankind—justifiably, if cautiously—in their analyses.[2,3,5] Quite understandably, at this point the debate about sociobiology becomes especially vigorous.

8   The Pollen Grain—
A Science in Itself

The Navajo have a strong feeling for plants, which they treat
with the greatest respect. The symbol for life and productivity,
for peace and prosperity, is pollen. Pollen symbolizes light.

Stephen C. Jett, "Navajo Wildlands," 1967

Is there any other plant product that serves so many sciences as
the pollen grain? In the special construction of its nearly inde-
structible wall lies information of interest not only to the systematist but also to the paleobotanist, the archaeologist, the geolo-
gist in search of oil, the climatologist, the allergy researcher, the
beekeeper. All of them make use of the pollen grain, learning from
its form and surface structure something about the plants to which
the pollen belongs—plants that inhabited the land in prehistoric
times, plants that tell us about the climate in times past, plants
with allergy-causing pollen, and plants at which the bees carry out
the business of collecting.

For us the information hidden within the pollen grain is more
important: the genetic information, which must be transmitted to
the stigma in sexual reproduction. And it is to transmit this information that the whole insect transport system has developed.
Therefore it is worth examining the pollen in detail.

Pollen grains are small miracles, tiny spheres with diameters
ranging from about 3 μm (forget-me-not) to 250 μm (pumpkin),
3- to 250-thousandths of a millimeter. Otto Gunnar Erdtman, a
Swedish researcher, measured 4,521 grains from no less than 2,452
species of angiosperm plants.[3] Most of the diameters were in the
vicinity of 34 μm. When they are ripe, the pollen sacs in the anthers split open along a preformed line or pore (Fig. 5) and release
the pollen into the open. The journey to the stigma can be long

and complicated. Once there, however, the pollen grain adheres
to the stigma; the surface of the stigma is covered with hairlike
papillae and is sticky in addition (Fig. 14). The transfer of the
male genetic material from the pollen grain to the egg cell in the
ovary at the base of the pistil can begin. It takes place as follows.

First the so-called pollen tube grows out through a special pore
in the pollen grain (Fig. 5). This structure has the remarkable
ability to digest its way through the cells of the style tissue, in case
there is no clear path; sometimes the style already has loose, easily
penetrated tissue or even a hollow channel. The pollen tube grows
very rapidly, as much as one to three millimeters per hour. Even
if the style is long, like that of the meadow saffron (15 mm), the
goal—the opposite sex—is reached after only half a day.

The ripe pollen grain contains two or three nuclei. Within each
are threadlike chromosomes, the male (in this case) genetic material. Having moved down the pollen tube to the ovary, one nucleus fuses with the egg cell. The product of this fusion gives rise
to a new embryonic plant. A second nucleus helps to produce the
endosperm, the tissue that nourishes the embryo.

In the Shelter of the Pollen Wall

The importance of the content of a pollen grain in sexual reproduction is rivaled by the remarkable complexity of the wall structure and its surface. The durability of the pollen wall, only about
a thousandth of a millimeter thick, results from the presence of
sporopollenin (a polyterpene) in the outer layer, the exine. An
entire science is based on the study of the pollen wall, searching
for clues to the vegetation and climate in earlier times. Especially
in bogs one can find pollen grains that have lain there for many
tens of thousands of years, with the distinctive characteristics of
their walls preserved.[2] The content of the pollen grain is not so
durable; it survives barely a few days.[2]

The surface structure of the wall is characteristic of each particular group of plants—in some cases, of a single species—and can

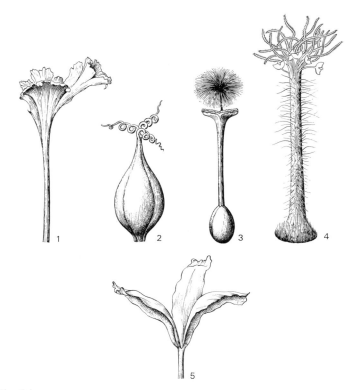

Fig. 14:
Stigma forms. (1) Crocus (*Crocus*); (2) alpine rush (*Juncus alpinus*); (3)
lesser periwinkle (*Vinca minor*); (4) dwarf mallow (*Malva neglecta*); (5)
iris (*Iris*); (6) rat's-tail fescue (*Vulpia myurus*); (7) yellow bristle grass
(*Setaria glauca*); (8) monkey flower (*Mimulus*).

therefore be used for identification. Irregularities in the deposition
of the sporopollenins cause projections of the wall in the form of
spines, warts, and angular or rounded ridges (Pl. 13). In the present context it is particularly interesting to learn that the most elab-
orately sculptured pollen surfaces are often found in the flowers
that are pollinated by insects. The rough structure increases the
chance that the pollen will cling to the insect's hairs and remain
attached throughout the aerial journey to the next flower. An-

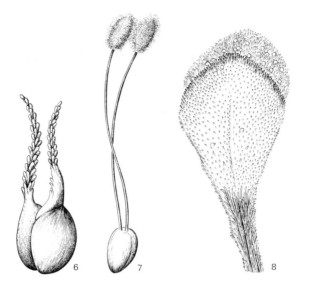

other, no less important, adaptation to the same transport problem is the "pollen glue" that makes animal-carried pollen sticky so that it clumps together. This clumping can go so far that the content of an entire half anther forms a solid mass. As we shall see again later, this happens in orchids. Botanists call such a mass a pollinium. Pollinia have special adhesive disks or clamplike structures by which they attach to the proboscis, the head or another part of the body of the visiting insect, so that they are transported as a whole (Figs. 64, 69).

In wind-pollinated plants, by contrast, the pollen grains separate from one another in the lightest breeze and fly away like dust. The clouds of pollen released by hazel bushes and blooming conifers are a familiar sight, and the amounts that sometimes drift about in the air become especially obvious when rain over a lake brings them down, to form a yellow sheet on the surface of the water. For an animal-pollinated plant such dispersal would be fatal; its pollen must be kept ready for the arrival of a suitable carrier.

2.6 Million Packets of
Concentrated Food

In addition to the transfer of male genetic information, the pollen grain has another, quite different function—it is food and attractant for the flower-seeking insects. It is useful as food because of its high protein content, 16 percent to 30 percent. It also contains 1 percent to 10 percent fats, 1 percent to 7 percent starches, almost no sugar, and many vitamins. In fact, then, it is a very high-quality food. There are "pollen flowers," which offer the insects pollen only, and no nectar. Flowers such as the corn poppy (Pl. 2) make it readily available in great quantities. So do members of the rose family and many of the buttercup family, though the latter also secrete nectar (Fig. 22, Pl. 12). Pollen flowers are easily identified by the large number of stamens, usually in colors that contrast strikingly with the petals. The stamens of the corn poppy produce no less than 2.6 million pollen grains per flower![7] Clearly, this is far more than would be required for pollination alone.

No wonder such a banquet attracts the insects, especially since it is set out openly. As we have heard, pollen is particularly important to the bees as food for the youngest larvae. Bumblebees also collect it in large amounts, and its role is by no means subordinate to that of the nectar. The two functions of a pollen grain—reproduction and the attraction of pollinators—are necessarily mutually exclusive. A pollen grain that is eaten is lost for reproductive purposes. Only the excess of pollen makes the dual function possible. Some plants maneuver themselves out of this situation by an elegant compromise, in that they produce two kinds of stamens, those with "pollination-anthers" and those with "food-anthers." The food-anthers contain cells that taste good but are of no use in reproduction. They are sterile (e.g., *Cassia* species of the family Caesalpiniaceae, tropical and subtropical woody plants; Fig. 15). Sometimes the food-anthers do not even contain sterile pollen, but rather a milky juice (*Commelina coelestis*). Scientists are currently discussing the possibility that these stamens no longer even have a nutritive function, but simply replace the true stamens

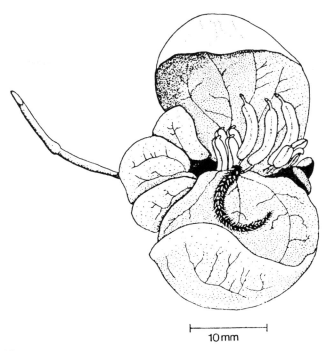

10 mm

Fig. 15:
The flower of *Cassia quiedondilla*, with four short food-stamens, three
short regressed stamens, and three long stamens for pollination.

to act as advertising signboards.[1,4] In any case, the insects take
care of pollination with the true pollen automatically while they
are devoting their hungry attention to the modified stamens.

In Chapter 16 problems related to this dual function of pollen
are treated further.

9 Baskets, Brushes, and Sweeping Machines

But science, which from the very beginning has been content
with knowledge and ascends to heaven when it appears in print,
leaves nothing out.

Erhart Kästner, "Die Stundentrommel vom heiligen Berg Athos,"
1956

Millions of years of "practical experience" during the long random
history of evolution have occasionally produced structures and
mechanisms of a perfection that astounds even modern technically
oriented minds. As far as the insects are concerned, there have
been not only morphological adaptations of body structure but
also adaptations of behavior, which will be described in later chapters. First we shall consider simply the mechanical apparatus used
by the insects to collect pollen. There is enough material here for
an entire book, so inventive has nature been. We must be satisfied
with a few examples, to give us at least some idea of their variety.
Again we begin with the honeybee.

A Complete Toolbox

The honeybee's pollen-collecting apparatus is a full set of tools for
picking up many thousands of tiny pollen grains, working them
into a substantial clump and attaching it to the hindlegs for safe
transport to the hive (Pl. 9). What happens to it there will be
described at the end of this chapter. Let us first see how the packet
of pollen comes into being.

Insects that collect pollen, at least those that do it routinely, are
typically covered with a dense coat of hairs. Seen at close range,

bees and bumblebees are quite woolly creatures (Pls. 13 to 15). Their hairs are exceedingly delicate threadlike projections from the cuticular exoskeleton, only a few thousandths of a millimeter thick. Usually there are a large number of teeth and hooks on each hair, to which the pollen grains—sticky with the greasy "pollen glue"— adhere when the insect contacts the anthers of the flower, either unintentionally or while digging out the pollen with its jaws and forelegs. After visiting a "pollen flower" (Chapter 8) a bee or bumblebee looks as though it has been wallowing in a tub of pollen. But as it is flying to the next flower it cleans the pollen up, using the hindlegs—which are specially equipped for this job— with the greatest agility. The first of the five segments of the foot (tarsus) of the hindleg is very wide, with several rows of bristles running perpendicular to the long axis of the leg on its inner surface. This is the "brush" (Pl. 16). With the brushes on its two hindlegs, the worker bee gathers the pollen out of its hairy pelt while still in flight. Then a "comb" at the lower end of the hindleg tibia (Pl. 17) is used to comb the pollen out of the brush. Obviously this maneuver requires both hindlegs; the right comb works on the left brush and the left comb, on the right. This, too, occurs during flight. So does the last part of this action, which finally brings the pollen into the "luggage compartment" known technically as the pollen basket. This is a hollow in the outer surface of the extra-wide tibia of the hindleg, a surface that is bare except for the sturdy bristles encircling the hollow. A spur juts out from the "heel" (the upper end of the first tarsal segment) of the hindleg, curving outward so that it can be pressed against the inside of the comb on this leg. As the comb scrapes downward, the pressure from this spur forces the pollen into the lower end of the basket. One load after another is pushed in, until the basket is full. A thick bristle helps to hold the mass in place (Pl. 18). The middle legs beat and compress the pollen clump, which—depending on what the flowers had to offer and on the demand at home—can weigh as much as ten milligrams and contain as many as a million pollen grains. This solid mass is so firmly attached that it is not lost even though the flight to the hive may cover a mile or more.

It helps, too, that while collecting the pollen the bee moistens it with some honey it has brought along.

The last station on the collecting tour is the beehive. Here the collector deposits its freight in a storage cell of the comb. The younger bees responsible for the housework nimbly break it up and pack it in. Eventually the nurse bees will eat the pollen, and in a special gland in the head it will be converted into the nutritious "mother's milk" (actually one should say "sister's milk") they feed the larvae (Chapter 6). The male bees—the drones—and the queen play no part in the business of collecting, nor do they have any collecting tools on their hindlegs.

Abdominal and Crop Collectors

Not all bees (in the broad sense) collect with their legs as the honeybees and bumblebees do. In other bees the brush is located on the underside of the abdomen; these are the abdominal collec-

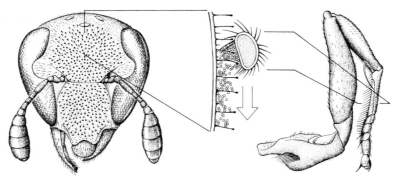

Fig. 16:
The pollen-collecting apparatus of the wasp *Celonites abbreviatus*. On the left is the head, with the button-ended collecting bristles on the front surface; on the right is the comb at the end of the forelegs with which the pollen is combed out of the head hairs (middle) so that it can be swallowed for transport. *Celonites* belongs to the family Masaridae, rare in Central Europe, which in collecting pollen as well as nectar is exceptional in the group of vespoid wasps.

tors. The abdominal brush not only collects the pollen, but also carries it to the hive. A number of solitary bees such as the mason bees and leafcutter bees operate in this way. Other bee species are crop collectors. These are nearly hairless, and simply swallow the pollen that is scraped together by the legs and mouthparts. At the end of their tour they spit it out again, together with the nectar they have collected.

Without question the honeybee (*Apis*), the bumblebee (*Bombus*), and the closely related stingless bees of the tropics (Meliponinae, the communication system of which will concern us in Chapter 28), are the most important pollen collectors—as one would expect from their brood care and social organization—and have the most highly perfected collecting apparatus. The hornets (*Vespa*), which are close relatives of these bees and also live in social groups, feed their larvae on animal materials (insects). An interesting exception among their close relatives is shown in Figure 16.

A Beetle's Pollen-Sweeping Machine

But pollen is not always gathered so altruistically, as community provisions. Many flower visitors eat some of it themselves, and the flies and beetles use it entirely as their own food. Because they do this with their mouthparts, it is no surprise that these structures also occasionally become specialized. A well-known example is the rose chafer (*Cetonia aurata*), a beetle up to 2 cm long of shimmering metallic green, having the same solid and sedate appearance as its relatives, the June beetle and dung beetle. In summer the rose chafer can be found sitting on all kinds of flowers. It is quite smooth, with very few hairs, so that (like most beetles) it is unlikely to be much use as a pollinator. But it is all the better equipped for eating the pollen. Its mouthparts, the maxillae, bear dense pads and tufts of hair that serve as pollen brooms (Fig. 17). Because beetles in general have typical chewing mouthparts, the rose chafer has no trouble crushing the pollen and sending it down the throat. The long-horned beetles (Cerambycidae), a group that

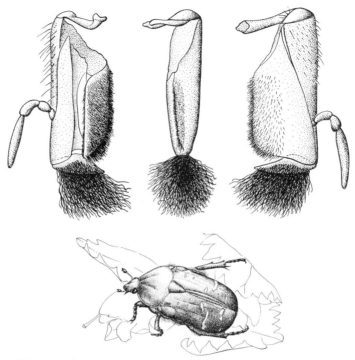

Fig. 17:
Pollen broom on the mouthparts of the rose chafer (*Cetonia aurata*).
Left: The maxilla from various sides.

includes the most regular flower-visitors among the beetles, have
quite similar tufts of hair; an example is *Strangalia maculata*.

But the most ingenious brush system awaits us in the beetle
Malachius bipustulatus (Malachiidae).[5] In the words of its discov-
erer, this is a real pollen-sweeping machine. Its basic components
are bristles with trumpet- or spoon-shaped ends such as have not
been found on the mouthparts of any other insect. Analysis of the
gut contents of *Malachius* revealed that the pollen of wind-pollinated grasses is its preferred food. This pollen is floury, with very
little adhesive material (Chapter 8). But the trumpet-bristles on
the outer appendage of the maxilla fit so tightly against this un-
sticky pollen that they can pick it up (Fig. 18). Then it is wiped

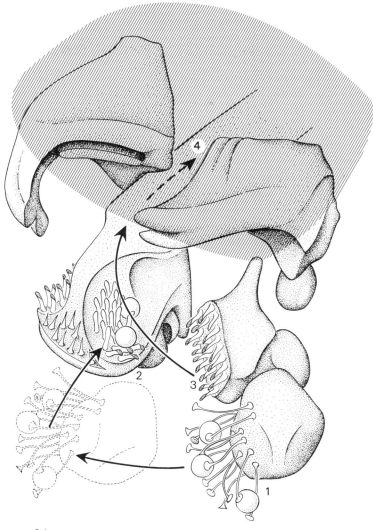

0.1 mm

Fig. 18:
The pollen-sweeping machine of *Malachius bipustulatus*. Trumpet bristles
(1) on the outer maxillary appendage take up the pollen and wipe it onto
the spoon bristles (2) of the labium. The spoon bristles of the inner maxillary appendage (3) then sweep it away, into the mouth opening (4).

off against the spoon-bristles of the labium, and eventually other spoon-bristles on the inner appendage of the maxilla sweep it out and pass it on to the mandible. There it is kneaded so that the beetle can swallow it.

Because their mouthparts are short, beetles are usually (a rare exception is described in Chapter 11) found on flowers with exposed pollen—for example, on flowers of the rose (Rosaceae) and buttercup (Ranunculaceae) families. Beetles can deal with flowers in which the food is less accessible (for example, because it is surrounded by a long tubular corolla) if they are small or slender enough to crawl into the flower or at least push their heads far enough inside. The only recourse of large beetles—and it is a method used often and not only by beetles—is to chew their way through to the hidden anthers or nectaries. Visitors of this sort do more harm than good to the plants.

A Moth That Eats Pollen, and Bees That Gather Oil

Two curiosities to end this catalog of specializations: a pollen-eating moth and a diet of oil. First the moth. That a moth should eat pollen seems self-contradictory, because a characteristic trait of the Lepidoptera is the long proboscis (Chapter 11), useful only for sucking up fluids. The exceptions to this rule are the primitive moths, the Micropterygidae. They have no proboscis at all, but well-developed chewing mandibles rather like those of beetles. The fingerlike maxillary palp ends in a kind of claw, which they use to scratch the pollen out of the anthers (Fig. 19a). And what they scratch out is their main food. In Central Europe the species *Micropteryx calthella* is often seen on the flowers of the marsh marigold (*Caltha palustris*).

And now to the oil. It has been known for only a few years that certain species of some plant families—the orchids, irises, and others—have flowers that offer the insects not nectar, but rather oil as food.[10] They produce it in special glands, and the females of certain anthophorid bees collect it with highly specialized absorbent mops and combs on the forelegs, and pack it in among long hairs on the hindlegs for transport. Mixed with pollen, this unusual flower product serves as food for the larvae (Fig. 19b, c).

Buzz Pollination

In 1959 John H. Barrett, of the Highlands Agricultural Experiment Station in Aiyura, New Guinea, described a method of collecting pollen that is rather like shaking the fruit out of an apple or pear tree. On his forays into the jungle he repeatedly noticed brief, low-frequency buzzing sounds. These proved to come from pollen-collecting bees, and were much louder than the normal flight sounds. Charles Michener, renowned bee expert of the University of Kansas, says that he has frequently used this sound as a guide while collecting bees. Barrett's report induced him to look further into the matter of these noisy bees, and he published his findings in 1962.[2,6] It turned out that the bees were doing something he aptly termed "buzz pollination."

The ripe anthers of most flowers release the pollen by splitting open lengthwise to a greater or lesser extent (Fig. 5). Then the pollen grains either fall out by themselves or can easily be scooped out by the insects. But some flowers have anthers with only a small opening at the end. The bees we are discussing here are undeterred by this obstacle; when they are unable to reach the pollen directly, they bend their bodies so as to clasp the anthers tightly and shake them (Fig. 20). The pollen comes pouring out and lands on the hairy ventral surface of the bee.

The buzzing noise, which can be heard as much as ten meters away, is produced by the shaking movements. Each vibration, lasting only a fraction of a second, results from contraction of the powerful flight muscles. This contraction sets the thoracic skeleton and the legs, attached to it, into oscillation, and the legs transmit the vibration to the flower. During all this the wings are folded over the back, moving hardly at all.

The indirect flight musculature, which is acting here, is encoun-

tered again and again in quite different contexts. It is called indirect because the muscles do not move the wings themselves but
rather deform the thoracic skeleton, which causes the wing movement. In the course of insect evolution this type of muscle has
become progressively more important. It provides the force for
the up- and downstrokes, while the direct muscles ultimately retain "only" a steering function. Important subsidiary functions of
the indirect flight musculature, in addition to pollen shaking, are

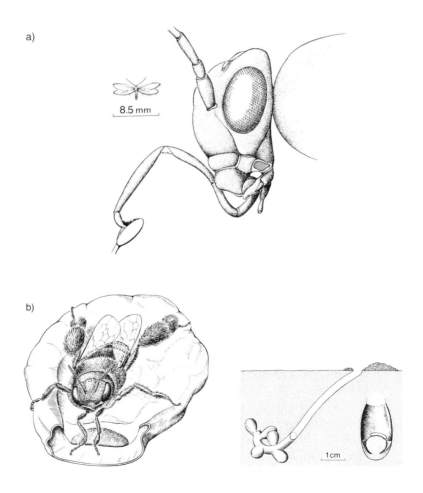

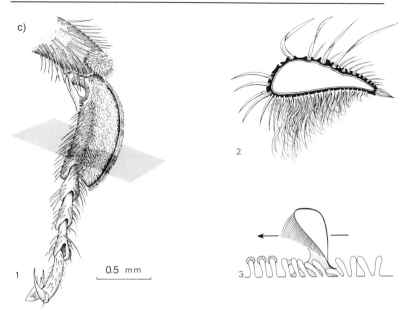

Fig. 19:
(a) The pollen-scratcher (maxillary palp) of the primitive moth *Micropteryx calthella*. (b) An anthophorid bee (*Tapinotaspis coerulea*) collecting the oil from an oil flower with the mops on its forelegs; note also the long-haired hindlegs, into which the collected oil is packed. *Right*: The bee carries the oil to its nest in the ground and supplies the larvae with a mixture of pollen and oil; the inset on the right shows a brood cell with the food mixture and an egg on top of it. (c) The oil-collecting apparatus of another anthophorid bee (*Paratetrapedia melampoda*). (1) The collecting mop on the foreleg with the scraping edge outward on the right. (2) Cross-section through the mop-bearing part of the leg; the mop is downward and the scraper on the right. (3) The scraper slides over the field of hairs in the oil gland and the mop absorbs the oil.

temperature regulation (Chapter 29) and the sound signal generated during the waggle dance (Chapter 27).

The number of pollen-shaking bee species is large, and from the most primitive to the most highly developed they are distributed throughout the group of bees in the broad sense. The honeybee, however, is not one of them.

The plant species with this kind of anther are also very common.

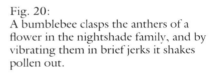

Fig. 20:
A bumblebee clasps the anthers of a
flower in the nightshade family, and by
vibrating them in brief jerks it shakes
pollen out.

The nightshade family, which includes the potato, is only one of
sixty-five families, which together comprise nearly four thousand
species.[2] Species of *Cassia*, which we have remarked upon because
of their diverse types of anthers, are also shaken by bees.[1]

Typically, such flowers produce no nectar and their pollen grains
are small (10 to 25 μm; cf. Chapter 8), with relatively smooth
surfaces and little pollen glue, which certainly helps them to be
shaken out so easily. Observations and experiments have shown
that it is unimportant for the pore in the anther to point downward during the shaking. In many cases it points upward, but the
pollen is flung out just as effectively.

One need not travel to a tropical forest to hear the buzzing of
pollen-shaking bees. I noticed it for the first time some years ago,
on a spring day when dozens of bumblebees were gathering pollen
from the first rhododendron flowers in my garden. Their stamens
stand upright in the flower, and the openings are at the upper
ends of the anthers. You can convince yourself of the effectiveness
of the bumblebees' behavior by trying it yourself; shake the anthers, and a slightly flocculent mass of pollen will fly out.

10   Nectar

Do not praise a man for his good looks, nor loathe a man
because of his appearance. The bee is small among flying
creatures, but her product is the best of sweet things.

Ecclesiasticus, or the Wisdom of Jesus the Son of Sirach, Chapter 11

The food from flowers is not just pollen; nectar is even more
important. Of course! But that was not always the case. In the
evolution of flowering plants (cf. Chapter 30) pollen has the longer
history. This should come as no surprise now that we have seen
what an important place the pollen grain occupies, not only in the
life cycle of the flowering plants but even—as microspores—in
that of lower plants such as the fern (Chapter 2). Pollen is indispensable, nectar is not. Even present-day flowers do not always
use nectar to lure the pollinating insects. Some of them are pure
pollen flowers (Chapter 8) and others, like the orchids, know how
to trick their visitors and attract them without food (Chapters 23
and 24). And there is something else: nectar secretion in the broadest
sense is by no means always associated with the flower and the
process of pollination. Nectar existed before the flowering plants
evolved. Curiously, botanists have reported that nectar is secreted
by the fronds of the European "eagle fern" *Pteridium aquilinum*
and attracts honeybees. Furthermore, even in flowering plants nectar is often secreted far away from the flower itself—on leaves and
their stalks, for example. Then it is called extrafloral nectar, because it has nothing to do with the flower. The function of this
extrafloral nectar is in debate, and we need not go into the theories
of the specialists here. It suffices to note that nectar secretion has
obviously been a development independent of the flowers, that

nectar can be interpreted physiologically as an excretory product of the plant's metabolism as well as more ecologically, as an insect attractant, and finally that the flower in a sense has simply added a further modification to an already existing principle.[4]

We are interested here in the floral nectar, the chief coin with which the flowers pay the insects for their visits. It has another rather resonant name, nuptial nectar, which reflects its close relationship to pollination. Christian Konrad Sprengel correctly deduced this relationship two centuries ago: "My studies convinced me more and more that many—indeed, perhaps all—flowers with juice are fertilized by the insects that feed on this juice, and hence that although from the insects' point of view this feeding is the ultimate goal, from that of the flowers it is only a means, and in fact the only means, to a particular end: their pollination."

Composition

Nectar is basically sugar-water. Its total sugar content amounts to about 40 percent, though it can fluctuate widely among different species. The spectrum of possible concentrations is indicated by two extremes: 8 percent for the crown imperial (*Fritillaria imperialis*) and 76 percent for the marjoram (*Origanum vulgare*).[1,2] In addition to the sugars (sucrose, glucose, fructose) other substances are present in relatively small amounts. Among them are amino acids, proteins, organic acids, phosphates, vitamins, and enzymes.

In any case, nectar is rich in organic substances, including the various kinds of sugar. It is not surprising, then, that the nectaries—the sites of nectar production—make close contact with the conduits that carry the organic substances the plant itself produces by photosynthesis (using the sunlight and its own chlorophyll) from the carbon dioxide in the air and the water in the ground. But nectar is not just the fluid in these conduits (the phloem). The nectar gland cells, which ultimately excrete the nectar, are active cells, selectively removing certain substances from this fluid and adding others to it. Only the total sugar content of the fluid remains nearly unchanged.[1]

Nectaries

Nectaries vary widely in appearance. Sometimes they have striking shapes, and often they are yellow-green in color. They can be found in all flower parts—the petals and sepals, the stamens, the pistil, and the axis of the flower itself (Fig. 21). As has been mentioned, in addition to these floral nectaries there are extrafloral ones. Because they have nothing directly to do with pollination, we shall ignore them here.

Let's look at a few flowers to get a concrete idea.

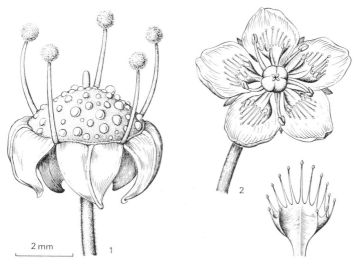

Fig. 21:
When the air is humid, the exposed nectar gland of the ivy (*Hedera helix*) becomes covered with droplets of nectar (1). The grass of Parnassus (2) (*Parnassia palustris*) attracts insects with sham nectaries, the stalked heads of which glisten like nectar droplets (Pl. 20).

Turk's-cap lily (*Lilium martagon*) (Pl. 19): Here the nectaries are recessed in six hair-covered grooves at the bases of the light violet, upward-curving petals. A hungry insect must push its proboscis into this groove, a difficult task because the petals of the lily are smooth and slippery, so that most insects cannot walk on them. The main insects that suck the nectar of the Turk's-cap lily are hawkmoths (Sphingidae, Lepidoptera), for they can hover above the flower while feeding.

Iris (*Iris variegata*) (Pl. 19): This flower also secretes nectar at the bases of the petals (the falls). The arrangement of the parts of the flower to ensure cross-pollination by the insects lured into its depths is described in Chapter 4.

Buttercup family (Ranunculaceae): A number of members of this family produce their nectar in special "nectar leaves" (Fig. 22). Those of the globe flower (*Trollius europaeus*) are five to ten narrow, light yellow, spoon-shaped petals within the flower. The blue, bell-shaped flowers of the alpine clematis (*Clematis alpina*) also conceal around a dozen nectar leaves of simple structure. More complicated nectar leaves are found in the monkshood *Aconitum napellus* and columbine *Aquilegia vulgaris*, two flowers that even at first glance appear highly differentiated. In the monkshood, two nectar leaves are hidden in the upper, helmet-shaped petal. Each has a long stalk, at the end of which is a small bowl-shaped structure that both produces and stores the nectar. In the columbine the nectar is found in conspicuous external structures, upward-pointing conical petals that taper to a hooked spur.

Sweet violet (*Viola odorata*): Not all spurs serve for both production and storage of the nectar. In the sweet violet, for example, the nectaries are set on the stamens and project only into the base

◊
Fig. 22:
Nectaries of flowers in the buttercup family. (1) Nectar scale at the base of the petal of *Ranunculus*; (2) in the columbine (*Aquilegia*) the conspicuously spurred nectar leaves stand up between the corolla petals; (3) conical nectar leaves of the hellebore (*Helleborus*); (4) the nectar leaf in the "hood" of the monkshood (*Aconitum*).

of the spur. The rest of the spur is used as a "syrup jug," into which the sweet juice flows as it is secreted.

Orchids (Orchidaceae): Yes, there are even spurs that contain no juice—for example, the lip spurs of *Orchis* species. But it would be wrong to conclude that this is a typical orchid characteristic. The spur of the fragrant orchid *Gymnadenia odoratissima*, with an odor like vanilla, and that of the broad helleborine (*Epipactis latifolia*) do indeed contain the nectar one would expect to find.

Roses (Rosaceae), gentians (Gentianaceae), and primroses (Primulaceae): Flowers in all these families, like many others, bear their nectaries at the base of the blossom, on its axis. Such nectaries are typically simple in structure.

Protection and Fraud

Although there are many cases of entirely exposed nectaries, an extreme example of which is the ivy (*Hedera helix*) (Fig. 21), there

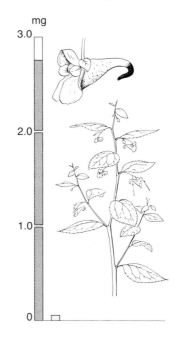

Fig. 23:
Nectar production by various types of flower. *Left*: orange balsam (*Impatiens biflora*); *middle*: rosebay willow herb (*Epilobium angustifolium*); *right*: goldenrod (*Solidago canadensis*). As a rule of thumb, nectar production increases with the size of the flower. The diagrams show the amount of nectar secreted per flower in twenty-four hours (tall columns left and middle, column on right) and the amount found in flowers to which insects had free access (short columns left and middle). The low rate of nectar secretion by single goldenrod flowers is compensated by the large total number of flowers, over 1,000 per plant. In the enlarged drawings of flowers the nectar is black.

are also a large number of flowers in which the nectar is hidden at the base of the flower, in a spur or in another container, closed off by a cover or a fringe of hairs. Such arrangements protect against evaporation, ensuring that the nectar does not rapidly thicken or even crystallize—in which case it could be taken up only by insects that can use their own saliva to dilute or dissolve it. On the other hand, they also shield the nectar from rain so that it is not so easily watered down or washed away altogether. The same thing is accomplished when the flowers close during bad weather or at night. Sometimes even brief shading by a passing cloud suffices to cause closing. Many a mountain climber has seen this behavior of the stemless gentian (*Gentiana acaulis*).

And when the time of nectar production coincides with the visit of a pollinating insect—as happens in many flowers pollinated by night, which may produce no nectar at all during the day—the flower ecologist is especially happy, because just such intimate relationships and sensible arrangements are the objects of his search (Chapter 26). The great differences in the amount of nectar pro-

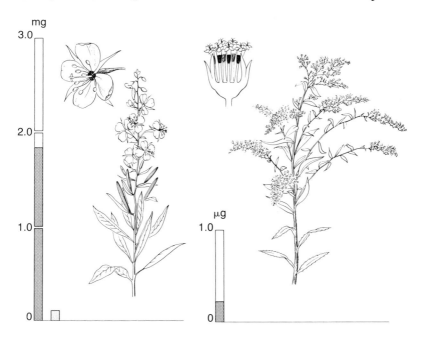

duced by various flowers are illustrated in Figure 23, which shows three quite different ecological flower types.

Not everything that looks like nectar is really nectar. In the flower of the grass of Parnassus (*Parnassia palustris*) (Fig. 21, Pl. 20) there is a circlet of small yellowish buttons that at first glance looks like a delicacy. But this impression is false. These structures are dry and have nothing to do with nectar; they are "sham nectaries." There have been reports, at one time questioned but recently confirmed, that flies can be attracted by them.[2] They tap the shining knobs with the proboscis, in vain of course. But the flower is not entirely fraudulent. Real nectar is secreted nearby, in the middle of the staminoids, the fingerlike outgrowths of which bear the sham nectaries.

11 Nectar-Collecting and the Biomechanics of the Lepidopteran Proboscis

Natural history is altogether based on comparison. External characteristics are significant, but not sufficient to distinguish organic bodies appropriately and reclassify them.

Johann Wolfgang von Goethe, "Zur Morphologie," 1820

How do the insects get the nectar inside their bodies?

It is not hard to guess that they use their mouthparts. Some lick the nectar up, and far more suck it in as though through a straw. This process is easy to observe when a butterfly flies up to a flower, unrolls its long proboscis, and inserts it precisely into the flower. But the whole process isn't quite that simple. A little thought about such observations raises many questions. Is there really a closed "drinking straw"? Which of the many mouthparts form it? Are there differences among bees, bumblebees, butterflies, moths, and flies? And furthermore, the straw alone is no good; where is the pump that creates the suction to pull the nectar into the pharynx? And finally: what can one do with a long straw when one is not using it—and perhaps even flying through the air with it?

The road leading to the answers may be a bit dry and stony for the unprepared reader. But the goal is worth the trouble. Constructed of an admirably adaptable and variable material, the cuticle, the mouthparts have made a great contribution to the remarkable success of the insects. Their manifold modifications range from hard toothed pincers to the elegant proboscises with which the butterflies draw nectar from the deepest flowers. Such modifications have enabled the insects to exploit almost all conceivable food sources. The proboscises used to suck nectar are part of this larger theme.

The Basic Material

Let us start with the basic structure of insect mouthparts, looking at a few fundamental principles in the classical, now rather unfashionable, method of comparative anatomy. First we consider the little-differentiated chewing mouthparts of a phylogenetically early insect. The cockroach, one of the favorite animals of the zoologist, is a good example (Fig. 24). From its mouthparts we can derive the special adaptations for the uptake of liquid food.

The actual chewing tools of a cockroach—and also of a beetle and a bee—are the paired upper jaws or mandibles. These are short, powerful cuticular structures that can be moved from side to side against one another. With their toothed edges, they make an effective pair of pincers. An insect uses its mandibles for biting and fragmenting.

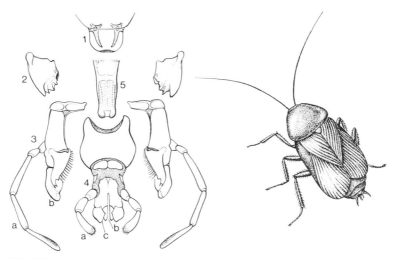

Fig. 24:
The mouthparts of the cockroach, a phylogenetically primitive insect. (1) Labrum (upper lip); (2) mandible (upper jaw); (3) maxilla (lower jaw), with a long maxillary palp (a) and the galea (b); (4) labium (lower lip) with the labial palps (a), the glossa (b), and the paraglossa (c); (5) hypopharynx.

As we look at the cockroach head from above, we find that the mandibles are followed by two more paired mouthparts, the lower jaws (maxillae) and the lower lip (labium), the basal parts of which have fused to form an unpaired element (mentum, submentum). Both the maxillae and the labium bear appendages—the palps, galea, glossa, and paraglossa.

All these parts are the raw material available to evolution for the construction of a sucking proboscis. It is fascinating to see how differently the different insect orders have made use of them.

The Bee Proboscis

In the honeybees and bumblebees both the maxillae and the labium are much longer than they are in the purely chewing type of mouth. The bee proboscis is certainly not an integral, completely closed structure. Rather, it consists of five individual elements, to which the zoologists have given the ponderous name "labiomaxillary complex." In the middle is the tongue (glossa). This is covered with long hairs and has a spoon-shaped end (Pls. 22, 23). With the tongue the bee reaches the nectar and licks it up, very like a cat licking milk. This is what happens: the nectar rises in the narrow spaces between the hairs of the extended tongue by capillary action, a passive process. Then the bee pulls its tongue back into the actual suction tube formed by the other four elements of the proboscis, which are grouped around the tongue (Fig. 25). (To be precise, they are the two sickle-shaped galeae of the maxillae and the two labial palps.)

This suction tube is joined by an airtight connection to a pump in the head, which allows the fluid that has risen passively between the tongue hairs and between the tongue and the tube wall to be actively pumped higher. The "motor" of the pump is a set of muscles attached to a cuticular framework in the pharyngeal region so that they can expand the pharynx. The whole thing works about like a bellows sucking in air. The increase in volume reduces the pressure in the pharynx, and the fluid follows the pressure gradient. Then the bee extends its tongue again and the process starts

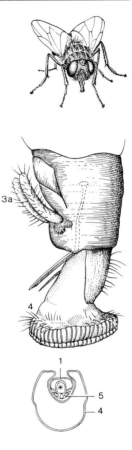

Fig. 25:
The variability of the mouthparts of insects, exemplified by the housefly (*Musca domestica*), the honeybee (*Apis mellifera*), and the cabbage white butterfly (*Pieris brassicae*). The numbers correspond to those in Fig. 24, so that the morphological modifications can be seen directly by comparison. *The actual feeding channel in the cross section.

over. When sucking up large drops the honeybee and bumblebee proceed more efficiently. They dip the suction tube itself into the liquid and the pump acts directly, without intermediate licking by the tongue.

When a honeybee or bumblebee does not need its proboscis, it folds it back like a clasp knife. This movement and the unfolding are easy to observe, if one is willing to take the trouble to wait by a flower a few minutes until a bee comes to visit.

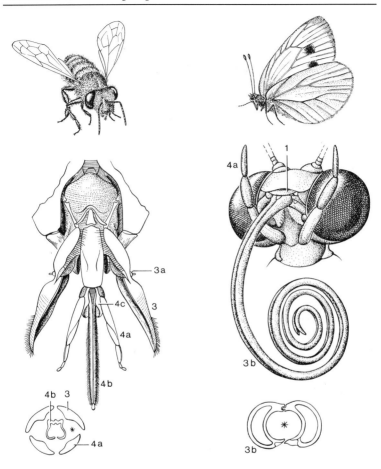

Despite all this specialization of the mouthparts for sucking, the mandibles of the bee are also well developed—unsurprisingly, for they are needed for eating pollen, building the comb, cleaning the beehive, and sometimes for fighting uninvited guests. Nicolaus Unhoch of Oberammergau put it well in his bee book of 1823: "Under the front of the mouth two large black teeth protrude; they are horny and sturdily built, because with them the bee gnaws at and builds everything."

The Suction Tube of the Lepidoptera

The lepidopteran proboscis, as a rule, is different (for the exception, *Micropteryx*, see Chapter 9). Lepidoptera are entirely dependent on liquids for food and pay no attention to the pollen. This is evident in various features; for example, the mandibles and labium have largely regressed, leaving only the middle appendages (the galeae) of the maxillae as functional mouthparts. These appendages form the proboscis, a small technical masterpiece (Pl. 24). If we cut it across like a salami, the cut surface (Fig. 25) shows clearly that it consists of two elongated tubes bent to form a banana shape in cross section, with the bananas touching one another at each end. This bending creates a central hollow space between the two. This is the space through which the nectar is sucked up. The two tubes around it contain muscles, nerves, and blood-filled cavities (Fig. 26).

The work of human hands appears more crude and less orderly the more closely one looks at it. In nature the situation is quite different; the orderliness remains and becomes progressively finer and more fascinating. Not until we look through the microscope do we discover how delicately and ingeniously the two tubes of the lepidopteran proboscis are coupled and interlocked.

On the inward-pointing edges of each half of the proboscis are dense rows of stable hooks, with practically no space left between them. Each hook has a small tooth on the inside of its broad base. Between this tooth and its associated hook on one side is inserted the tip of a hook of the other proboscis half, forming an intimate

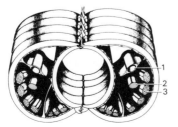

Fig. 26:
Lepidopteran proboscis in cross section. The actual suction tube in the middle is surrounded by the two crescent-shaped halves of the proboscis, which are complexly linked at top and bottom (1, air-filled tracheae; 2, proboscis nerve; 3, muscle bundle).

linkage. This arrangement has several technical advantages. First, it is watertight, so that the valuable nectar is not lost. Second, it prevents the two halves of the proboscis from springing apart when the pressure in the suction tube rises and the musculature changes the proboscis cross section. And third, like a zipper it is quite flexible in the longitudinal direction, so that the insect can extend the proboscis and roll it up again.

The dorsal coupling of the two halves of the proboscis is less stable than the ventral one. Basically it serves only as a closed roof over the feeding tube. Two rows of lancetlike plates overlap like shingles, and between the plates are the openings of the secretory ducts of gland cells. L.E.S. Eastham and Y.E.E. Eassa, zoologists at the University of Sheffield who have made the most thorough study of the structure of the lepidopteran proboscis[2]—they studied the cabbage white (*Pieris brassicae*)—have good reasons to suspect another ingenious mechanism in this arrangement. The secretion of the gland cells, so the hypothesis goes, is squeezed out as though from a toothpaste tube when the pressure in the blood-filled cavities on either side of the feeding tube rises as the proboscis is extended, and it then lubricates the "shingles" as they slide past one another and seals the gaps between them.

Resilin Saves Energy

The typical method of rolling the proboscis into a spiral is an invention unique to the Lepidoptera. The rolling is done with mathematical precision; the rolled-up proboscis is a perfect biological example of what the mathematicians call a spiral of Archimedes.[3] Zoologists have long known that the rolling of the lepidopteran proboscis occurs passively, without use of the musculature. The driving force is the elastic restoring force exerted by a rod in the outer wall of each proboscis half (galea). The principle is simple: if we take a curved steel spring and straighten it out, as soon as the external force is removed the spring snaps back into the original curved shape.

That the rolling-up process basically has nothing to do with muscles can be demonstrated by a simple experiment. The proboscis rolls itself together even when the muscles have first been destroyed. Indeed, it is possible to dissect out the elastic rod and show that it still rolls up—but the rest of the proboscis does not.[2]

The British zoologist H. Randall Hepburn, in recent studies in the Department of Zoology at the University of Bristol, found that the cuticular spring of the lepidopteran proboscis consists of resilin.[3] The discovery of resilin, about twenty years ago, aroused excitement and enthusiasm among all biologists and technical experts with an interest in useful materials. Here nature has produced a substance with properties closer to those of an ideal rubber than are possessed by any known artificial material. Resilin, then, is a rubberlike substance, a protein, with unusual elastic properties. What use can an insect make of such a thing?

So far resilin has been found in wing joints, tendons, and jumping joints. These are all places put under mechanical stress countless times during an insect's life; that is, they are exposed to shape-altering forces. It is an advantage that they return passively to their original state as soon as these forces cease to act. That saves energy. Physics classes in school have taught us that a body stores kinetic energy with less loss, and releases it again with less loss, the more elastic it is. Resilin meets this requirement excellently. Some loss, of course, it unavoidable. A certain percentage of the energy is always lost as heat associated with deformation and by the inevitable friction. Nevertheless, a system with a highly elastic component has the great advantage that it practically oscillates by itself when once set into motion.

The virtues of the high elastic efficiency of resilin are especially clear in the context of insect flight. On its long migratory flights, the desert locust stores in the wing suspension a large part of the energy in the downstroke of the wing, and makes use of the stored energy during the upstroke. And the same thing occurs during the upstroke; again a considerable fraction of the energy invested remains available for the downstroke. The wing suspension stores no less than 96 percent of the kinetic energy it acquires. The wing musculature must contribute only a small amount, giving the system a sequence of little "pushes" during flight to compensate for the energy losses due to friction and heat formation. The energy saving is enormous, in an animal that beats its wings twenty times a second, in some cases for hours at a time. Without resilin, the long flights of the locust would probably be quite impossible.

Now the advantages of resilin in the lepidopteran proboscis are also easily seen. Even a butterfly that lives for only a few warm summer months will unroll its proboscis some hundred thousand times to insert it into a flower, and just as often roll it up again when flying to the next flower. According to Bastian J. D. Meeuse,[7] a hummingbird hawkmoth (*Macroglossum stellatarum*) was seen to visit 194 violet (*Viola calcarata*) flowers in less than seven minutes! This is a notable achievement, even though we know that the moth is not so industrious all day long—and need not be, for it is feeding only itself.

The frequency with which the proboscis is extended and rolled up again is only one aspect of the miracle material resilin. It seems to be well placed in the proboscis for a second reason: a fine suction tube that must pass into the narrow corollas of flowers has no room for powerful muscles.

How Is the Proboscis Unrolled?

The lepidopteran proboscis is not entirely free of muscles, though. Muscles are involved in extending it. They are positioned in the two halves of the proboscis (Fig. 26), and their action is reinforced by a hydraulic mechanism—the pumping of blood into the cavities of the two proboscis halves.

After long controversy, beginning over a hundred years ago, about the mechanism by which the proboscis is unrolled, in 1955 Eastham and Eassa[2] proposed an explanation based on their studies of the cabbage white. Its central points are the following. The proboscis is not extended by hydraulic forces acting directly when blood is pumped into the cavities of the two proboscis halves.

That is, it is not like the familiar party toy with a paper tube that unrolls when one blows into the mouthpiece and then—in this regard very like the proboscis—snaps back into a roll because of the elasticity of a wire glued to the tube. Instead, the process is initiated by the fine muscle bundles set at an angle in the proboscis. When they contract they deform the proboscis cross section in such a way that the proboscis is forced to extend (Figs. 27 and 28). A prerequisite for extension is pressure within the cavities of the proboscis halves, which are permanently closed off at the end away from the body and can be transiently closed at the head end by a muscular valve. Such pressure has been shown to exist; it is produced when the animal pumps blood into its proboscis and closes the valve.

But why is this pressure so important? The situation can be visualized in terms of a piece of bicycle inner tube closed at both ends. First imagine it only slightly pumped up, so that it is limp. If we press this tube between two fingers we produce only a local deformation. The air can be displaced practically without resistance because the internal pressure is so low. But if we pump more air in and raise the internal pressure so that the tube is almost fully blown up, the same local force, or the reduction in cross section it produces, raises the pressure in the tube sufficiently to stretch its wall and straighten the tube. The inner tube is equivalent to the wall of the proboscis and the externally imposed force of the fingers, to the contractile force of the muscles attached within it.

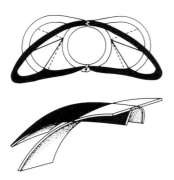

Fig. 27:
Above: Cross section of the proboscis when rolled up (white) and unrolled (black). *Below*: A diagram of the effect produced on a longitudinally curved piece of elastic material by pressing the sides together.

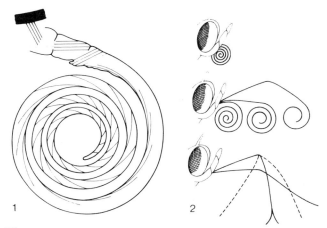

Fig. 28:
(1) Lepidopteran proboscis in longitudinal section, showing the internal muscles, and (2) in various positions before and during sucking.

In the Lepidoptera, as in the Hymenoptera, the suction pump operates on the principle of muscular expansion of part of the pharynx. The nectar moves down the pressure gradient toward the head, finally flowing into the digestive canal.

The Intricate Proboscises of Flies

Haven't we all swatted mosquitoes on warm days and secretly enjoyed this revenge for their bites? And doesn't every coffee drinker react just as strongly when he sees a fly licking his sugar cube? But hardly anyone gives a thought to what he is destroying, or even to the perfection of the apparatus with which his victims bite and lick. Our relationship to these hastily and unjustly condemned creatures could be considerably better. Take a lesson from the zoologists who, in obvious admiration, have given flies such prestigious names as "famous golden fly" or "royal glittering fly."

The mosquitoes and flies present us with a third variant of proboscis construction. A glance at the cross section reveals the essential features (Fig. 25). There are no less than three tubes, one within the next. The innermost is the actual food-sucking tube. Outside it is the saliva tube through which saliva flows out to dissolve food such as the coffee drinker's sugar cube, or to prevent coagulation of the host's blood where the mosquito has bitten. These two tubes are enclosed by a third. The comparative anatomy of the mouthparts has revealed that the feeding tube is a modification of the labrum (an "upper lip" above the mandibles), whereas the saliva tube is an elongation of the pharynx and the third tube is formed by the labium.

What has become of the mandibles and maxillae? In female mosquitoes they take the form of minute piercing spines. The males do not need them, for unlike the bloodthirsty females they are content to suck nectar.

In the housefly and its licking-sucking relatives (which include the hover flies) again we find that the mandibles and maxillae are nearly undetectable. The externally predominant structure is the massive labial tube with two terminal pads, the labella. (In case you are interested, these are a special modification of the labial palps.) Viewing them in the microscope, one is struck by the artful arrangement of transverse grooves and channels. These form an ingenious system of tubes slit along the outside—that is, open—and stiffened by hard skeletal rings so that they do not collapse. Their fine ends are only hundredths of a millimeter in diameter. The fly uses this tube system to take up fluid food, including nectar. The fine channels open into larger collecting channels, from which the food is transported into the digestive tract by the pharyngeal pump.

The fly labellum is covered with sense organs, which provide information about the food—its mechanical consistency and in particular its chemical composition. About 250 long hairs are especially conspicuous. All of them are innervated; they tell the fly, for example, how concentrated is the nectar into which it has just dipped its proboscis. Chapter 22 goes into more detail about this.

On the inner surfaces of the labella, around the mouth opening, are little teeth. These are used to scrape pollen out of a flower,

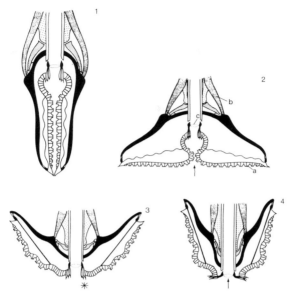

Fig. 29:
Various positions of the fly proboscis. (1) Resting position; (2) filter position; (a) System of fine canaliculi; (b) muscles; (c) mouth opening; (3) scraping position, in which the teeth (*) around the proboscis opening are exposed; (4) position in which the food can be taken into the feeding channel directly.

and by grating movements they can break down large food particles. And that is not all. The fly can employ its labella in quite different ways. Depending on how they are spread apart they can filter fluid food, soak it up with the tube system described above, or assist direct sucking through the mouth opening (Fig. 29).

The Rank Order of Sucking Proboscises

The length of a sucking proboscis plays a large role in view of the diversity of flower structures and the often hidden position of the nectar. It is a critical determinant of the kinds of flowers an insect can profitably visit—apart from the flowers that offer their nectar openly.

A few numbers will soon show how broad the spectrum is.[5]

Hymenoptera (worker individuals)
Honeybee (*Apis mellifera*)	6.5 mm
Bumblebees: *Bombus terrestris*	8-9 mm
Bombus hortorum	14-16 mm
Other bees: *Halictus* spec.	1.5-6 mm
Anthophora pilipes	19-21 mm

Lepidoptera
Cabbage white (*Pieris brassicae*)	16 mm
Hummingbird hawkmoth (*Macroglossum stellatarum*)	25-28 mm
Privet hawkmoth (*Sphinx ligustri*)	37-42 mm
Cocytius cluentis	250 mm

Diptera
Hover flies: *Syrphus*	2-4 mm
Volucella bombylans	8 mm
Drone fly (*Eristalis*)	4-8 mm
Bee fly (*Bombylius discolor*)	10-12 mm

The honeybee is by no means the star; this honor belongs to the lepidopterans, in particular the hawkmoths (Sphingidae). Many of them have exceedingly long proboscises, and those of the record-holders are 25 or even 30 cm in length: *Cocytius cluentis* of South America and *Xanthopan morgani* of Madagascar.

Xanthopan has been given the additional name *forma praedicta*, and Charles Darwin was behind it. For a long time botanists were mystified by the orchid *Angraecum sesquipedale*, which grows in the humid heat of the Madagascan jungle. It has a spur 20 to 30 cm long, which contains nectar at the end. The astonished botanists knew of no animal that could make use of this food source. Around the middle of the last century, when Darwin was shown the large, ivory-colored flowers, he prophesied to the botanists that there must be an insect with a proboscis long enough to reach the nectar at the bottom of the spur. Forty years later *Xanthopan morgani*, the predicted one, was discovered. It is very likely that it

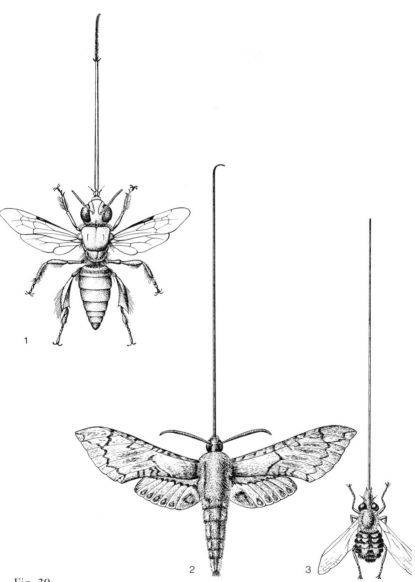

Fig. 30:
Particularly long sucking proboscises. (1) South American orchid bee
(*Euglossa cordata*); (2) South American hawkmoth (*Cocytius antaceus*);
(3) South African tangle-veined fly (*Megistorhynchus longirostris*).

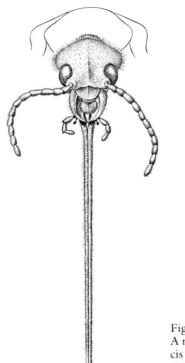

Fig. 31:
A rare case: a beetle with a long proboscis for sucking nectar out of deep flowers (*Nemognatha*).

feeds on this orchid and thereby pollinates it. Darwin had recognized the complex relationships in a process today called coevolution, and in so doing he was far ahead of most of his contemporaries (see Chapter 30).

In temperate latitudes there is no proboscis of comparable length. Even the monumental proboscis of the hummingbird hawkmoth, which measures 25 mm, is only a tenth as long. But it is enormous compared with the 6.5-mm-long proboscis of the honeybee, which is exceeded by all the temperate-zone bumblebees and many bee flies.

Exceptions within the group of bees are the orchid bees (Euglossinae) of the Central and South American tropics. Their proboscises are up to 30 mm long, and they are always extended as the bees fly about (Fig. 30, Pl. 35, and Chapter 23).

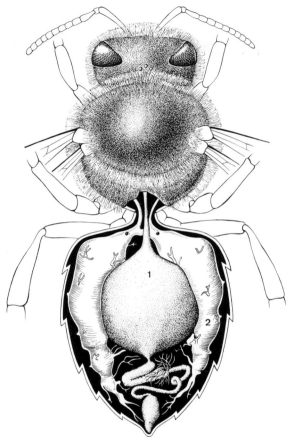

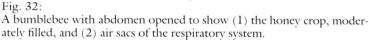

Fig. 32:
A bumblebee with abdomen opened to show (1) the honey crop, moderately filled, and (2) air sacs of the respiratory system.

Nectar and Honey

"The honeycomb is made from flowers, and the materials for the wax they gather from the resinous gum of trees, while honey is distilled from dew, and is deposited chiefly at the risings of the constellations or when a rainbow is in the sky."

When speaking of nectar people usually already have honey in their minds, and the two terms are sometimes, though incorrectly, used synonymously. Honey is what the bees make out of the nectar. It is not distilled from dew, as Aristotle erroneously assumed in the fifth volume of his *Historia animalium*. But how do the bees make the honey?

The first step is rather unappetizing. The bee vomits the collected nectar out of its honey crop (actually one should say nectar crop) (Fig. 32). Fellow members of the hive quickly take up the ejecta, only to regurgitate it themselves. Thus the nectar is repeatedly exposed to the warm air of the hive, and as its water slowly evaporates the nectar thickens. Finally it is stored in open honey cells of the comb. During this process a glandular secretion added by the bees has split the sucrose of the nectar into glucose and fructose, which are easier to digest. When the honey is ripe, the bees cover the honey cells with a thin layer of wax.

But there is a little truth in Aristotle's assertion that honey comes from dew. In addition to flower honey there are also "leaf honey" and "forest honey." The substance from which these are made is not nectar but rather honeydew, which—as though it had condensed out of the air like real dew—sometimes covers thickly the needles and leaves of trees. Its origin, again, may seem rather unappetizing to the squeamish; it is the excrement of aphids and scale insects. These insects pierce the sap conduits of the plants, suck out the juice with its concentrated sugars and proteins, and excrete the surplus in chemically modified form. The bees collect these excretions.

The manna of the Bible—the bread that God rained down onto the Jews in their journey through the desert—was honeydew, chiefly from scale insects that live on a species of tamarisk.

12   Insects See Colors

The corolla (except in a very few species) is colored—that is, colored other than green—so that it stands out clearly against the green color of the plants.

Christian Konrad Sprengel, "Das entdeckte Geheimnis der Natur," 1793

The pale yellow of the first primroses at the edge of a wood, the rainbow of color in a spring meadow, the radiant blue of the cornflowers against the gold of a ripe grain field—who could help thinking that the hues of the flowers must also be perceived by the insects? After all, are not the petals like bright banners surrounding the reproductive organs, to show the insects the way to food and to pollination?

"That most flowers secrete nectar, and that this nectar is protected from the rain, would be of no help to the insects if there were not some means of ensuring that they can easily find this food intended for them. Nature, which does nothing by halves, in this case again has found the most effective devices. First she has made sure that the insects discern the flowers from afar, either by sight or by smell or by both senses together. All nectar flowers are therefore decorated with a corolla, and very many emit a scent that to humans is in many cases pleasant, often unpleasant, sometimes unbearable—but always pleasant to the insect for which the nectar is intended. The corolla (except in a very few species) is colored—that is, colored other than green—so that it stands out clearly against the green color of the plants." So, almost two centuries ago, thought Christian Konrad Sprengel.[16]

But no matter how plausible insect color vision may be, there is no substitute for proof. Moreover, there is no way to find out whether insects perceive the colors in the way humans do; their perceptions may be quite different. With regard to scent, which is treated in later chapters, the same can be said.

Let us follow the development of experiments on these questions in the course of this century, to see how they—and hence the answers they provide—have become more refined and precise. In so doing, we can learn a great deal about the problem of color vision itself.

In 1910 Sigmund Exner, Professor of Physiology at the University of Vienna, described a quite simple experiment in a paper on the physical bases of flower colors.[5] Let him speak for himself:

"It was on a mountain slope covered with many flowers and low shrubbery, where all kinds of insects fluttered about from one blossom to another, that I amused myself by deceiving the insects with crumpled cutouts of colored paper, choosing a color that corresponded approximately to one of the many flowers in bloom and fixing the cutout to a stalk of grass or the like. An insect flying from one of these flowers to the next relatively often directed its route toward my cutout, apparently deceived. As far as I can remember, no insect ever settled on the paper, but they flew to within centimeters of it, and perhaps within fractions of a centimeter. These deceptions can only have been brought about by the color."

Much earlier, beekeepers had agreed that bees have color vision. It is an old custom to mark beehives—especially when they stand close together—with color to assist the bees in finding their way home. And in Exner's time there were a number of other good indications that bees see color. But there were also dissenters, probably the most famous of whom was the director of the Munich Eye Clinic, Carl von Hess. On the basis of a considerable number of experiments, he regarded fish and all invertebrates as colorblind. His most important finding was that when these animals were stimulated with light in the various spectral regions, the curve of stimulus effectiveness versus wavelength so obtained matched the curve representing the brightness distribution of the spectral colors for a totally colorblind human.

The First Experimental Proof

At this time (1914) the late Karl von Frisch, then only twenty-eight years old, produced the first unambiguous proof that bees have color vision. His experiments were demonstrated at a meeting of the German Zoological Society in Freiburg.[6] The result was unequivocal and clearly contradicted the world-famous authority Carl von Hess: the bees really see the colors and not the differences in brightness.

Karl von Frisch, who became a Nobel laureate in 1973 for his pioneering work in behavioral physiology, cleverly exploited a basic feature of bee behavior that enables the bees to be trained. Collecting bees do not fly randomly from one kind of flower to another, but rather keep returning to the accustomed kind until they no longer find food there; only then can they be induced by the dance of a collector from another group in the same colony (see Chapter 27) to turn to a new kind. Two days before the meeting of zoologists von Frisch had begun to feed his bees with sugar-water on a table with a checkerboard pattern. The feeding dish first stood on a blue square surrounded by squares in different shades of gray, ranging from black to white. After sufficient training the bees continued to fly to the blue paper even when its position on the "checkerboard" was changed and no more food was to be found. To make sure that olfactory sensations are not involved, one can cover the whole table with a glass plate. Of course von Frisch made sure that the mere presence of the feeding dish could not serve as a landmark; during the color test there was a dish, empty and cleaned, on each square. Moreover, during the training period von Frisch changed the position of the blue field every twenty minutes, to prevent the bees' being trained to a particular site.

In other experiments it turned out that the bees could not be trained to the gray fields or to a white or black one. The compelling conclusion: they really see and identify the blue as a color and not as a shade of gray. This result also disposes of an objection to the first experiment, that the ability of the bees to discriminate brightness might be so great that the shades of gray chosen were too far apart—that is, that the bee was being trained to brightness because none of the shades presented was identical in brightness to the color.

In this first epoch of experimentation, however, the bees seemed not to distinguish colors as well as humans do. Orange-red, yellow, and yellow-green papers were confused with one another, as were blue, violet, and purple-red. Finally, they could not distinguish pure red papers from black or dark gray: that is, the bees proved to be red blind.

In his *Erinnerungen eines Biologen*, published in 1962, Karl von Frisch wrote with great admiration about his famous uncle, the Professor Sigmund Exner mentioned above:[8] "The most important thing I learned from Sigmund Exner himself—to do clear-cut experiments and be cautious about drawing conclusions." Elsewhere in the book he gave a vivid description of Exner's help in the bee experiments. "In the summer of 1913 I was very anxious to bring the investigation to a successful conclusion, and therefore I sometimes trained my bees to colours at as many as four different places at once, rushing round from one to the next the whole day long in a frenzied effort to keep them all going. This stage I could just manage on my own. But for the experiments proper it was necessary after due preparation for all bees alighting on the various cardboard squares to be carefully counted. For this I needed helpers, and the members of our family group rose cheerfully to the task. My two gray-bearded uncles, the Professors Franz and Sigmund Exner, volunteered at once, and I could not have wished for better or more reliable observers."

The Spectrum of Colors

About a decade later the zoologist Alfred Kühn, together with the physicist Robert Pohl,[12,13] made a crucial methodological improvement in the training experiment, which in particular allowed him to find the limits of the spectrum visible to the bee. His training colors, unlike the pigmented papers used previously, were of very well defined wavelengths—either lines in a mercury spectrum or clearly delimited sections of a continuous spectrum.

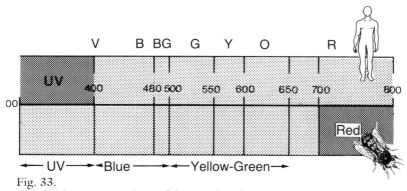

Fig. 33.
Color vision; a comparison of the wavelength spectra visible to humans and bees. Unlike the bee, the human cannot see ultraviolet (UV); unlike the human, the bee cannot see red (R). V violet, B blue, BG blue-green, G green, Y yellow, O orange. The numbers give the wavelengths of the light in nanometers.

The result: the spectrum of colors seen by the bee is about as broad as our own but is shifted toward the shorter wavelengths. The bee, then, is indeed insensitive to red (red is at the long-wavelength end of our spectrum), but it sees far into the ultraviolet region (ultraviolet is beyond the short-wavelength end of our spectrum) (Fig. 33). As a result of this difference, the bee sees the variegated world of flowers in color, but not in the colors we see. We shall hear a good deal more about this in Chapter 14.

Now let us cast a glance at some other insects; bees, after all, are not the only flower visitors.

Bee Fly and Hummingbird Hawkmoth

Between 1921 and 1926 Fritz Knoll[9] published, in the *Proceedings* of the Zoological-Botanical Society of Vienna, a number of very extensive experiments on a bee fly (*Bombylius fuliginosus*) and the hummingbird hawkmoth (*Macroglossum stellatarum*). Bee flies, like the housefly, are dipterans; the name comes from their compact furry appearance. Outdoors one's attention is immediately drawn to a bee fly when it stops still in the air, like a hover fly. The hummingbird hawkmoth is unlike most of the other moths in that it flies in the brightest sunshine.

First the bee fly. With its long sucking proboscis, visible even during flight because it cannot be folded up or retracted, the fly draws up nectar, preferring yellow, blue, and violet flowers. Fritz Knoll carried out many of his experiments in the maquis of the southern Dalmatian coast. He was especially concerned with the dark blue flowers of the grape hyacinth (*Muscari racemosum*). Because he wanted to learn whether the blue color attracts the bee fly from a distance, he first had to show that the intense scent of the grape hyacinth is not the decisive signal. It soon became apparent that the straight flight of the bee fly from one flower to the next is not simply upwind in scented air. As in the bees and bumblebees, the direction of the wind is irrelevant. Moreover, *Bombylius* also flies to odorless blue pieces of paper—and not to paper of other colors—when it is in the process of sucking from grape hyacinths. Finally, Knoll inverted glass tubes over the flowers. The bee fly circled around the tube just at the level of the blue flowers; even if there was a gap at the open end of the tube through which the scent could emerge it did not crawl into the tube from below. If a tube made of yellow color-filter glass was used in this experiment, *Bombylius* paid no attention at all to it, even if it was open at the bottom.

The conclusion: here the *long-range* action is visual, not chemical. Odor is important in *short-range* orientation (Chapter 29).

Knoll also succeeded in extending the gray-field experiments of von Frisch to the bee fly, using blue paper. The individuals attracted to the color had evidently been "trained" by nature itself, to the blue of the grape hyacinth (Fig. 34).

The hummingbird hawkmoth is also attracted visually by flowers a long distance away. The first evidence, again, comes from

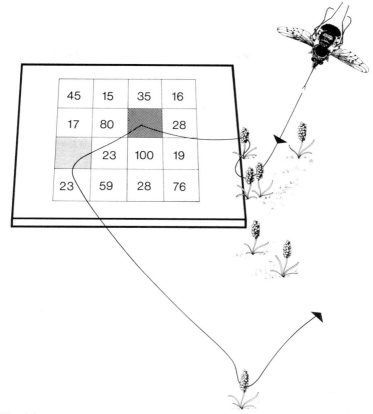

Fig. 34:
Bee fly (*Bombylius fuliginosus*) in an experiment. After visiting the blue
grape hyacinths (*Muscari racemosum*) it flies to the two blue squares (dark
and light blue) on the otherwise gray board, and only to them. The numbers in the other squares show the darkness of the gray.

experiments with flowers under a glass bell. These were supported
by Knoll's gray-field experiments; he used animals that had previously been sucking from flowers of the common toadflax (*Linaria vulgaris*) and were therefore presumably trained to yellow.
When he presented an orange, a yellow, and a blue paper together
with various shades of gray, they flew almost exclusively to the

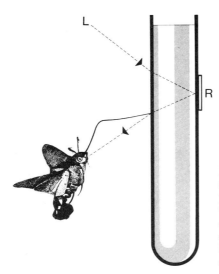

Fig. 35:
Hummingbird hawkmoth (*Macroglossum stellatarum*) in an experiment. It flies up to a reflector tube filled with colored liquid, and brings the tip of its proboscis to the spot where the beam of light emerges (L light source; R reflector).

yellow—again a successful demonstration of color vision. In the laboratory Knoll obtained more precise evidence by testing captured moths with colored artificial flowers, with colored solutions in the test tubes (Fig. 35), and even with spectral lights. The end result: these animals are very like the bees and bee flies in that they can discriminate two major color groups but confuse hues within each group; there is a blue group with pure blue, indigo, violet, and purple and a yellow group with pure yellow, reddish yellow, greenish yellow, and yellow-green. Another striking similarity to the bees is their red blindness, their inability to distinguish red from black.

Red Blindness and Ultraviolet Vision

Red blindness has also been demonstrated for bumblebees[10,11] and wasps.[3,14,20] The German wasp *Paravespula germanica*, a familiar uninvited guest whenever plum cake is served outdoors, can distinguish yellow and blue from one another. It also sees ultraviolet. Here, again, is a color sense consistent with that of the honeybee.

It now seems quite certain that red blindness is a feature typical of insects. But it is not an immutable law; as always in biology, one must be prepared for exceptions, for special adaptations, for "nature's playfulness"—things so often falsely regarded as unimportant curiosities of life, which nevertheless were and are of great elementary importance in the process of evolution (Chapter 30).

In the eye of the dragonfly larva (*Aeschna cyanea*) Hansjochem Autrum and Gertrud Kolb of the University of Munich[1] found red-sensitive sense cells. There is also evidence that New World tropical butterflies in the genus *Heliconius* and *Papilio troilus*, a relative of the swallowtail, can see red.[17-20] The cabbage white (*Pieris brassicae*) can distinguish red from gray, and when in search of food it flies spontaneously to red, yellow, and blue-violet flowers. And recently Gary Bernard[3] of Yale University showed that red vision is very likely in nine of the seventeen lepidopteran species in four families he studied.

Certainly further studies of other insects will bring to light more with red vision. Nevertheless, the other end of the insect color spectrum, the ultraviolet (UV), is certainly more important. That these wavelengths are detected by insects—though not by people—has been established in many very diverse species (Chapter 13). Often sensitivity is especially high in this region. In the case of flower-visiting insects, this sensitivity has its counterpart in an important and widespread feature of flowers, UV guide marks for visual short-range orientation. To us, these marks on the flowers are invisible. For the insects, however, they are like restaurant signs, leading to a meal that cannot be detected at a distance by either sight or smell (Chapter 15).

13 Visual Cells Dissect the Spectrum

Science advances but slowly, with halting steps. But does not therein lie her eternal fascination? And would we not soon tire of her if she were to reveal her ultimate truths too easily?

Karl von Frisch, "A Biologist Remembers," 1967

Although ultimately only a behavioral experiment—reflecting the performance of both eyes and brain—can show whether an animal discerns colors or not, investigation of the entrance portal—the eye—with the modern methods of neurobiology has brought fundamental advances in our understanding of the mechanisms of color vision. Study of single cells has elegantly demonstrated that the "applied" principles are astonishingly uniform throughout the animal kingdom. Given the need to deal with the physical properties of light, which are always the same, evidently the same "tricks" have developed repeatedly and independently in the course of evolution.

Enormous achievements have resulted. A human who is not color-blind can distinguish millions of hues and shades of color.[1] And the honeybee, which has become one of the best-studied objects of visual physiology, is hardly inferior in hue discrimination, at least in the spectral region to which it is most sensitive (blue-green to green).[5]

All these colors, at the moment they strike the eye, are not yet colors but rather physical signals having certain wavelengths or mixtures of wavelengths. One might think, then, that the eye has a separate receiver for each wavelength mixture. But that is not

so; the eye solves the problem much more ingeniously and economically. It manages with three types of receivers, visual cells that
in a sense dissect the light into three components. Their visual
pigments absorb light from particular regions of the spectrum especially strongly—different regions in each case.

The brain processes the messages arriving from each of these
three cell types and, so to speak, reassembles the components. All
our subjective color sensations are determined by the relative proportions of the three components and by what the brain makes of
them.

Trichromatic Color Vision

Thomas Young, the extraordinarily gifted Englishman—linguistic
genius, physician, physicist and decipherer of Egyptian hiero-
glyphs—inferred a three-component mechanism as early as 1801.
Hermann von Helmholtz, the greatest German physiologist of the
nineteenth century, who also did more than anyone else to advance research into the mechanisms of hearing, confirmed Young's
proposal in his investigations of anomalies in human color vision
and the colored afterimages in the eye. He concluded that the eye
contains the following three types of visual cells: type 1, most
sensitive to long-wavelength light (red to green); type 2, most
sensitive to light at intermediate wavelengths (orange to blue-green);
and type 3, most sensitive to short-wavelength light (yellow-green
to violet). According to Helmholtz, the selective stimulation of
cells of types 1, 2, or 3 gives rise to the color sensations red, green,
and violet, respectively.

Since the early 1970s we have known that there are indeed three
kinds of color-sensitive visual cells in the human eye. Because of
differences in their visual pigments they are particularly sensitive
in three different regions of the color spectrum: the yellow region
(at c. 570 nm), the green region (at c. 530 nm), and the blue
region (at c. 440 nm). A nanometer (nm), in which light wavelength is usually expressed, is equal to a millionth of a millimeter.

Back to the bee! Apart from the shift of the visible spectrum toward shorter wavelengths (UV vision, red blindness), it is not the differences from the human eye that are astonishing, but the similarities to it.

It was a notable success when, in the early 1960s, the zoologist Hansjochem Autrum, who took over Karl von Frisch's professorship in Munich, with his colleague Vera von Zwehl[2] first demonstrated directly that the color-analyzer properties of single visual cells long demanded by theory are actually present in the bee eye. This achievement required extensive technical preparation and the development of the most delicate methods, for it was necessary to insert a microcapillary with a tip diameter of at most a thousandth of a millimeter into a visual cell itself only about seven-thousandths of a millimeter in diameter, while keeping the cell functional as long as possible.

To understand why this was done, one must know that there is an electrical potential of about 70 millivolts across the membrane of a sense cell (inside negative). When the sense cell is stimulated by illumination of the eye, this potential changes. In the case of the bee eye it becomes smaller the stronger—that is, the brighter—the light stimulus (Fig. 56). The microcapillary mentioned above is a fine glass tube drawn out to a point at the end. The physiologist fills it with a potassium chloride solution or some other electrically conducting liquid and uses this electrode to measure the voltage across the cell membrane and to see how it changes. Some of the difficulties encountered in such electrophysiological experiments are associated with the production of the electrodes, accurate penetration of the cell by means of a precision micromanipulator, and the avoidance of even the smallest vibration. And, of course, with the presentation of stimuli having exactly the physical properties desired. It is no wonder, then, that it sometimes takes years before such experiments succeed, and that the zoologist attempting them relies on the collaboration of physicists, electronics experts, and, not least, a highly qualified mechanical workshop.

Many things that were exceedingly laborious twenty years ago have now become simpler because of improvements in apparatus and extensive advances in technical know-how. At that time such experiments were exciting crossings of new frontiers. I remember very well the day when I first witnessed one. I had just begun my studies in Munich and was overjoyed when the grand master, Hansjochem Autrum, under whose tutelage I eventually completed my doctoral thesis, opened to this young, ignorant student the door to the inner sanctum. The room was dark; I had to step softly in it. Now and then a colored light flashed. A mountain of apparatus. There could be nothing more suspenseful, even though the bee—no, the isolated bee head—was hardly to be seen.

To work out the properties of the visual cells as color analyzers, Autrum and his colleagues stimulated the eye with monochromatic (pure) spectral lights. All the colors had to have objectively identical intensities. This uniformity is crucial to the experiment, because the effect of wavelength alone was of interest, and not that of intensity. The amplitude of the voltage fluctuation measured across the cell membrane indicates the spectral sensitivity of the visual cell. It is greatest when the wavelength of the stimulus light is that most strongly absorbed by the visual pigment.

The result: Over 150 years after Thomas Young postulated that the wavelength continuum is broken up into several inputs, the diversity of the color-sensitive cells in the bee eye was shown directly. At first four cell types were found, but later studies, including training experiments, are consistent with the hypothesis that only three types of sense cell participate in the color-evaluation system of the bee (Fig. 36):[4,5,10]

Type 1—UV receptor (340 nm);
Type 2—blue receptor (463 nm);
Type 3—green receptor (530 nm).

That is, the postulated trichromatic system is indeed present.

The Discrimination of Hues

The agreement with the behavioral observations described in the preceding chapter is striking. UV vision and red blindness can be

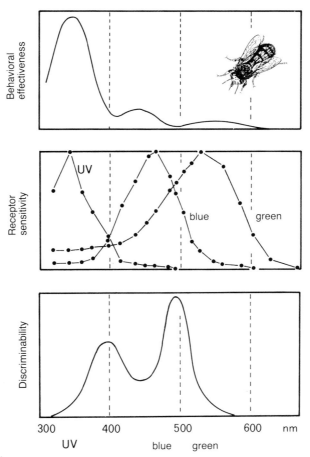

Fig. 36:
The color sense of the honeybee. A comparison of the effectiveness of
light stimuli of different wavelengths on behavior (*top*), the sensitivity of
the three visual-cell types (*middle*), and the ability to discriminate wavelengths found in behavioral experiments (*bottom*).

explained at the very first stage of the sensory process, by the
presence and absence of cells sensitive to these wavelengths. An
analysis by the Freiburg zoologist Otto von Helversen in 1975[5]
shows considerably more. Von Helversen, in extending the older
work of Alfred Kühn[8,9] and Karl Daumer[4] by training experi-

ments, found a very precise answer to the question: In which spectral regions can the bee distinguish different hues, and how well? In terms closer to nature: How well can the bee discriminate flower colors?

To find this out, von Helversen trained the bee to a spectral color; then he presented this color together with an alternative wavelength brought closer to the training wavelength at each trial, and measured the degree to which the two colors were confused (Fig. 36). The bee distinguishes the training and test colors especially well at two places in the spectrum: in the violet region (around 400 nm) and in the blue-green region (around 500 nm). Discrimination is particularly poor near the three wavelengths to which the three cell types are most sensitive. There is a plausible explanation for this. Two colors can be distinguished only if at least two types of visual cell are activated by them. The ability to discriminate is greatest when the change in wavelength most strongly alters the relative excitation of the two cell types. In the bee eye, this situation exists just at the two wavelengths at which the curves of spectral sensitivity cross. There could be no clearer result.

In the blue-green, the region of best discrimination, the bee can tell the difference between wavelengths only 4.5 nm apart. The best value for human discrimination is 1 nm. The bee comes very close to it.

The Ommatidium

Even without magnification one can see that the bee eye, like other insect eyes, consists of many subunits, each with its own lens (Pl. 25). These subunits are the ommatidia, so called from the Greek *omma*, eye. In the honeybee eye there are about 5,500 of them, and each contains nine visual cells arranged in a circle around the long axis (Fig. 37). At the center of the circle the membranes of the visual cells are deeply folded to form a fringe of densely packed projections, called microvilli. Here the visual pigment is located. The microvilli of all nine visual cells together form an axial rod,

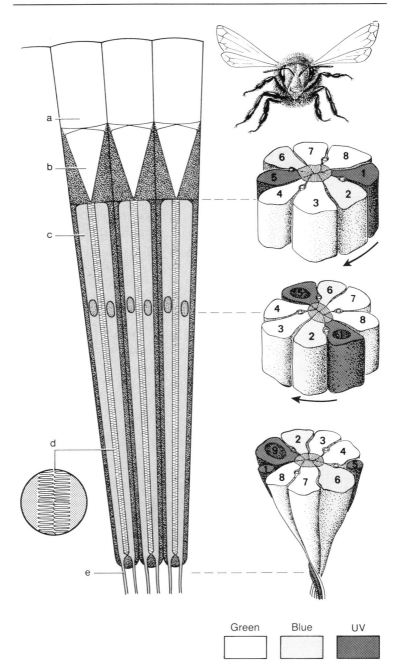

a

b

c

d

e

Green   Blue   UV

the rhabdom. The light collected by the lens passes through the rhabdom. In doing so, it alters the visual pigment, which in turn causes the change in the voltage across the cell membrane described above. The optical properties of the rhabdom and the surrounding cells are such that the light is transmitted efficiently, as in fiber-optics technology.

All three visual-cell types are represented in each ommatidium. That is to say, each point in the visual-field mosaic is simultaneously trichromatic.

Modern analyses of visual-cell optics have shown that the visual cells within an ommatidium are not just a group of independent receivers. In addition to sharing a common lens, they exert profound physical influences on one another. One of the important new findings is the lateral color-filter effect. The fringe of microvilli along each visual cell in the bee eye acts as an absorption filter set in front of the microvillar fringes of the other cells. The consequence is a greater wavelength selectivity of the cells, with no loss of sensitivity in their spectral region.[13]

The Way into the Brain

We would also like to know about the network of nerve cells that lies behind the sense cells and processes the signals from them, to remove the ambiguity unavoidably present at this level. That is, the signal from a visual cell depends not only on wavelength, but also on the intensity of the stimulus. Therefore the *relative* contri-

◊

Fig. 37:
Individual ommatidia in the eye of the honeybee. (a) Lens; (b) crystalline cone; (c) visual cell; (d) the central rhabdom formed by fine membrane projections of the individual visual cells and containing the visual pigment; (e) fiber from the visual cell that conducts its signals to the next processing station. On the right are cross sections of one of the ommatidia at different levels. It is constructed of nine sense cells, which except for the short cell number 9 are twisted about the long axis. Each ommatidium contains all three types of visual cells: green-sensitive (3, 4, 7, 8), blue-sensitive (2, 6), and ultraviolet-sensitive (1, 5, 9).

butions of the visual-cell types to the total activity must be determined, so that color can be separated from brightness. Sensory physiology is still far from a complete explanation of the processes in the optic ganglia and the brain that underlie color vision. But the discoveries that have already been made in the bee are exciting enough.[11]

The visual pathway in the bee brain comprises nerve cells of functional types that—like the sense cells themselves—have also been found in higher vertebrates such as the rhesus monkey. Even more interesting, the way they are connected to one another also resembles the vertebrate organization. Here, again, the similarity of the problem in the two cases has evidently resulted in comparable solutions.

An important principle is the determination of the relative contrast in pairs: brightness as compared to average brightness (broadband neurons), and UV as compared to long-wavelength light (opponent-color neurons). That is, whereas the events in the visual cells themselves are consistent with the Young-Helmholtz component theory, the brains of both higher animals and bees contain mechanisms not incorporated in that theory. They do, however, fit very well into another theory, now 100 years old—the opponent-color theory of the Leipzig physiologist Ewald Hering. Hering based his theory on psychophysical results, in particular the finding that in our sensations certain colors exclude one another—red and green, for instance, or yellow and blue. The responses of the central nerve cells that are excited by one color and inhibited by the other are quite consistent with this idea.

Often there is a long and arduous road to travel before very old theories can ultimately be established beyond all doubt. The seemingly simple question as to whether or not the flower visitors can perceive their colors has been refined step by step. Thanks to brilliant, but also patient and persistent experimentation, color vision has now become one of the best-studied areas of sensory physiology.

Plate 13   127

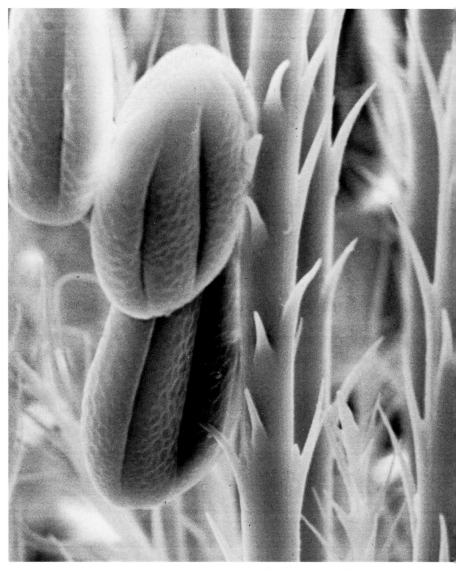

Pollen in the hairy coat of a bumblebee head. Small hooks act together
with the pollen glue to ensure that when the bee visits a flower and is
powdered with pollen, the valuable food sticks to the hairs. Magnification
1,450 ×.

The hairs covering almost the entire body surface of the bee constitute an important organ for pollen collection. Feathery hairs of this type make a dense fuzz in several places, as here on the leg of the honeybee (*Apis mellifera*, femur of the hindleg). Magnification 325 ×.

Plate 15 129

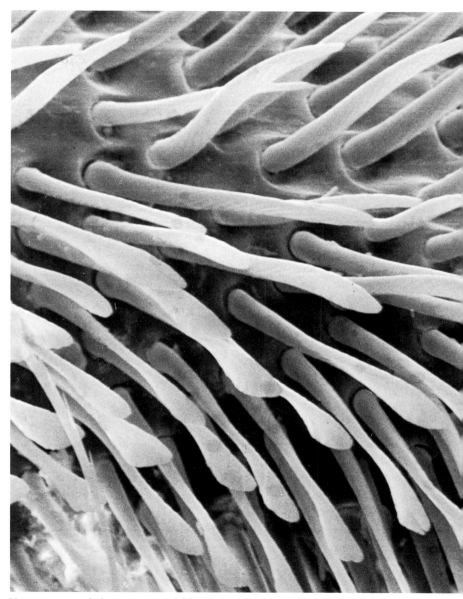

Hymenopteran hairs are very variable. These are found on the foreleg
(tarsus) of the bumblebee *Bombus lapidarius*. Magnification 450 × .

The first tarsal segment on the hindleg of the honey bee is especially large and especially important in pollen transport. On the inner side is a regular brush, made of ten rows of stiff downward-pointing bristles. With this the bee, while flying to the next flower, brushes the pollen out of the hairs covering its body. Magnification 87 ×.

Plate 17   131

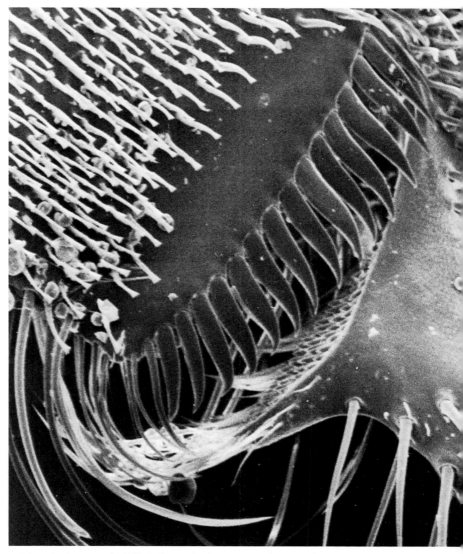

With a single row of stiff bristles at the lower end of the hind tibia the bee combs the pollen out of the brush (see Pl. 16) on the opposite hindleg. The pollen compressor or tarsal spur, situated directly opposite the comb, pushes the pollen from the comb onto the outside of the tibia and up into the basket (see Pl. 18). Magnification 130×.

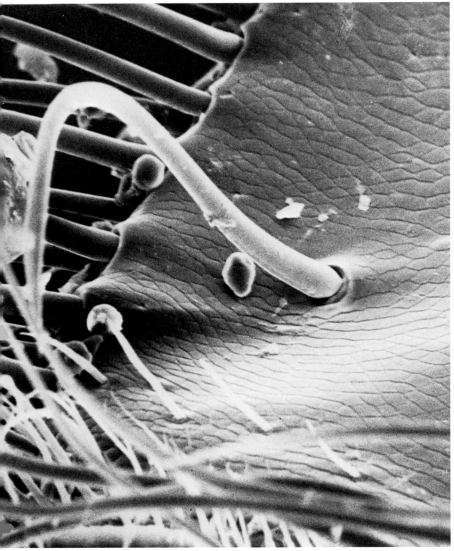

The organ in which the pollen is ultimately loaded for transport in bumblebees and honeybees is the basket on each hindleg, a smooth, hollow on
the outside of the tibia. It is fringed by sturdy inward-bending hairs. In
our picture, of the honeybee basket, a thick, curved bristle for anchoring
the pollen packet is clearly visible (cf. Pl. 9). Magnification 325 × .

Plate 19   133

The Turk's-cap lily (*Lilium martagon*) takes its name from the turban shape of its flowers. Here the nectaries are in a hair-covered groove on the upper surface of each of the six petals. A hungry insect must push its proboscis into this groove—a difficult feat for small insects, which slip on the smooth surface of the petal. Thus the main pollinators seen here are hawkmoths, which hover under the flower while sucking with their long proboscises. The anthers of the Turk's-cap lily hang down on flexible stamens, swinging in the air, and dust the moths with pollen from above. Hawkmoths usually fly in the evening hours, when the odor of the lily is particularly intense.

The iris *Iris variegata*. To the Greeks Iris was a goddess of light, the rain-bow suspended between heaven and earth as a messenger from the gods to humans. The iris flower has several features to assist pollination. Its structure is clearly visible here: (1) three large, spreading outer petals (the falls) with a highly contrasting pattern of brownish-red stripes, (2) three pure yellow inner petals (standards) inserted between the outer ones, (3) a petal-like style arm over the inside of each fall, beneath which are the stamens. Like the striped pattern, the long-haired beard of the falls proba-bly helps the insects find the way to the nectar. But it is also thought to have a second function: it forces the visiting insect, often a bumblebee, to contact the stigma on the underside of the style arm on its way to the hid-den nectar. Finally, the beard is also thought to attract insects by its re-semblance to pollen.

Plate 20   135

The wreath of small, glistening, yellowish buttons in the flower of the grass of Parnassus (*Parnassia palustris*) is a sham nectary. The buttons are dry. They attract mainly flies, which explore them in vain with their proboscises. The insects are led to the real nectar in the depth of the flower by the honey smell. The thick anthers ripen before the stigma; the grass of Parnassus is a protandrous plant. Ultraviolet photography has shown that the petals reflect UV only weakly. But the longitudinal stripes do not reflect it at all, creating for the insect a contrast invisible to us.

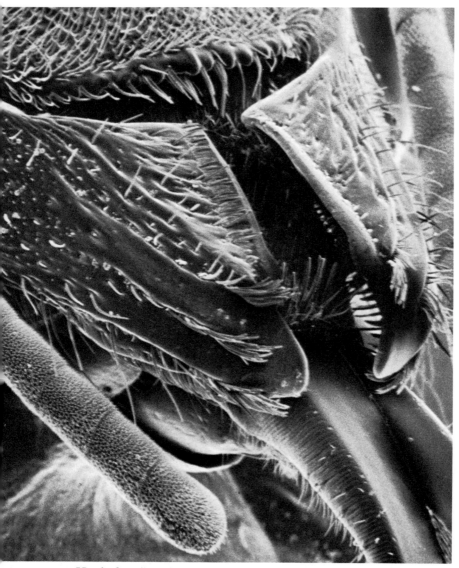

Head of a solitary bee in the group of abdominal collectors (Megachilidae). The most conspicuous structures are the two segmented antennae and the powerful mandibular pincers, beneath which the proboscis emerges. Magnification 120 ×.

Plate 22   137

The tongue (glossa) of the proboscis of a bumblebee (*Bombus agrorum*).
Note the dense hairs covering it and the spoonlike tip, both of which are
important in sucking nectar. Magnification 200 ×.

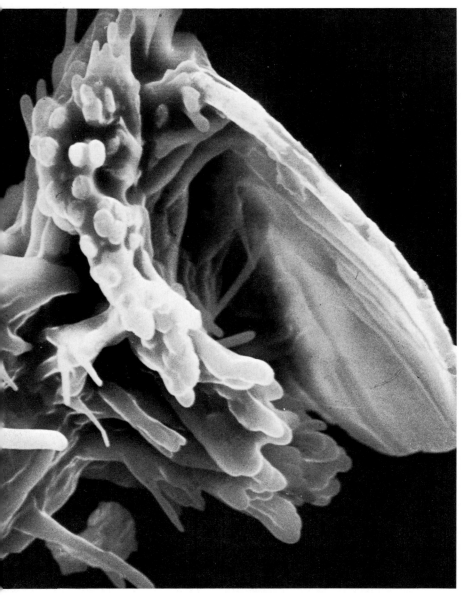

The spoon at the end of the tongue of the proboscis of *Bombus agrorum* magnified 1,080 ×.

Plate 24   139

The proboscis of the numphalid butterfly *Vanessa urticae*, rolled up in a spiral. Magnification 55 ×.

14   Bee Colors and Flower Colors

The data-processing system thus operates with physical and chemical processes, but it provides something quite different from a physical analysis of what is seen.

Hansjochem Autrum, "Die biologischen Grundlagen des Farbensehens," 1964

The shift of the bee spectrum by about 100 nm as compared with our own (Fig. 33) means that the honeybees—and probably most of the other flower visitors as well—see colors very different from those seen by humans, although the underlying principles are surprisingly similar. The colorful summer meadow is also colorful to the bee, but the picture is not the same.

As for humans, the spectrum of light visible to the bee can be

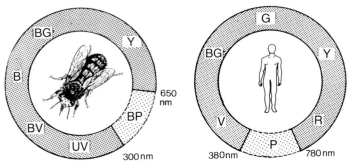

Fig. 38:
The color circle of the bee and that of humans (cf. Fig. 33).

represented as a circle in which all the colors are joined to one another by intermediate hues (Fig. 38). The intermediate hues can be produced by the additive mixing of three primary color regions. In humans these are blue-violet, green, and red, whereas in the bee they are ultraviolet, blue, and yellow. In color television, by the way, the primary colors are blue, yellow, and red. Sectors of the color circle opposite one another form complementary color pairs. In the bee, these are blue-green and ultraviolet, yellow and violet, and bee-purple and blue.

The color circle is closed by mixing the ends of the spectrum; in man, with the purple hues produced by mixing violet and red, and in the bee with bee-purple, a mixture of ultraviolet and yellow.[2] The bee does not confuse bee-purple with any other color. Of course, we cannot know how bee-purple looks to the bee, but we do know that the bee perceives as distinct colors not only ultraviolet itself but also mixtures of ultraviolet with other colors.

Another of these mixtures is bee-white. It is produced by mixing all three of the primary colors or complementary colors in a particular ratio. If we filter out the UV component of bee-white light, the remaining light appears to the bees in the complementary color, blue-green. When other colors are removed, corresponding results are obtained.

Bee-Black and Bird-Red

Such color mixtures can be created, by rather elaborate methods, in the laboratory of the sensory physiologist; but of course they do not exist only there. Mixed colors also occur naturally in flowers, and in very many cases they include UV. Because it is invisible to us, we have many surprises in store when we try to look at flowers as though through a bee eye. Karl Daumer[3] studied no fewer than 204 flowers closely in this regard. His method: the flowers were photographed through three color filters in succession; the transmission bands of the filters corresponded to the three primary color regions of bee vision. The blackening on the photograph in each case was then compared with a calibrated gray scale so as to quantify the reflection in each color band.

A few examples will show what happened.

1. Yellow and yellow are two different things. The auricula (*Primula auricula*) (Pl. 26) and the globeflower (*Trollius europaeus*) reflect almost exclusively in the yellow, with at most 1 percent in the UV. Therefore their flowers are also yellow to the bee; to be cautious, we say "bee-yellow" because we cannot know what subjective color sensations the bee has—we cannot even be absolutely sure about those of our fellow man. The marsh helleborine (*Epipactis palustris*) also reflects mainly in the yellow region. Despite the additional but much weaker reflection in the blue-green, it counts as another bee-yellow flower. But the situation is quite different in the case of the marsh marigold (*Caltha palustris*), which appears such an unsurpassable yellow to us (Pl. 26). It is one of the bee-purple flowers, for the light it reflects contains up to c. 5 percent UV in addition to the yellow. In other bee-purple flowers the UV component can be as great as 40 percent. Examples are the mullein (*Verbascum*) (Pl. 30) and the rock-rose (*Helianthemum nummularium*) (Pl. 3).

2. Blue can also be more than one color to the bee. Whereas the stemless gentian (*Gentiana clusii*) (Pl. 4) reflects by far the most strongly in the blue region and therefore is also blue to the bee, bee-blue, the blue of the birds-eye speedwell (*Veronica chamaedrys*) contains considerable UV and is therefore bee-violet.

3. Finally, many flowers that look white, pink, or mauve to us look different to the bee eye, namely bee-blue-green. These reflect strongly in the yellow and blue regions but not in the UV, so that they appear to the bee and other insects as its complementary color. The mountain avens (*Dryas octopetala*), the foxglove (*Digitalis purpurea*) (Pl. 30), and the wild cherry (*Prunus avium*) are examples.

4. The differences among the red flowers are particularly easy to understand. If no UV is reflected, the color is bee-black. But red flowers that reflect UV are bee-ultraviolet. The brilliant red corn poppy (*Papaver rhoeas*) (Pl. 2) is a typical bee-ultraviolet flower.

Its central pollen guide is bee-black (Chapter 15). Otherwise, bee-ultraviolet is a rather uncommon color. The color that looks pure intense red to our eye is also rare in temperate latitudes. There are many red flowers, but their red almost always contains a considerable blue component. Therefore they tend to look purplish red to us—in any case, not pure red.

In the tropics pure or yellowish red is much more common, and it is thought to be associated there with pollination by birds such as the humingbird (Trochilidae). Because most insect pollinators do not see pure red as a color, such flowers are to a certain extent an unoccupied ecological niche, available to the birds that do see red. As early as 1931 Otto Porsch[11] made an extensive study of the occurrence of "bird-red" flowers. His findings show that glaring, often yellowish red is indeed found in all families of flowering angiosperms for which bird pollination has been demonstrated. On the other hand, not every flower known to be pollinated by birds is bright red. But it is certain that "bird-red" is a particularly valuable color for long-range attraction. It stands out starkly from all the colors of the background and is clearly visible even in the early morning and late afternoon—at times when many birds prefer to fly.

The extreme scarcity of bright-red flowers in the temperate-zone flora can be explained by the red blindness of most of the pollinators there. This assertion is supported by the fact that temperate plants do produce bright-red fruits. Barberries, rose hips, strawberries, the fruits of the mezereum and the yew—all these are meant for the eyes of the birds that eat them and thereby assist distribution of the seeds.

The Bee-Gray Background

Let us return to the insects. First, training experiments have demonstrated directly that the bees in fact see all the bee colors just mentioned and can distinguish them from one another. Now consider another thing: the visual conspicuousness of a flower to a foraging insect clearly depends not only on the color of the flower itself but also on the contrast with its surroundings. To our eyes, this background is predominantly green. But the insects see it as bee-gray slightly tending to bee-yellow, for the following reason. A leafy expanse that looks green to us reflects about equally intensely in all regions of the bee spectrum. In other words, the achromatic component of the reflection is large.[3] Therefore the flowers stand out optimally, as colored spots on a colorless background. And now we also understand why it is no disadvantage to the bees that they have difficulty in distinguishing yellow, the color of so many flowers, from a narrow-band green stimulus. Conversely, it is no longer surprising that the many greenish flowers as a rule are not insect flowers but, like the grasses, are pollinated by the wind.

Favorite Colors

When an inexperienced insect is offered a choice of various colors, it soon becomes apparent that the insect has certain favorites. Put more precisely, certain colors are more effective; they have a higher stimulus value.

For the bee, ultraviolet is especially attractive and blue-green, least so (Fig. 36).[2] Day-flying butterflies find little attraction in greenish blue to blue-green models, and some species fly spontaneously most often to red and purple.[5] The hover fly *Eristalomya tenax* and the blowfly *Lucilia* have a strong preference for yellow, even when they are no longer choosing without previous experience but have been trained, for example, to blue.[8,9] For bumblebees, colors in the blue-violet-purple region are particularly effective stimuli.

Countless observations have been made in this area of research, but for our purposes the above examples should suffice. I find much more interesting the findings that indicate a direct relationship among flower color, stimulus value, and natural selection. Consider an example from the very recent literature.

The wild radish (*Raphanus raphanistrum*), a bothersome weed to the farmer, in England grows in wild populations with a white and a yellow variety. The yellow form reflects ultraviolet in addition to yellow and hence is bee-purple to the insects. The white form reflects uniformly over the entire visible spectrum, and hence is one of the quite rare bee-white flowers.[6] Do these differences have any adaptive value to the plant? Do the insect visitors prefer one of the two flower colors? Q.O.M. Kay, at the University College of Swansea, tested this possibility very thoroughly and directly in field experiments.

The most frequent visitors of the wild-radish flowers were bumblebees and, to a lesser extent, bees. Cabbage white butterflies (*Pieris*; especially *P. rapae, P. napi,* and *P. brassicae*) routinely accounted for up to 15 percent of all visits, and hover flies (*Eristalis arbustorum, E. tenax*), for 5 percent. Both the cabbage whites and the hover flies showed a clear preference for the yellow flowers as opposed to the white. In one of the populations studied by Kay 60.8 percent of the flowers were yellow. Of the total visits by cabbage whites and hover flies, 87.7 percent and 100 percent, respectively, were to the yellow form. The question of the stimulus value of a flower color, then, is not only of academic interest. Flower-color polymorphism can have an adaptive value, keeping evolution in progress by reducing the reproductive chances of a competing variant. Conversely, one can easily imagine that the difference would persist, that the one variant would not drive out the other, if the pollinating insects belonged to different species, with different favorite colors.

In a later chapter we shall be concerned with the learning of colors, the ability to relate food and color to one another. Under natural conditions this ability, at least in the case of bees, plays a greater role in the choice of flower color than does the inherent preference for a particular color, to which the insect flies spontaneously.

The Chestnut Lowers the Flag

All this imaginative diversity in the color, shape, and scent of flowers is the method by which the individual species keep themselves distinct from one another. Each combination is special in the true sense of the word, and causes the food-seeking insects to remain true to that particular species as long as possible, carrying the right pollen to the right stigma in an energy-conserving and reliable way. Herein lies the great difference from the random nature of wind pollination.

Once pollination has occurred, however, the special signal of the species becomes an encumbrance. Usually pollination is followed by rapid fading of the flowers. When bumblebees collect food from horse-chestnut trees (*Aesculus hippocastanum*), they can often be seen to avoid the older flowers. The yellow nectar guide on the upper petals of the young flowers gradually becomes discolored, turning first orange and eventually carmine. Only in the yellow and initial orange phases does the flower secrete nectar.[7] Bees and bumblebees rapidly learn the difference. Success teaches them to associate food with yellow, which they can readily distinguish from carmine. The advantage: greater economy in the work of collecting. The corresponding advantage to the chestnut: more frequent visits to—and hence pollination of—the younger flowers. Incidentally, the discoloration is accompanied by a change in the scent of the flower.[10]

15 Visual Signposts on the Flower

It turns out that these patterns and forms are peculiarly restricted, that the immense variety that nature creates emerges from the working and reworking of only a few formal themes. These limitations on nature bring harmony and beauty to the natural world.

Peter S. Stevens, "Patterns in Nature," 1974

"Now, when an insect attracted to a flower, whether by the beauty of its corolla or by its pleasant smell, alights: it will either detect the nectar immediately or it will not, because the nectar is located in a hidden place. In the latter case Nature comes to its aid, with the nectar guide. This consists of one or more spots, lines, dots, or figures of a color different from that of the corolla as a whole, so that it stands out more or less strongly against the color of the corolla. It is always just where the insects must crawl in if they want to reach the nectar." So far we have spoken of colors only in the context of long-range orientation by insects. But once one has arrived at the restaurant, one must still find the door. This was also clear to Christian Konrad Sprengel, as the quotation shows. His "nectar-guide theory" greatly advanced the understanding of the reciprocal relations between insects and flowers.

Many flowers bear visual guide marks that show the visitor the way to the food once it has landed. Occasionally the nectar and pollen guides for this short-range orientation are very conspicuous to our eyes. In other cases we can see them only by making the ultraviolet visible.

Petals are frequently multicolored, and in such cases the entrance to the flower is often colored in distinct contrast to the surroundings. Let us go outdoors and look at some examples; they can be found on all sides.

Rings: The birds-eye primrose (*Primula farinosa*) and, very similarly, the forget-me-not (*Myosotis*) (Pl. 27) are decorated by a yellow ring in the midst of the pink or blue of the petals.

Corona: In the poet's narcissus (*Narcissus poeticus*), the corona is yellow and red, contrasting conspicuously with the white perianth.

Spots: The white-blossomed alpine butterwort (*Pinguicula alpina*) bears an intense yellow spot on the lower lip. In other cases whole groups of such spots are found at comparable sites. Think of the purple corolla of the foxglove (*Digitalis purpurea*; see also the yellow *Digitalis*) (Pl. 30) with the many white-bordered dark-purple spots on the inside, and the Turk's-cap lily (*Lilium martagon*) (Pl. 19) with its dark-purple spots and a green nectar groove. In the marsh gentian (*Gentiana pneumonanthe*) rows of light green dots point the way to the nectar, and in the yellow monkey flower (*Mimulus guttatus*) (Pl. 5) there are orange spots.

Stripes: Striped guides are found in the wild pansy (*Viola tricolor*), the mallow, the meadow cranesbill, species of saxifrage, and many others.

Invisible Patterns

We already know that what looks like a solid color to us can appear distinctly patterned to the insects. Again, ultraviolet plays a major role—still another biological proof of the great ecological significance of the ultraviolet vision of the flower visitors. No elaborate apparatus is required to demonstrate ultraviolet marks. A simple camera with a filter that passes only ultraviolet shows us on black-and-white film how common they are. They are even more common than the marks visible to us; they coincide with places within an ultraviolet-reflecting area where the UV is not reflected but is strongly absorbed. Among the large number of examples are the following (see also Fig. 39).

Marsh marigold (*Caltha palustris*) (Pl. 26): the center of the flower absorbs ultraviolet much more strongly than the periphery; in the UV picture we see a large black spot.

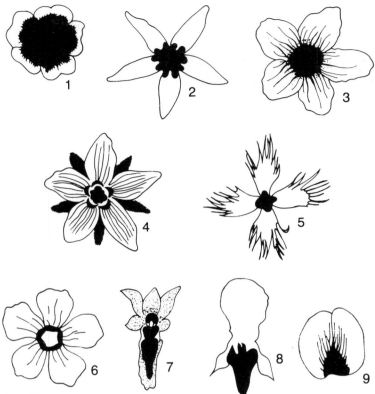

Fig. 39:
Ultraviolet marks of flowers. (1) Golden cinquefoil (*Potentilla aurea*); (2) marsh felwort (*Swertia perennis*); (3) white bryony (*Bryonia dioica*); (4) borage (*Borago officinalis*); (5) pink (*Dianthus arenarius*); (6) lesser periwinkle (*Vinca minor*); (7) Jersey orchid (*Orchis laxiflora*); (8) yellow archangel (*Galeobdolon luteum*); (9) broom (*Cytisus canariensis*).

Stemless carline thistle (*Carlina acaulis*) (Pl. 28): the tubular flowers do not reflect UV, but the surrounding silvery rays do.

Cornflower (*Centaurea cyanus*): only the infertile display florets reflect UV.

Gentian (*Gentiana germanica*): the fringes at the entry to the nectar of the German gentian are a UV-free nectar guide.

Broom (*Cytisus*) (Fig. 39): as in many butterfly flowers, the standard bears a UV-free mark at its base; in lip flowers the mark is on the lower lip.

A number of flowers have combined guide marks, spots that are both UV-absorbing and visible to us. To pick out a few more from the cornucopia of examples: the yellow spot of the alpine butterwort (*Pinguicula alpina*) and the green dots in the tube of the marsh gentian (*Gentiana pneumonanthe*) are combined guideposts of this sort. Conversely, the visible patterns of the Turk's-cap lily (*Lilium martagon*) (Pl. 19) are not visible in ultraviolet, for the entire surface of the petals reflects no ultraviolet.

Pollen and Nectar Guides Wherever We Look

These discoveries are mainly due to the work of two people, Hans Kugler[5] and, in particular, Karl Daumer,[1] a student of Karl von Frisch. F. E. Lutz[7] photographed flowers in UV as early as 1924, though he could not fully appreciate the patterns he observed. Still earlier, Karl von Frisch[3] noted in the course of his famous studies on bee color vision that the most common color combinations of flower marks and the surrounding area (in ninety-four cases he examined) were yellow-blue and yellow-purple, orange-blue and yellow-violet, or white combined with various colors. Thinking back to Figure 38, we remember that these are all highly conspicuous color contrasts for bees.

From Hans Kugler's[5] extensive studies we know in detail how extremely widespread pollen and nectar guides are. In disk, funnel, and bell flowers (see Chapter 3) he found guide marks in about 50 percent of the 259 species examined, and in stalked-plate, head, and lip flowers, in about 70 percent of 281 species. Of 57 species of butterfly flowers, no less than 88 percent had such a mark. When no UV mark is present on the petals, as a rule at least the pistil and stamens are conspicuous by their UV absorption. Flowers with no UV mark at all, such as the field rose (*Rosa arvensis*), the alpine snowbell (*Soldanella alpina*) (Pl. 4), and the garden monkshood (*Aconitum napellus*) (Fig. 22) are indisputably in the minority.

These numbers support the hypothesis that the nectar and pollen guides are functionally significant to the pollinators. The more complicated the structure of the flower, and the more hidden the nectar, the more likely it is that some such mark will be present. So what else could it be but a guide for the insects?

But even this evidence is not a proof of the correctness of Sprengel's nearly two-hundred-year-old theory; however plausible, it all comes down to the experiment.

The Demonstration of Function

Adherents of Sprengel's ideas were long opposed by people who thought that flower marks were a functionless whim of nature. Clear proof of the relationship Sprengel correctly discerned so early was slow in coming. In 1926 Fritz Knoll,[4] a professor at the University of Vienna, showed that the hummingbird hawkmoth (*Macroglossum stellatarum*), the day-flying hawkmoth with a broadened hind end, points its long proboscis toward the deep yellow nectar guide when it is hovering over flowers of the common toadflax (*Linaria vulgaris*). It seems obvious that the moth is trying to find the way to the nectar in the spur of the flower at just this point. The experiment to demonstrate this was a simple one, and its result was correspondingly convincing (Fig. 40).

Between two spikes of the flowers Knoll set up a few single flowers in their natural position, sandwiched loosely between glass plates. The gap between the plates allowed the odor of the flowers to escape at the edges. When the moth had emptied the spurs in one flower spike, it started toward the other. On the way it passed by the mounted flowers, at which it immediately pointed its proboscis in an attempt to push it into the flower. With the glass in the way, of course, it failed, and eventually it flew on to the second spike.

The behavior of the hawkmoth shows, for one thing, that its approach to the flower is visually controlled. The scent of the flowers would have attracted it to the edge of the glass plate, where the odor could emerge. But this never happened. For another thing,

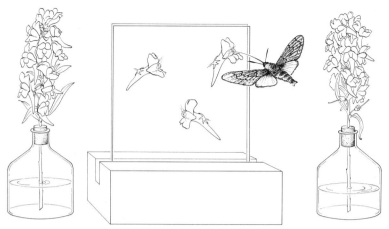

Fig. 40:
The hummingbird hawkmoth (*Macroglossum stellatarum*) in an experiment to demonstrate the effectiveness of the nectar guides of the common toad-flax (*Linaria vulgaris*). The moth's proboscis leaves traces exactly over the nectar guides of the flowers mounted between the panes of glass.

the tip of the proboscis, still damp from the preceding flower visit, left traces on the glass plate. They were exactly over the nectar guides—even when Knoll did the control experiment of cutting the nectar guide out of the flower and attaching it to the flower at another place. And the same thing happened even when instead of a real flower he presented artificial ones, elliptical objects with nectar guides attached.

The Bumblebee's Approach

In the case of bumblebees, it is much more difficult to evaluate the goal-directedness of their activities on flowers. Having landed on a flower, the bumblebee often covers most of it with its massive body. Therefore Aubrey Manning of Great Britain[9] worked with greatly enlarged models of flowers. These models were 12-15 cm in diameter, and as a rule were blue with a yellow mark of various shapes.

We ask ourselves: do bumblebees pay attention to flower marks?

Again, the strategy of the experiment is quite simple. Manning first accustomed his bumblebees to a training model, in the middle of which they were rewarded by the discovery of sugar syrup. After about an hour the bumblebees had accepted the model well enough that it could be replaced by test models. Then the bumblebees flew to these, even though they were not identical to the training model in the features of interest—their outlines and markings—and had no food. Observation of the bees' behavior at the test models provided a number of important results.

1. The bumblebees are initially attracted most strongly by the edge of a model flower. They fly directly to it from a distance as great as c. 60 cm. This is their first detectable reaction to the model flower. They steer toward the edge even though they had previously been trained with the feeding dish in the center of the training model, and they do it even when a nectar guide clearly indicates the middle of the test model. With large real flowers such as the poppy (*Papaver*) the same thing can be observed in the field.

2. From a distance, the bumblebees fly equally often to models with and without nectar guides. But once they have arrived above the flower, the nectar guide evidently becomes quite attractive; the bees hover longer over models with guide marks, land on them more frequently, and then often follow the nectar guide to the center of the model. In Manning's opinion, the nectar guide as an overall pattern has no significance to the bumblebees. He thinks they find their way to the middle of the flower because once they have reached the edge they follow converging lines. In the case of circular nectar guides, according to Manning, it is their colored contour that distracts the bee from the attractive edge and leads it to the middle.

The pioneer of bumblebee pollination ecology, Hans Kugler,[6] draws different conclusions from his own experiments with small models. He finds that the stimulus value of real flowers in long-range attraction is increased by the guideposts. In his observations, the bumblebees visit bluish asters with yellow central disks more frequently (62 percent) than asters of a single color, and small disk models with darker radii more frequently (71 percent) than those with none. He obtained similar results with blowflies (*Lucilia*).

Work on these questions is still in progress, and certainly more discoveries will be made. In a recent study the Englishman J. B. Free[2] confirmed that flower marks are also attractive to the honeybee. His models were yellow and had a diameter of 30 mm. The bees landed in considerably larger numbers on models with a blue nectar guide than on pure yellow models (Fig. 41). Dotted lines

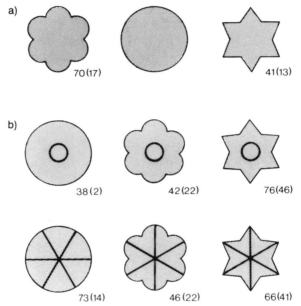

a)

70(17)   41(13)

b)

38(2)   42(22)   76(46)

73(14)   46(22)   66(41)

Fig. 41:
On which flower models does the honeybee land most often? (a) First the bees were trained to the round model in the middle (diameter 3 cm). Then in the test they were confronted with the round model and one of the two others; they clearly preferred each of the two alternatives to the round model. The number of landings is shown below the models, with the value for the round model in parentheses. (b) In the second series of experiments the bees had to choose between the pure yellow model with no marks and a model of the same shape with blue marks. They preferred the model with the nectar guide. The number of landings is given under each model, with the value for the model without a nectar guide in parentheses.

increased the attractiveness of the models more than solid lines; similarly, a group of dots was more effective than a ring. Lines pointing toward the middle caused the bees to land especially often in the middle if they had previously been trained to look for food there, but not otherwise. A black spot in the middle made the model clearly more attractive to the bees.

Although there are still a number of open questions in the details of the problem, it is now certain that the guide marks are biologically significant, as can be demonstrated by the behavior of the insects. This relationship can be a crucial feature in evolution biology, if mutants without marks or with relatively unattractive ones have a reduced chance of reproducing because of ethological isolation. There are concrete examples of such a phenomenon. Bees and wasps stayed away from markless mutants of *Monarda punctata*, a lip flower, when they were growing among "normal" plants.[10] The lower lip of the "normal" flower bears a row of dots.

The Head-Proboscis Reaction of the Bee

Let us close with an experiment that shows directly and convincingly that the bees also notice UV patterns on flowers and use them for short-range orientation to the nectar. When a honeybee reaches the nectar guide it stops abruptly, jerks its head down and unfolds its proboscis to suck. Zoologists know this as the head-proboscis reaction. Is it actually elicited by the guide mark? A simple deception experiment proves that it is.

The ray florets of a species of sunflower (*Helianthus rigidus*) with the typical open round inflorescences absorb ultraviolet at their inner ends. Together they form one of the characteristic UV marks (Fig. 42). Now we can pull these florets out one by one, turn them around and put them back together to make a flower shape in which the UV-free parts are around the outside. Then something very curious happens.

The bee walks from the middle outward to the nectar guide and there, at the edge of the UV-free spot, extends its proboscis.[1] It

Fig. 42:
In an experiment on the head-proboscis reaction the ray florets are
plucked out and put back together in the reverse orientation, so that the
UV-absorbing marks (black) point outward.

has been deceived, revealing to us that it expects to find food
where the nectar guide is, even if the way to it—in this case, by
the trick of a clever zoologist—leads in the wrong direction. Because even untrained bees behave in this way, we must count the
head-proboscis reaction as a form of innate behavior. The bee does
not need to learn to associate a UV-free area on the flower with
the nectar source.

The bee is not the only insect that must extend its proboscis at
the right moment. Flies and lepidopterans also have a proboscis
reaction. For them, though, the trigger is not visual but chemical.
Bristlelike sense organs on the tips of the feet signal to the brain:
"I am standing in sugar." The brain understands the message and
commands the muscles: "proboscis out!" (see Chapter 22).

16 Do Guide Marks Imitate Pollen?

> . . . But I have painted a series of color studies, simple flowers,
> red poppies, blue cornflowers and forget-me-nots, white and
> red roses, yellow chrysanthemums—and in them sought for
> contrasts of blue with orange, red and green, yellow and
> violet, sought the broken and neutral tones, in order to
> harmonize the brutal extremes. Tried to achieve intensive
> color and not a gray harmony.
>
> *Vincent van Gogh to H. M. Levens, 1887*

In recent years the interpretation of guide marks has been interestingly and, it seems to me, very importantly enriched. In this
new view they are not only signposts and notice-boards. Rather,
the hypothesis goes: many guide marks can be understood as pollen models, imitations of an original pollen signal.[2,4,5]

The idea is based on the following. In the evolution of the
flower, pollen was the original form of food for the insects. Only
later was nectar added. The primitive magnolia blossom is a pollen
flower; no nectar can be found there. Pollen itself, and still more
the anthers, are usually conspicuous in the flower because of their
color, shape, and position. Is the flower advertising with it? Do
pollen and anthers function as signals to the insects? That they do
is revealed by many different observations.

One is that there is often a striking color contrast between the
pollen/anthers and the petals. A frequent combination is yellow
anthers (which as a rule reflect no ultraviolet) against a blue, violet, or purple background. As we remember, these are complementary colors for the bees. Three examples: the pasqueflower (Pl.
12), the African violet (Pl. 29), and the blue-flowered iris.

Saving and Signaling

Further evidence of the signal function of the pollen is associated with the fact that not all flowers are so generous with their pollen as the poppy (Pl. 2) or the pasqueflower (Pl. 12). In fact, there is a general tendency to offer visitors as little as possible. But pollen conservation is a good policy only as long as the flower nevertheless remains attractive to the insects. To achieve both at the same time, various methods have developed.

One possibility is to offer "food pollen" in addition to the fertile pollen, the latter often being hidden. Food pollen looks like fertile pollen but is infertile. The insects are readily deceived, for they find the food they are looking for, and from their point of view its infertility is irrelevant (Fig. 15). Another possibility is to reduce the number of stamens and make the few that are left especially large and conspicuous. Think of the tulip and the African violet, and the potato flower, in which the gaudy yellow stamens form a narrow cone that juts far out of the flower (Fig. 20). As it happens, even European nobles once found potato flowers so beautiful and exotic that they adorned themselves with them.

Finally, flowers can resort to genuine deceit, swindling the insects altogether. Long hairs and knobs on the stamens give the impression of masses of pollen where in fact there is only a little, as in the flowers of the mullein (*Verbascum*) (Pl. 30). Even the stigmas, female parts of the flower, are sometimes used to imitate pollen. In female begonia flowers the stigma looks like a bunch of stamens; the insects come, but find no food at all. This is a particularly interesting case, for it shows us what an advantage hermaphrodite flowers have. One good reason for their evolution must have been that in plants with unisexual flowers only the male flowers were attractive, because only they had food—pollen—to offer. In bisexual flowers the presence of the pollen signal nearby ensures pollination of the stigma.

The greatest tricksters in their relation with the insects are the orchids. Often lacking nectar, and having pollen packets that cannot be used as food, they attract their pollinators with elaborate deceptions—real crime stories, to which two whole chapters will be devoted (Chapters 23 and 24). Here we shall mention only one of their ploys. It consists of exploiting the signaling action of pollen by the production of pollenlike powder, which comes from distended hairs and papillae on the lip.[1,3] Günther Ritter Beck von Mannagetta und Lerchenau, of the Royal and Imperial University of Prague, in 1914 gave the first detailed description and interpretation of this phenomenon.

Enough about pollen as a signal.

Concealing and Signaling

Now another factor enters. In addition to the increasing pollen parsimony in evolution, one finds a tendency to change from open flowers, equally accessible on all sides, to flowers of complicated structure (Fig. 94). Such modifications provide protection of the food from rain, wind, direct solar radiation, and unhelpful visitors, which eat without pollinating. The consequence: if the pollen itself is no longer visible, some visible evidence of its presence is required for the insects. And now we are back to the guide marks. They can often be interpreted as pollen models, especially in cases in which the real food is hidden in the flower. Even where nectar is the chief attraction for the insects, the signaling action of the anthers and the pollen (or the structure imitating it) is retained. This hypothesis has recently been very clearly formulated and confirmed by the Freiburg zoologist Günther Osche.[2] Abundant examples corroborate it. We need consider only a few of them to understand the basic points (Pl. 29 and 30).

Foxglove (*Digitalis purpurea*): there are only a few stamens, hidden in the flower; the reddish lip is marked with striking white-edged spots. Interestingly, these spots are lacking in the yellow foxglove; instead, at least in older flowers, anthers peer out of the corolla tube.

Alpine butterwort (*Pinguicula alpina*): again the stamens are hidden; glowing yellow spots, actually slightly elevated, imitate anthers.

Common toadflax (*Linaria vulgaris*): the lower lip bears orange-yellow spots, distinctly raised from the surface.

Broomrape (*Orobanche gracilis*): on the reddish brown style is a dumbbell-shaped brilliant yellow stigma, which along with the imitation of anthers by the begonia stigma is one of the best examples of "three-dimensional" mimicry. It looks like the two halves of an anther and is located directly in the opening of the corolla tube, concealing behind it the unprepossessing true anthers.

Not the least of the things that make biology such an attractive science is that it appeals so directly to our senses in so many areas. It would be rewarding to take a closer look at the colorful patterns on the flowers during one's next country stroll.

17 Form Vision

> In general, the problem is to selectively throw away most of the information.
>
> *Rüdiger Wehner, "Pattern Recognition," 1974*

Funnels, spheres, disks, spurs, gullets, lips, flags, large and miniature, smooth or jagged. Why are there flowers with such different shapes? Couldn't they all look the same?

Put in this way, the question sounds rather philosophical. But in the light of what we know about evolution, we can expect to find specific biological answers; from the fact that so much diversity exists it follows that some advantages for reproduction are involved. Diversity is not a luxury of nature, but rather one of its essential features, fundamental to the process of evolution (Chapter 30). Our excursion into color vision has made it seem plausible that the pollinating insects also detect shape and pattern and use them, as they do the colors, to distinguish species. The colors, after all, are not floating formlessly in the air.

Research on form vision and pattern recognition is a difficult undertaking, not only in the practical details of the experiments but even more with regard to the theoretical foundations. The difficulty is illustrated by the fact that technology, despite great effort and expense, has not yet succeeded in mastering pattern-recognition processes that seem quite simple in comparison with what a bee can do. Such research is well underway, and it will continue to occupy many laboratories for quite a while.

But shapes and shape recognition have such fundamental implications in the biology of the encounter between insects and flowers that, in spite of the problems that remain, I want to give at least some idea of the kinds of questions asked and the methods of answering them.

Mosaic Eyes

The many facets of the insect eye—3,300 in the housefly, 5,500 in the honeybee, 750 in the wood ant—all have their own small lenses, each with seven to nine visual cells in a conical arrangement below it (Fig. 37). Does the insect see a thousandfold world with its thousand lenses? No, the lenses break up the visual field into many small areas. For this reason the specialist speaks of mosaic eyes and vision.

The spatial resolution of an eye is entirely comparable to the "graininess" of a film, if for the moment we disregard the sensory and nerve cells and think only of the optics. The grain depends on how densely the ommatidia are packed. Two parameters determine resolution: the divergence angle and the acceptance angle. For short, we shall call them $\Delta\phi$ and $\Delta\rho$. Their significance is easy to grasp (Fig. 43a). The divergence angle is the angle between the optical axes of neighboring facets; it sets the limit of resolution. The acceptance angle tells us the size of the part of the visual field from which light enters each receptor. It is given as the width (at half its height) of the bell-shaped curve obtained when one moves a light source past an ommatidium and measures the incident light on the other side of the lens (Fig. 43a, 1). The absolute magnitudes of these angles in the housefly and the bee have been found to vary between 1.4 and 3.9 degrees.

The practical consequence of these angles? If we imagine that a striped pattern is passed in front of the eye, we can see how $\Delta\phi$ and $\Delta\rho$ limit what is perceived (Fig. 43). If the wavelength of the pattern (λ, equal to the distance between the leading edges of two adjacent black or white stripes) is smaller than $2\cdot\Delta\phi$, the brightness distribution is no longer represented correctly. Then the pattern seen has dark regions further apart from one another than they are in the actual pattern (c2 in Fig. 43). The contrast seen also does not always agree with the actual contrast, because each visual field $\Delta\rho$ measures only an average brightness. The part of the visual field in front of and below the animal, which is sure to

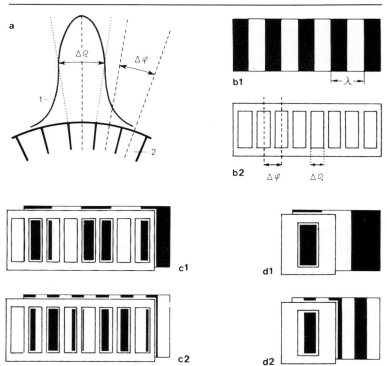

Fig. 43:
Aspects of spatial resolution by an insect eye. In (a) several ommatidia (2) are shown with their optical axes (dashed lines) and acceptance angles (dotted lines). (b1) A simple striped pattern, as a schematized example of a natural stimulus. (b2) Diagram of the receptor array. When the striped pattern is moved past the receptor array (c), the period λ of the pattern is transmitted accurately if it is above the resolution limit, whereas periods below the resolution limit seem to be larger than they actually are (c2). The limit of resolution is at λ = 2Δφ. Because each visual field Δρ measures only an average intensity, in the second case (d2) the measured brightness of each is also lower; the measured contrast, then, depends on the ratio between the acceptance angle and the wavelength of the pattern.

be especially important during visits to flowers, has an especially "fine-grain" representation. Here the angle between the visual axes of neighboring ommatidia is especially small.[15]

The Brain Produces the Picture

So far we have only scratched the surface of the problem of form vision—both metaphorically and literally. It cannot simply be a matter of reproducing the mosaic generated by the superficial array of receptors in all parts of the visual pathway, from the sense cells through the following stations of nervous processing. It would be exceedingly uneconomical to try to distinguish as patterns all the multitude of brightness distributions in the world entirely on the basis of the color and intensity of each element in the mosaic. There are countless combinations of them! In fact, pattern recognition involves processes of generalization and classification—the recognition of geometric correlations. The visual system does not discriminate all possible patterns from one another; the most biologically important ones must be sorted out from the crowd. The same is true of the other senses—the point is not to see everything, smell everything, or hear everything, but to reduce the superabundance of information to what is biologically important. A grasshopper listening to the symphony of chirps on a mild summer evening must be able to pick out the song of its conspecifics. A male silkmoth must pick out the alluring scent of his female from all the other odors.

In principle, the same thing holds for humans. It has been estimated that every second a quantity of information amounting to ten billion bits flows in through our sense organs, and from it the brain selects only about a hundred of the biologically most important.

The picture that an insect ultimately has of its surroundings is not produced in the eye itself any more than it is in humans. It is not simply a passive image. Therefore one should be careful not to take the analogy with a camera too far; like the idea of mosaic vision, it applies only to the most peripheral processes in seeing. The brain produces the picture.

The processes by which this is achieved in the insect brain are very hard to analyze, because the nerve cells are minute and lie close to one another in a small space. At first the arthropod brain was thought to be a comparatively simple apparatus, because it contains relatively few nerve cells. After all, there are only a few hundred thousand of them, as compared with a hundred billion in humans. But it has now become clear that the cells can be interconnected in a highly complex way, and that the word "simple" is quite inappropriate.

Behavioral Experiments on Pattern Recognition

First consider what insects can recognize, and how they behave when presented with patterns. The experiments are based on two different principles; in one case the animals make a spontaneous selection from a choice of patterns, and in the other they are first trained to a particular pattern (at which they are rewarded with food) and then their ability to discriminate patterns is tested, usually without a reward.

Many insects move directly toward black figures, choosing one of them when several are presented at the same time. The stimulus value of a figure is said to be greater, the more frequently this figure is approached as compared with others. Stick insects (*Carausius morosus*) approach a model more frequently, the more closely it resembles a food plant—that is, the more similar it is to a shrub.[10] Ants (*Formica rufa*) given a free choice prefer vertically oriented stripes to diagonal or horizontal stripes.[16] This immediately calls to mind the fact that they normally climb up trees to reach aphids and milk them. Insects living on the ground, such as some crickets (*Nemobius silvestris*), respond in just the opposite way, approaching a horizontal stripe pattern much more often than a vertical one.[11] For the blowfly *Calliphora erythrocephala*, dark contrasting areas, vertical contrast boundaries, and subdivided figures are attractive. Rudolf Jander, in these and many similar experiments, developed the concept of special neurosensory detector mechanisms that respond selectively to elementary characteristics of an optical pattern—for example, an edge at a certain angle, a figure contrasting with the background and oriented in a certain way, and so on.

Similarly, it seems reasonable that the honeybee (*Apis mellifera*) prefers highly subdivided figures when it is foraging for food—a checkerboard pattern, for example, rather than a black disk.[5] But when it is ready to return home, its preference reverses. Then the bees fly to the lowest-contour figures, which obviously bear the greatest resemblance to the entrance hole of the beehive.[9] Corresponding responses have been observed in the hornet *Dolichovespula saxonica*.[13]

Figural Intensity, Figural Quality, and Position in Space

That shapes are evaluated by insects according to entirely different "viewpoints" than are used by us was shown as early as 1915 by Karl von Frisch, in bee-training experiments. Remarkably, the bees could not distinguish a filled circle from a filled square or triangle, nor an X from a diamond or a pattern of four vertical stripes (Fig. 44). But each of the filled figures was readily distinguished from all the open figures, and conversely!

Total contour length is without doubt particularly important here. The term "figural intensity" is applied to this quantity, the "edginess" of the figure, whereas the nature of the pattern—whether round, square, composite, etc.—is termed the "figural quality" (Fig. 45). We have since learned that figural intensity loses significance when the contrast between figure and background is too great ($>$ 1:10). In this case, the filled figures are preferred spontaneously.[14] And it is also known that the discrimination of figures is based not only on the absolute contour length, but on the contour density—that is, the ratio of contour length to enclosed area.[2]

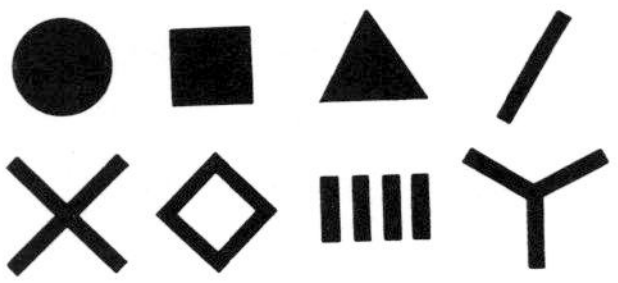

Fig. 44:
Whereas honeybees easily learn to distinguish each of the upper figures from any of the lower ones, they cannot discriminate within the upper or the lower group.

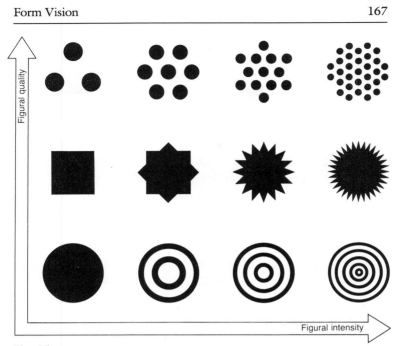

Fig. 45:
"Figural intensity" and "figural quality." The figures in a horizontal row differ in their figural intensity, and those in a vertical column, in their figural quality.

This is all rather complicated, and it shows that we are still far from a comprehensive understanding of form vision in insects. Very recently evidence has accumulated that in addition to richness of contour other properties are important in pattern discrimination. For example, bees can distinguish figures identical in area and shape, and hence in contour, by their orientation in space; vertical bars or crosses are distinguished from those at an angle. Tilting a cross by only four degrees is sufficient for the bee to tell the difference. Moreover, when trained to a cross at a particular angle, the bee will continue to prefer crosses at that angle even though their arms are shortened, reducing their total contour length.[17] Even a single bar can be shortened or subdivided optically, and if its inclination is unchanged it will still be preferred to a bar neither shortened nor geometrically altered but set at an angle different from that of the training pattern. The bee recognizes stripe inclination regardless of contrast, accepting white stripes on a black background as equivalent to the black stripes on white background to which it was trained. Reduced to a common denominator, these ingenious experiments—a remarkable achievement of Rüdiger Wehner at the University of Zurich—show that the orientation of a pattern is not only important but can even be successfully played off against its geometry.[18]

But if we throw these findings into the same pot with the results of the many other attempts to discern rules about the ability of insects, especially bees, to generalize, we must admit that the situation is not entirely clear. There are indeed a number of important pattern features such as contour length, inclination, size, and contour density, which in a given experimental situation allow one to predict which of a set of patterns of a certain type the bee will choose. But a comprehensive function, by means of which the experimenter could predict the response to any arbitrary pattern, has not yet been found. Those particularly interested in the problems of spatial vision in arthropods in general are referred to an extensive recent review by Rüdiger Wehner.[22]

Flowers as Visual Patterns

So far, the many natural flower shapes have not been studied specifically with regard to insect form vision. Here is a broad field for future research. But laboratory categories such as figural intensity and quality are not just snatched out of thin air. A carline thistle (*Carlina acaulis*) (Pl. 28), for instance, has high figural intensity while that of the corn poppy (*Papaver rhoeas*) (Pl. 2) is low. A funnel-shaped gentian (*Gentiana acaulis*) (Pl. 4) has a different figural quality from a butterfly flower like those of clover, sainfoin, or broom. Nectar guides also vary in these respects.

The comparison of laboratory experiments with field data can be fascinating, as the English zoologist Alan Anderson[1] showed a few years ago. He discovered that when the configurations of the natural nectar guides of many flowers are expressed in terms of the product of stripe width and stripe spacing, the value obtained comes very close to that found to be most attractive to bees in laboratory tests with various striped patterns.

What the Flying Insect Sees

When watching a movie, why do we not see the black strips between the individual frames of the film? If our eye is illuminated with single light flashes, we see them as separate events only if they come at a rate of no more than twenty per second. At a frequency above 20 Hz the stimuli "fuse," as seen by our eye. The so-called flicker fusion frequency has been exceeded. The real question here is: does a flying insect see the contours flashing past as individual brightness changes or as a long smear? Electrophysiological experiments indicate that the insect eye is quicker than ours. The moving surroundings do not cease to flicker until the rate of stimulus change reaches 200 Hz.[4] The response of a visual cell to a stimulus dies out rapidly; that is, it has a short time constant. This property increases the contrast, because the next stimulus does not overlap with remnants of the response to the one it follows.[23] In the insect brain, as in that of vertebrates, there are neurons that respond specifically to moved objects, and for some the movement must occur in a particular direction. This should not surprise us, for a rapid change of scene must be a stimulus situation of particular importance to flying insects.

Very recently research on pattern-recognition processes has taken an interesting new direction, with the precise analysis of insect flight behavior. When bees approach a vertically mounted pattern, they fly slowly around, one or two centimeters away from the pattern, before they land.[2,3,20] The flight path roughly copies the pattern; evidently the bees are scanning it visually and using this behavior to determine the resemblance between the training and test patterns. It may be that the bee can also make use of information about its own flight movement. The bee's on-board computer would work out something like this: narrow pattern, because short horizontal flight. That a comparison of the perceived picture with stored information shortly before landing can be important is also evident when one watches a bee approaching a plexiglass bottle containing food and a visual pattern; while still in flight the bee adopts a constant fixation position before landing at the opening of the bottle.[21] Whenever it flies up to the bottle, it fixates the pattern presented behind the tubular opening in such a way that the pattern falls on the same parts of the eye. This strategem, apparently, simplifies considerably the comparison of a stored picture with an actual picture.

18 Scent and Smelling

> But the irises I carried with me were more strongly scented in the mild coolness of the falling night; with a scent at once more penetrating and more vague, for one could not see the flower from which it flowed—a flower made entirely of scent, which in the shadowy solitude intoxicated body and soul.
>
> *Juan Ramón Jiménez, "Platero y Yo," 1965*

Odors are powerful forces in human life. From the fragrance of a familiar perfume to the stench of a sewer, they can awaken deep emotional responses and profoundly influence behavior.

In the animal kingdom, odors act in many different functional contexts: in acquiring food or attracting a sexual partner, in everyday social interactions, in marking off a territory, in repelling an enemy, in warning others of danger.

From the insect's point of view, the scent of flowers basically falls into the category of food acquisition, and that is what this chapter is about. For the time being we shall disregard the fact that there are also stinking flowers, sought out by flies as egg-laying sites, as well as flowers with a female-bee scent that causes male bees to try to copulate, and perfume flowers, from which male Brazilian bees collect a supply of an odor substance—probably in order to use it to label a courtship territory (see Chapter 23).

Scent Patterns

There is a very simple way to find out whether a flower has olfactory as well as visual guide marks—not a general scent perceptible to our nose, but rather characteristic odor spots, odor gradients, or an odor mosaic. One has only to cut the flower up neatly into the parts of interest and put each part into its own small closed glass container. After about ten minutes an experimenter makes an olfactory test of these samples, judging the quality and intensity of the smell. It is astonishing what Therese Lex[6] and Alexandra von Aufsess[1] managed to learn by such a simple procedure.

A brief summary:

1. Scent marks are even more common than visual marks. Of eighty flowers tested, no less than seventy-seven had one.

2. It is not only the nectar marks visible to us that are specially scented; the UV patterns also have an odor distinct from that of their surroundings.

3. Even flowers with no visual nectar guide usually have the approach to the food source marked by odor.

4. The human nose—and the brain behind it—can distinguish three kinds of differentiation in flower scents: *A* smells different from and stronger than *B*, *A* smells different from and just as strong as *B*, or *A* smells the same as but stronger than *B*.

Again, a few examples:

Marsh marigold (*Caltha palustris*) (Pl. 26): We have noted already that this flower, so brilliantly yellow to our eyes, on closer examination proves to have a very distinct UV nectar guide (Chapter 15). In addition, it has a scent mark. The odor of the basal part of the flower is of the same quality as that of the rest of the flower, but it is stronger. There is an odor gradient, increasing in the direction of the site of nectar secretion—in the marsh marigold, two depressions at either side of the ovary.

Spreading bellflower (*Campanula patula*) (Pl. 34): The situation here is the same; the intensity of the scent increases toward the base of the flower.

Horse chestnut (*Aesculus hippocastanum*): The striking yellow nectar guide smells stronger but with the same odor as the rest of the corolla as long as it is yellow. The conversion to red (see Chapter 15) is associated with a qualitative change in the odor.

Thus the flower visitors are informed not only visually but also chemically that nectar production has ceased.

Auricula (*Primula auricula*) (Pl. 26): The nectar is secreted at the base of the ovary. The bright yellow entrance to the corolla tube smells no stronger than, but different from, the tips of the petals and the tube they form.

Corn poppy (*Papaver rhoeas*) (Pl. 2): The nectar guide smells stronger than and different from the other parts of the flower. The same is true of the narcissus (*Narcissus poeticus; N. pseudonarcissus*), the nasturtium (*Tropaeolum majus*), the German iris (*Iris germanica*) and the pansy (*Viola tricolor*).

The food sources themselves, the nectaries and the pollen, are also usually marked by more intense or different scent.

Human Nose and Bee Nose

So far everything that has been said has been based on the responses of the human nose! How do insect noses compare? As the first step in answering this question, it is worth casting a glance at flowers pollinated not by insects but by birds. This is particularly interesting because the flower-visiting birds in general do not have a very well developed sense of smell.

To humans, bird flowers have little or no scent.[8] The various parts of the flower may be differentiated, but in contrast to the insect flowers the outer part of the flower smells stronger than the inner part just as often as the reverse. The pollen of bird flowers also has a fainter scent than that of insect flowers.

The older literature contains claims about the extraordinary performance of the bees' sense of smell. Whether they experience sensations similar to those we describe as, say, flowery or fruity will always remain a mystery. The experiments must be directed to different questions. The one that first attracts our attention is whether the insects recognize the same odor differences as are perceived by humans. That bees can be trained to odors has long been known.[3] Von Frisch, in 1965, in his delightfully simple language, described delightfully simple experiments:

"For training I used cardboard boxes with a hinged top and a flight entrance in the front. One box was supplied with the training odor and a feeding dish; beside it three others remained empty. Frequent change in the position of the training box prevented the bees from becoming acquainted with a definite location. For the test, four clean (usually new) boxes were set out in a different order, one of them with the fragrance but none with food, and the number of bees entering was counted. The intrinsic odor of the cardboard itself was not a disturbing factor, as control experiments with earthenware boxes showed. As odorants I used partly the fragrance of natural flowers in mineral oil (obtained by means of enfleurage), and in part essential oils, and as a control fresh-cut flowers also. In a test the trained bees would fly even to a clean perfumed box without food. That shows that they perceive the odor and use it as a cue."

To explore the bees' ability to discriminate scents, von Frisch set up whole batteries of boxes; for example, one box would contain the scent to which the bees were trained, and twenty-three others would contain twenty-three other scents. The bees pick out the training scent particularly readily when it has a flowery, fruity, spicy character to the human nose. Other odors, including those unpleasant to us—for instance, putrid odors like skatol—are difficult or impossible for them to learn. But they do detect such odors, for a flowery training scent is spoiled, as far as the bee is concerned, when such an unpleasant perfume is mixed with it. If they are trained to a mixture of two "pleasant" scents and then tested with the components separately, they fly to both.[4]

Of 1,816 odor pairs tested, the bees could distinguish the components in 1,729[12] (Fig. 46). We are dealing here with an extraordinarily fine nose.

Now back to the flowers and their scent marks. Are they really a mosaic of smells to the bees, the minute elements of which can be recognized individually at close range? Or is it more like a well-stirred odor soup? It is a mosaic. For the bee, too, the scent mark stands out from the rest of the flower.[1,6] Without question, then, there is a partner capable of noticing with what, how strongly, and where a flower perfumes itself.

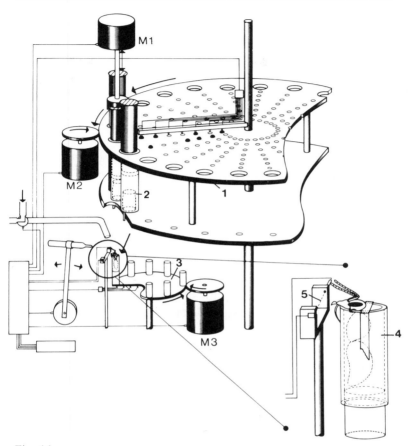

Fig. 46:
An automatic testing device, to determine whether the bee can discriminate the odor to which it has been trained from various alternative odors.
In the upper wheel (1), rotated by motor M2, there are twenty-seven sy-
ringes (2) each containing a different odor substance; in the lower wheel
(3), driven by motor M3, eight test bees are mounted in special bee hold-
ers (4). Each bee is presented with the various test odors one after the
other; the motor M1 depresses the plunger. When the training odor or
one mistaken for it comes up, the bee extends its proboscis, interrupting a
light beam (5) so that the response is automatically recorded. The turning
of the two wheels also occurs entirely automatically.

Olfactory Acuity

There is much to indicate that the olfactory sense of the bee performs very like that of humans. We have heard that bees are attracted by scents that smell flowery, fruity, and pleasant to us. And they are repelled by scents that we find unpleasant. Training experiments have shown that flowers odorless to us also have no odor to the bees.

But how about the acuity of the sense of smell? More precisely, how high must the concentration of an odor substance be for it to be just detectable? To anticipate the results: the olfactory acuity of the honeybee is not much different from that of man.[2,9,10] An experiment to demonstrate this goes as follows. For some time the bee is presented with sugar-water together with the training scent—for example, by placing the scent source in an open glass tube beneath the feeding dish. A test is then carried out to see how little of the training scent is just enough to cause the bees to prefer the dish under which it is placed to other, odorless dishes. The same thing can be done with people for comparison; this is simpler, because the subject can say in which of a series of samples the "training scent" is detected.

The thresholds in each case are between 1.9×10^9 and 4.5×10^{11} scent molecules per cubic centimeter.[10] The bee can detect lavender at a dilution of 1:500,000, rosemary at 1:100,000, and jasmine at 1:20,000.[2] It discerns flowery scents somewhat better than humans do, but with fatty acids its performance is worse.

These numbers are interesting in comparison with other animals. The peak performances in the animal kingdom are found in neither bees nor people. The list of champions is headed by the dog, the eel, and the silkmoth.

A dog can smell butyric acid at a concentration as low as 6,000 molecules per cubic centimeter.[7]

The eel detects β-phenylethyl alcohol at a concentration of 1,800 molecules per cubic centimeter.[11]

The male silkmoth, with its gigantic antennae (Pl. 31), smells the sexual attractant of the female when air containing only a thousand molecules per cubic centimeter is blown over the antennae. Then he begins to flutter his wings in sexual excitation, and starts out in search.[5]

These almost incredible achievements can be made still more vivid by other examples. German shepherd dogs, for instance, smell the butyric-acid odor of humans buried under meter-deep snow and can be trained to signal the presence of avalanche victims; even the odor left by a rubber boot when it touches the ground briefly can put a dog trained for tracking onto the trail. About the eel, Teichmann[11] makes the remarkable statement that it can detect a test substance even when it is diluted by an amount equivalent to mixing a single milliliter of the substance with fifty-eight times as much water as is contained in Lake Constance! Male moths find their way to females over a distance of kilometers, guided by the odor plume drifting out of the females' attractant glands.

By anyone's standards, such feats are surely wonderful.

19 Pore Plates and 3-D Smelling

> How, then, I thought: can this be believed, has the almighty
> Creator denied the industrious bee a nose? . . . How happy I
> was then, when all my own effort and industry were not in
> vain, for I had found a real nose with two nostrils.
>
> *Nicolaus Unhoch, "Anleitung zur wahren Kenntnis und
> zweckmäßigsten Behandlung der Bienen," 1823*

Forty Thousand Sensors on the Bee Antenna

Where is the nose of the bee?

The sensors with which the insects detect odors are located on
the hard exoskeleton—where we would expect them, for it is the
boundary between the animal and its environment. If we think
about it a little, we will also come to the correct conclusion that
these, like the sensors for other stimuli, are found in the greatest
numbers on the head. For an animal with a front end, which always makes the first contact with new terrain when the animal is
exploring, it makes sense to "follow one's nose."

Although sensilla are found on practically all parts of an insect
exoskeleton, their density on the movable feelers of the head is
unparalleled. These are rightly called antennae; they are teeming
with biological measurement devices. Most of these sensors are
minute hairs.

Forty thousand sensilla on the antennae of a worker bee—quite
a sensational discovery![1] Almost 6,000 of these organs are olfactory sensilla. These are not hairs; their shape is reflected in their
name: pore plates, or sensilla placodea. When the anterior surface
of an antenna is viewed in the microscope, they are immediately
discernible as oval, slightly concave plates with a long diameter of
only 12 μm, twelve-thousandths of a millimeter (Pl. 32). But this

microcosm has cost sensory physiologists years of work. Each pore plate is associated with a number of sense cells, eighteen on average. These cells are directly under the plate, connected to it by way of fingerlike processes, the dendrites (Fig. 47). As the name implies, the pore plate has pores—about 3,500 of them, arranged in a ring around the edge of the plate. It is to these that the dendrites run. The diameter of a pore is 150 Ångstrom, only 150 × 10[-7]mm.[5,12,13,14] This is sufficient, however, to allow the scent to diffuse through to the membranes of the sense-cell dendrites, where it gives rise to a nerve signal.

Neurophysiology of the Pore Plates

The sense organs are the point of departure of a continuous stream of information to the brain. The first step is that the physical and

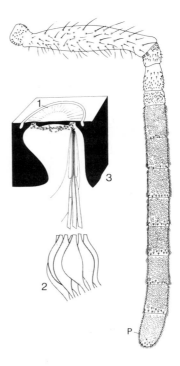

Fig. 47:
The pore plates (P) of the honeybee; distribution on the antenna and diagram of their structure. (1) Annular field of pores; (2) sense cells; (3) exoskeleton of the antenna.

chemical conditions in the surroundings, and changes in these conditions, are translated into the language of the nervous system—into so-called nerve impulses. Remember that across the membrane of the cell there is an electrical potential of around seventy millivolts. Nerve impulses are brief changes in this voltage, each lasting for about one millisecond. They are conducted along the nerve fibers to the brain. The more intense the stimulus, the more closely they follow one another. These nerve impulses, discussed further in Chapter 21, and the language of the nervous system, of which they are the elements, are the same for all types of stimuli. The impulses produced by a light stimulus to the eye do not differ from those produced when the scent of a flower reaches the sense cells of a pore plate.

Dietrich Schneider, of the Max Planck Institute for Behavioral Physiology in Seewiesen, Germany, and his student Veith Lacher were the first to record such signals from the pore plate of the honeybee with electrophysiological methods; the details of their experiments, done in 1963, were published a year later.[7] The technical principles are the same as for the insect eye (Chapter 13); I shall describe them again here, because electrophysiological methods are so important in answering the questions we ask about the sense organs and the nervous system.

The bee is first attached to a little table, and its antennae are fixed in the position most convenient for the experiment. If the bee is fed regularly with sugar-water, it will survive under these conditions for several days. An electrode (in this case it is best to use a tungsten wire sharpened to a fine tip, about 1 μm in diameter) is brought up to a pore plate by means of a precision micromanipulator so that the edge of the plate is pierced slightly. In this position it makes electrical contact with the sense cells. The manipulation must be accurate to within thousandths of a millimeter; therefore it is done under microscopic control with 550-fold magnification. A second electrode is inserted into the tip of the antenna and is grounded. The latter provides the reference potential, the "standard" by which the sense-cell signals detected by the first electrode are measured. The electrical circuit formed

by the electrodes and the measurement apparatus is closed in the
animal by the electrically conducting tissue between the electrodes,
in particular the blood. In the recording part of the circuit, the
signals are amplified and displayed on the screen of an oscilloscope. Usually a loudspeaker is attached to convert the electrical
pulses to a series of ticks. With practice, one can tell a great deal
about the response of the sense cell from the nuances of this sound.
Finally, a tape recorder and a computer can be used to put the
data into the form in which they ultimately appear in a journal.
Enough about the techniques; they are always only the means to
an end. What do the nerve impulses from the pore plates tell us?

1. Even when the sense cells of the pore plates are not being
stimulated they send nerve impulses to the bee brain. When a
scent-laden stream of air is blown over the antennae, this resting
activity either increases or decreases or does not change, depending on the odor substance. That is, there are excitatory, inhibitory,
and ineffective odor substances.

2. The palette of odors to which a sense cell responds is large,
and it is different for each sense cell.

3. Usually the response spectra of different cells overlap greatly.
This feature provides us, in theory, with a physiological basis of
the masterly ability of the bee to discriminate odors in behavioral
experiments. Each scent or, more realistically, each mixture of scents
corresponds to a quite specific pattern of unexcited, excited, and
inhibited sense cells. A limitless number of distinct patterns can
be so produced. According to the new findings of Ekkehard
Vareschi[15] mentioned above, the response spectra can be assembled in six major categories with hardly any overlap, but the cells
within each such group differ greatly from one another in their
responses.

Orientation in an Odor Field

"How, then, I thought: can this be believed, has the almighty
Creator denied the industrious bee a nose, when smell is the main

organ by which it detects honey an hour's flight away? . . . But each time I found, next to the teeth, a marked elevation with more than sufficient length and width for a nose. . . . I persevered with this thought, and decided to look for the nostrils in the place where I hoped to find them. . . . Finally I discovered, about in the middle of the nose on both sides, two small elongated and barely discernible openings. How happy I was then, when all my own effort and industry were not in vain, for I had found a real nose with two nostrils." It is just as well that Nicolaus Unhoch never realized how wrong this discovery made 160 years ago actually was.

The ability of the insects to detect odors and discriminate among them, the demonstration that flowers bear scent patterns, and the location of the olfactory receptors on two movable antennae together lead us inevitably to the next question: How does the short-range orientation of the bees in a floral odor field function? Do they perceive stimulus differences only by sampling the odor field at sequential moments with their antennae? Such a method is called klinotactic orientation. Or are the animals capable of orienting by the difference between the stimuli to the two antennae at each moment (the technical term for which is tropotaxis)? To what extent does the mechanical exploration of the flower with the antennae that accompanies the olfactory exploration enable three-dimensional smelling? Again a whole bundle of problems!

Auguste Forel, in the first decade of this century, postulated such a three-dimensional olfactory sense.[2] That would indeed be something special, for it would mean that a nectar guide would give the animal the impression, say, of an elliptical geraniol odor. Nothing of the sort is possible for our nose, because the pattern of odors reaching our olfactory mucosa contains no information about the distribution of the odors on the object emitting them. The most we can do is to sniff at the various parts of the object one after the other, which is another thing altogether.

Decisive experiments on these questions were done by Martin Lindauer[8] and Hermann Martin,[9] his former student, who in 1964 completed an extensive doctoral thesis on "The Close-Range Ori-

Plate 25   183

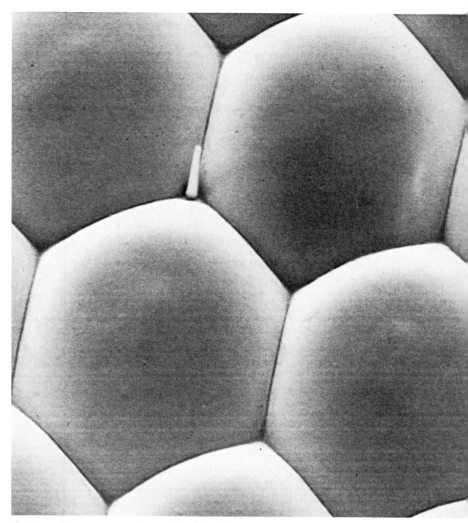

Surface of the compound eye of the blowfly *Calliphora erythrocephala*.
Each element in this "honeycomb" arrangement is the lens of an ommatidium. Magnification 1,900×.

The marsh marigold (*Caltha palustris*) appears yolk-yellow to us but quite different to insects; they see a "bee-purple," because the flower reflects ultraviolet in addition to yellow. Moreover, the center of the flower bears a guide mark visible to the insects, because in this region no ultraviolet is reflected. The marsh marigold attracts the most common European species of primitive moth, that remarkable group of Lepidoptera with sharp teeth on the mandibles, which they use to eat pollen (see Fig. 19).

The auricula (*Primula auricula*) was given its first Latin name for its early blooming and its second because of its ear-shaped leaves. The flowers reflect only in the yellow and thus are "bee-yellow." The strong, fresh scent, together with the glowing color, is particularly attractive to lepidopterans. The auricula is a typical representative of the alpine rock flora.

Plate 27   185

The birds-eye primrose (*Primula farinosa*), like the related auricula, belongs to the pollination-ecology category of "stalked-plate" flowers. The entrance to the corolla tube is so narrow that only lepidopterans and bee flies can push their slender proboscises in to suck nectar. The yellow, ring-shaped nectar guide presumably makes it easier for them to find the minute opening. The same is true of the flower shown below it, the sky-blue alpine forget-me-not (*Myosotis alpestris*), the gullet of which is constricted by five yolk-yellow scales.

Plate 28   187

◊

Above: The complex structure and coloration of the bee orchid (*Ophrys apifera*), unlike that of its closest relative (see Pls. 38 and 39), has lost its significance for pollination, at least in the northern parts of its range. There the bee orchid is independent of insects; in southern England self-pollination is the rule for this flower. The pollen packets protruding from the green anthers at the very top are clearly visible in the picture. They fall down, adhering to the sticky stigma of the same flower without the help of insects.

Below: One might easily take the stemless carline thistle (*Carlina acaulis*) for a single flower. In reality it consists of several hundred blossoms in a basket arrangement. Unlike the brown-rayed knapweed (see Pl. 6), this thistle has only one kind of tubular floret. The display function is taken over by the bracts, which encircle the shallow basket like a halo with a silvery-white sheen. These, unlike the tubular florets, reflect ultraviolet. Contour-rich figures of this sort, especially when radially symmetrical, were approached by bees particularly often in spontaneous-choice experiments.

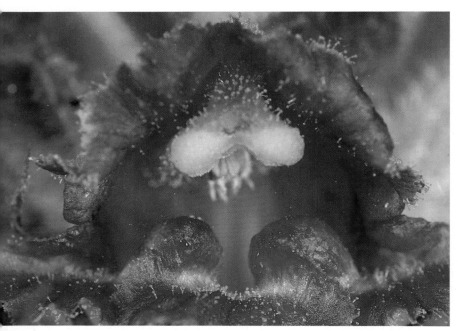

In the entrance to the corolla tube of the broomrape (*Orobanche*)—an entirely parasitic plant which germinates only if its host plant is in the vicinity—there is a dumbell-shaped structure of intense yellow. It looks like the two halves of an anther, but actually it is the stigma, evidently imitating the original pollen signal in three dimensions and in the correct color. The real anthers have completely lost their visual attractiveness; they are inconspicuously located within the corolla tube.

The flower of the African violet (*Saintpaulia*), a native of eastern Africa, is a particularly nice example of the visual signaling action of the anthers. Against the blue of the petals their yellow color stands out sharply, for bees and bumblebees as well. Even after they are empty the anther walls retain this shape and color, and hence their signaling action. As a result there is a greater probability of pollination of the stigma, which like the style is so inconspicuous in shape and color that it can barely be distinguished from the petals.

Plate 30 189

Four examples of the evolution of flower signals. *Above*: On the left the mullein *Verbascum nigrum*, the anthers of which are made more attractive by their colorful hairs. On the right a species of *Iris* with a mock-anther in bold relief, accented by the yellow-blue contrast. The real anthers are hidden in the gullet of the flower and are invisible, or nearly so, from outside.

Below: Left, a blossom of the foxglove (*Digitalis purpurea*); the spots on the lower lip are interpreted as visual imitations of anthers. Here, again, the real anthers are concealed in the corolla tube. Right, the common toadflax (*Linaria vulgaris*), with a raised orange pad in the middle of the lower lip. These pads look like abnormally large imitations of anthers, and are therefore perhaps especially attractive to insects. They block the entrance to the corolla tube and hence to the nectar, large amounts of which collect in the massive spur. The insects—probably mainly bumblebees—must push the lips apart to reach the food they seek.

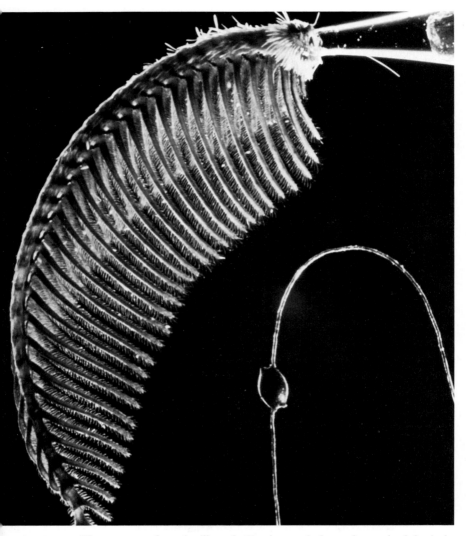

The antenna of a male silkmoth (*Bombyx mori*), in an electrophysiological experiment. Through a glass tube (not visible here) a scented airstream is blown over its many sensilla. Their summed response can be recorded with the two capillary electrodes at the tip and base of the antenna, appearing as a voltage change. The fine U-shaped wire on the right is a thermistor, which monitors the onset and duration of the odor stimulus. Magnification 33 ×.

Plate 32   191

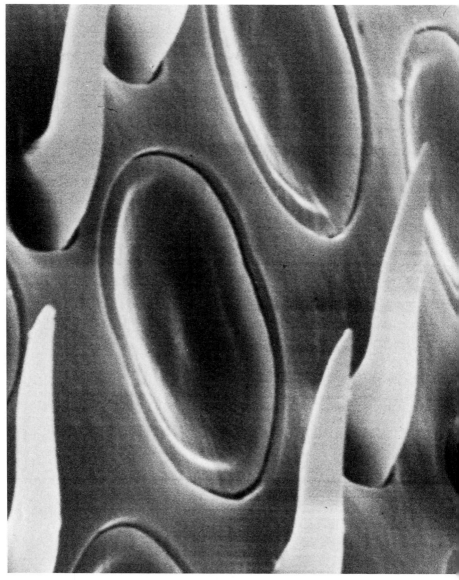

Pore plates, the olfactory organs on the antenna of the honeybee (*Apis mellifera*, worker). They account for about 75 percent of all the sense cells in the antennae. Magnification 6,000 ×.

entation of the Bee in an Odor Field, with a Demonstration of
Osmotropotaxis in Insects." Another important contribution has
recently been made by Ernst Kramer, of the Max Planck Institute
for Behavioral Physiology in Seewie^sen, Germany.[4]

The first thing to be shown experimentally is that the two antennae really do detect the odors separately, and that the bee can
perceive odors separately and localize them correctly. For this purpose the bees are trained to walk down the stem of a Y-tube and
at the fork choose to enter the branch labeled with anise odor (the
right one, for example). This they learn quickly. After they have
been trained, just before the actual experiment, the antennae are
crossed one over the other and firmly fixed in this position (Fig.
48). Then when the bees reach the fork they run without hesita-
tion into the odorless left branch of the Y-tube, making the "wrong"
choice. The information coming from the right antenna now says
"odorless" and is still interpreted by the bee's brain as associated
with the right side, even though the antenna now actually points
to the left. Normally no bee crosses its antennae, and as we have
heard each sense organ has its permanent private line to the brain.
The brain knows this, and identifies the sense organ by the line
over which its information arrives. Therefore in this situation, one
that nature has not allowed for, confusion results. The bee brain
gives the musculature an erroneous command. But to the scientist,
this mistake by the bee proves its ability for tropotactic orientation. Normally it turns around until the left antenna is also in the
region of high odor concentration, so that the right and left antennae are in balance.

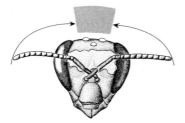

Fig. 48:
Bee with antennae crossed and glued
down. If they are fastened in such a
way that the tips lie in the shaded
middle region, the bee cannot distinguish between the stimuli to the two
antennae.

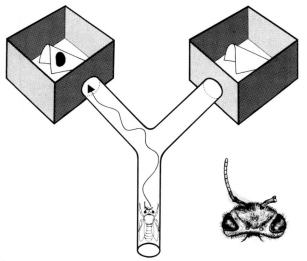

Fig. 49:
A bee without a right antenna and with left antenna fixed, in a choice experiment. It follows a typical oscillating path to the scented paper.

But what does the bee do when one of its two antennae is
removed? Then the remaining antenna continually swings from
side to side, and with it the bee finds its way into the correct
branch of the Y, to the odor source. That is, it is then able to
orient klinotactically, by rapidly sampling the two sides of its antennal field in alternation, with the single antenna. If the one remaining antenna is then fixed mechanically in position, the bee
still manages by turning the whole body, walking on a wavy course
(Fig. 49). This oscillating locomotion also appears when the antennae are crossed in such a way that their tips are less than 2 mm
apart. The odor differences are evidently no longer great enough
then for the two to be perceived as distinct (Fig. 48).

How large the difference must in fact be for the bee to detect
it is shown by a further ingenious experiment.

Hermann Martin,[9] then at the Zoological Institute of the University of Frankfurt, loaded fine glass tubes with odors at different

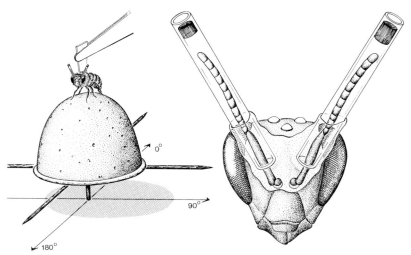

Fig. 50:
Experiment for measurement of difference threshold. Fine glass tubes
containing odor substance are fitted over the bee's antennae. The bee is
held fast but tries to turn. In so doing, it moves the light cork hemisphere
beneath it.

concentrations and pushed them over the antennae of a honeybee
that had previously been trained to just this odor (Fig. 50). What
does the bee do? Hypothesis: it will try to walk in the direction
of the higher concentration as long as it can detect the concentration difference. The result: at high odor concentrations the two
sides must differ by a factor of ten or more, whereas at low concentrations a factor of 2.5 suffices for tropotactic resolution of the
difference.

Do differences of this magnitude occur on flowers? Walter
Neuhaus[11] has worked on this problem. On the basis of theoretical considerations he draws the important conclusion that the pre-
requisites for tropotactic orientation over a distance of 1.5 to 2
cm from the odor source can be met as long as no wind is blowing.

Another Mechanism

In the case of chemical long-range orientation, in which the differences in the odor concentration are necessarily small, something different happens.

In the experiments of Ernst Kramer[4] bees found their way to the odor source even when tropo- or klinotactic mechanisms could not have been involved because the concentration differences in the odor field were too small. Evidently another mechanism is operating here. Kramer concluded that the animals can remember odor concentrations very well and that they orient to the odor source by following a path on which the odor concentration is equivalent to that associated with a reward during training. In this kind of orientation, according to Kramer, a major factor is that the bee (like other animals) turns into the wind that brings the odor to its nose.

So it often goes: a curious biologist asks a question that may at first seem quite simple. In the very first experiment the animals show us that it isn't as simple as we think. They may answer one question for us, but at the same time they raise ten new ones. Hardly ever is a real end in sight. The fascination of the marvelous world the biologist enters, in which humans are by no means the standard for everything else, unceasingly spurs research on to new goals.

Let us return to the bee on the flower. The question as to whether it can in principle detect a spatial odor pattern has been largely answered by the demonstration that the bee can distinguish different concentrations applied simultaneously to the two antennae.

After the landing on the flower, the antennae smell various odors on the way to the nectar. Can the bee's nose, together with the interconnected nerves behind it, discern their sequence as such? Even this achievement is not beyond its powers. Let us follow through the experiment that demonstrates such sequence discrimination.

Stage setting: a system of passages, four tubes (Fig. 51), in each

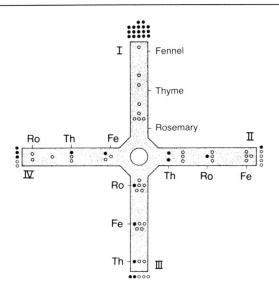

Fig. 51:
An odor arena; the bees enter through the opening in the middle. Then most of them (68.5 percent of runs) proceed through Passage I, with the combination "rosemary-thyme-fennel" to which they were trained. They have learned to break down a sequence of neighboring odors into its components, in the right order. The symbols in the passages indicate reversal points, where the run was interrupted. ○ one event, ● five events.

of which the same three odors—rosemary, thyme, and fennel—are placed in sequence. The critical point is that the sequence is different in each tube. Prerequisite: that the bee be trained to one of the sequences. Procedure: the trained bee enters the arena in the center—where does it go? And the result: most often, into the passage with the sequence to which it has been trained. Who would not applaud this performance?

20 The Noses of Flies, Beetles, and Butterflies

For whenever an animal is attracted to a thing by perceiving its smell, it is sure to like the taste of it.

Aristotle (384-322 B.C.*), "Historia animalium"*

Pore plates are not an exclusive invention of the bees, nor are they the only type of olfactory sensillum to be found in insects. Hairs are more common. They vary in length and are anchored to the skeleton in various ways. Such diversity demands classification, and indeed zoologists distinguish several basic types (Fig. 52).[4,14] This chapter presents a few examples to illustrate both the differences and the similarities in insect olfactory senses.

Flies

Flies, too, have a nose. From their behavior it can easily be deduced that in their everyday life they encounter at least two important categories of odors.

1. Flower scents, which attract them to a food source. Brief observation reveals that flies tend to throng about umbelliferous flowers, which are particularly rich in essential oils.

2. Meat aromas, which are important inasmuch as many flies search for meat in which to lay their eggs, so that when the larvae hatch they will be surrounded by food.

Fifty-six years ago a zoologist mowed a whole area of meadow down to the ground except for one plant of cowbane (*Cicuta virosa*), just to do an experiment on a few flies. The flowers of the cowbane are arranged in large umbels, which he hid from sight under leaves; then he seated himself nearby, and patiently watched his experimental animals.[9] The flies soon told him what he wanted to know: they can smell. From a distance of two meters they flew to the flowers, and they even crawled under the concealing leaves to get at the nectar. Perhaps they had identified the cowbane plant by sight, and knew from experience where the flowers were? They soon refuted this suggestion themselves. They flew straight to the plant only when they happened to come downwind of it, so that the wind carried its scent to their "noses." From the work of Hans Kugler[6,7] we know that quite a number of flies (*Lucilia, Calliphora, Sarcophaga*) approach otherwise identical flower models much more often when they are scented. And it is particularly interesting that *Calliphora* and *Sarcophaga* prefer yellow models to dark purple ones when both have a flowery smell, whereas the preference is reversed when both smell like dung. This correlation between sight and smell seems almost too good to be true.

Experiments of this sort are certainly interesting and important. But they tell us very little about the underlying mechanisms, which are what the researcher really wants to understand. A considerable advance in this direction was made only recently, when Manfred Kaib,[3] at the University of Regensburg, went to the heart of the matter by recording the activity of the olfactory sense cells involved. He wrote a paper on "The Meat- and Flower-Odor Receptors on the Antenna of the Blowfly *Calliphora vicina.*" Kaib identified the sensilla to be expected on the fly antenna by their physiological properties. They are hairs, situated either within a furry mass of other sensilla on the surface of the antenna or recessed in small pits from ten to fifty thousandths of a millimeter in diameter[9,18] (Fig. 52).

Again it was the electrophysiological method that put speculation on a factual footing. Again the sense cells could be categorized in terms of response types, each type giving the same kind of response—an increase or decrease of impulse activity—to the same spectrum of stimuli. So far a total of six types of meat-odor receptors and three types of flower-odor receptors are known.

The species of fly studied here searches for fresh animal cadavers in which to lay its eggs; some of its relatives prefer the stench of

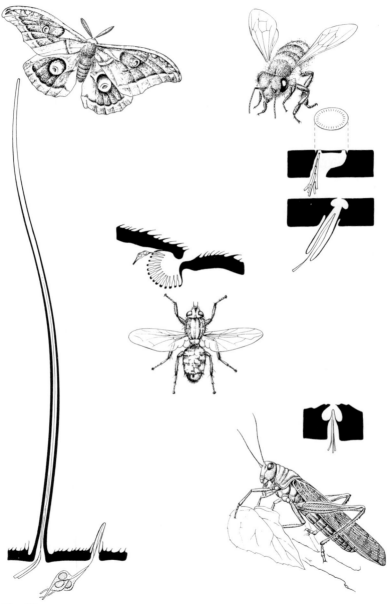

Fig. 52:
Typical olfactory sense organs on the antennae of lepidopterans (long and short hairs), bees (pore plates above, sunken pegs below), flies (composite pit organ), and grasshopper (simple pit organ).

Table 2. Response of fly chemoreceptors to the smell of meat of
increasing rottenness

Stimulus	Response
Meat, fresh	10 impulses per second
Meat 1 day old	19 impulses per second
Meat 2 days old	33 impulses per second
Meat 3 days old	136 impulses per second
Meat 20 days old	>200 impulses per second
Rotted meat, liquefied	124 impulses per second

advanced decay. Among their meat-odor receptors are some that
respond especially strongly to the odor of fresh meat and others
that give the strongest responses to stinking carrion, weeks old.
By the vigor of the reaction of its various sense cells, the fly can
detect the state of decay. For example, a cell of the second kind
behaves as shown in Table 2.

After about three weeks, then, the meat odor has the greatest effect on this fly sense cell.

The next step: what specific substances have an effect on this
cell? When pure synthetic odors are used as stimuli, it turns out
that this receptor type responds to compounds with a chain length
of five to seven carbon atoms, containing an alcohol, aldehyde, or
keto group. But the most effective fraction of the natural odor is
still unknown.

Among the flower-odor receptors, one type responds particularly strongly to anethole or 1-octanol, a second to 1-decanol, and
a third to terpenes such as pinene and camphene. All this will
mean little to the general reader, so we shall not bother here with
the many other technical terms we would need to understand
thoroughly either the chemical relations or the special characteristics of certain odor sensations. Even a zoologist who has not
specialized in odor chemistry may well find it difficult to follow
the explanations of a specialist. He would be more likely to feel
like the person newly arrived in Israel whose problem Ephraim
Kishon has so perceptively described: "Hebrew can be learned

relatively easily, almost as easily as Chinese. After only three or four years the newcomer is able to say to a passerby in the street, in fluent Hebrew, 'Please tell me the time, but if possible in English.' "

Attractive Stenches

For many years I have had a plant in my laboratory that each year is the scene of a remarkable performance. The star-shaped flower of this plant stinks of carrion. Soon after it has opened and allowed its unpleasant smell to flow out, flies arrive, scrabble around for a while, and finally lay their eggs in the middle of it. This cactuslike African plant (*Stapelia*) has played a trick on the flies (Pl. 34). With its dark-red color, the flower also looks rather like rotting meat, and it is entirely conceivable that its covering of hairs contributes to the success of the imposture as well. For the fly, this encounter has a fatal outcome; the larvae that hatch die of starvation. But the plant is pollinated by the fly as it crawls about. Here there is no question of life together for mutual advantage, of symbiosis. The plant is effectively a parasite of the fly.

Other plants also have a putrid smell, which attracts insects looking for food on cadavers, dung, and the like. One of them, the wild arum, is familiar to many people from their school days, because of its clever trapping mechanism. The unprepossessing ivy flower is also in this group; in the autumn its amine-containing odor of decay covers it with flies. And one rarity should be mentioned, a champion in a sense. In a copy of the German magazine *Umschau* from 1925 I found a headline for flower-lovers: "The Largest Blossom." The photograph that went with it has been redrawn for this book (Fig. 53). *Amorphophallus titanum* is a huge flower from the Indo-Malayan wonderland. Description: similar to the calla in structure; spathe a meter in diameter; spadix up to two meters high; odor appalling, fills the tropical night and stinks so very like rotting meat that people whose curiosity draws them too close have been known to faint. Pollinators: beetles which,

Fig. 53:
The gigantic inflorescence of *Amorphophallus titanum.*

having landed in the goblet, have difficulty climbing out because of a projecting collar around the spadix.

Beetles

First let us return briefly to the pore plates. Pore plates have also been found in aphids[17] and their structure has been well studied in the lamellicorn beetles,[10] a group including the cockchafer (*Melolontha melolontha*) and the scarab, the sacred beetle of Egyptian antiquity. Lamellicorn beetles have a typical "flag" on the antenna, formed by the leaflike expansion of the terminal segments. It bears olfactory sensilla in large numbers, in the cockchafer as well as its flower-visiting relatives such as the rose chafer (*Cetonia aurata*), and *Hoplia farinosa*, which has no English name (Fig. 54, Pl. 11).

Not all the olfactory sensilla of lamellicorn beetles take the form of pore plates. They can also be hairlike structures. According to Carl-Christian Meinecke, who in 1975 wrote a doctoral thesis on this subject, most of the many variants of lamellicorn olfactory sensilla can be regarded as modifications of three basic types: re-

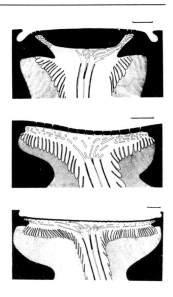

Fig. 54:
Pore plates of flower-visiting beetles; from top to bottom: rose chafer (*Cetonia aurata*, cf. Fig. 17), *Hoplia farinosa* (cf. Pl. 11), *Trichius fasciatus*. Scale 1/1000 mm.

cessed pore plates, pore plates on sockets, and hairlike sensilla. Comparison of fifty beetle species has shown that the groups set up on the basis of the structure of the olfactory sensilla fit remarkably well into the evolutionary tree worked out for the lamellicorn beetles on the basis of entirely different characteristics. Obviously, then, intermediate sensilla structures are the manifestation of genetic mixing—that is, kinship.

Lepidoptera

What can we say, finally, about the butterflies' and moths' sense of smell? There are quite a few reports to the effect that many lepidopterans use olfaction to find their food.[2,5,8,16] Some of these are in the family Nymphalidae, which includes the most gloriously colored butterflies of temperate latitudes—the large tortoiseshell (*Vanessa polychloros*) and the peacock (*Vanessa io*), for instance, as well as the purple emperor (*Apatura iris*) and the red admiral (*Vanessa atalanta*).

Again, the antennae are the site of the olfactory sensilla. So far, research has concentrated on a few species from quite different parts of the world. For example, the moth *Oraesia excavata* has the unusual habit of piercing grapes and sucking their juice. The way to this sweet reward is pointed out by the olfactory hairs on its antennae.[19] The queen butterfly (*Danaus gilippus berenice*) of Florida extends its proboscis when it smells honey.[11,12] Its olfactory hairs resemble those of another lepidopteran, the moth *Antheraea pernyi* (Saturniidae), the response spectra of which have been studied in some detail.[15] These sense cells respond to flowery, aromatic, and certain other odors. As in the pore plates of the bees, although their reaction spectra differ they are all large and they overlap, so that the cells are of the "generalist" type. This assignment is made with some reservations, since it has been found that even such relatively large spectra can be quite specific (Chapter 19); but there is still a clear difference between these and the type of olfactory sensillum termed "specialist" in the literature. The function of the "specialist" is to respond exclusively, or at least very much more sensitively, to one or a few selected substances. "Specialists" cannot be used like an array of "generalists," to discriminate a large number of substances. Instead, they are highly selective filters, amounting to narrow gates that allow signals from only one or a few odors entry to the central nervous system. Such odors must be of great biological importance, and include especially sexual attractants, alluring perfumes that play a major role in the lives of many lepidopterans.

Alluring Perfumes

The best known example is the silkmoth (*Bombyx mori*). When the male moth detects even the most minute quantities of the attractant bombykol, produced by the female in special abdominal glands, he begins to search for her. If the wind is blowing favorably, male moths in the wild can fly to the conspecific females, following their noses, over distances of several kilometers. But the laboratory silkmoth—the same animal that is used for silk production—has lost this ability. It can no longer fly, and would certainly not walk so far.

Dietrich Schneider and his coworkers at the Max Planck Institute for Behavioral Physiology in Seewiesen, Germany—in particular Karl-Ernst Kaissling—have been working for two decades to learn about the olfactory sensilla of the silkmoth. Their primary goal is to understand a mechanism at the core of receptor physiology, the conversion of the stimulus into a neural signal. In this process, called transduction, the chemical energy at the input is converted into the electrochemical signals that are sent out. The questions in this area are very complex, and lead far away from the biological phenomena easily perceptible to the nonbiologist. There are few types of receptor for which anyone has more than a rudimentary idea of these events. The best known are the light receptors—the eyes of vertebrates and insects—and, in fact, the olfactory receptors of the silkmoth. The latter is a good example to show the kinds of questions that interest the sensory physiologist, even though these questions themselves have no direct bearing on the encounter between flowers and insects. The silkmoth did not become a laboratory animal by accident. Its sensitivity and degree of specialization in the detection of the attractant substance are so pronounced that the underlying mechanisms may well be expected to be present here in a highly perfected, and therefore relatively clearly discernible, form. We shall consider them in the next chapter.

21   Elementary Processes in Sense Organs

Dream apart, numerical precision is the
very soul of science.

D'Arcy Wentworth Thompson, "On Growth and Form," 1917

A male silkmoth (*Bombyx mori*) looks like a helpless creature. Its
wings are feeble stumps, their fluttering much too weak to lift it
into the air as the wings of other moths do. The silkmoth is a
domestic animal; for millennia it has been kept to produce silk,
and it is only under these unnatural conditions that it could reproduce despite this handicap.

In the wild, butterflies and moths must often cover several kilometers in order to reach a sexual partner. How do they find their
way? When the female is ready to mate she releases a perfume that
guides the male to her. Aphrodisiacs and route markers together,
these messenger substances resemble the hormones except that their
coordinating action does not operate within the body but serves
for communication among individuals. Such substances are called
pheromones. The female silkmoth has two glands in her abdomen
that are protruded when it is time to reproduce, so that the se-
ductive fragrance is wafted out. In the laboratory, one can place a
female in this state on a table and blow air at her with an ordinary
household fan. When the airstream, loaded with attractant, reaches
a male he immediately begins to beat his stumpy wings and runs—
if he could, he would fly—straight to the female and copulates
with her. This interaction has become famous in zoological circles
as the Sex Show of the department of Professor Schneider in the
Max Planck Institute for Behavioral Physiology, Seewiesen (Fig.
55).

The experiment can also be done by replacing the female with

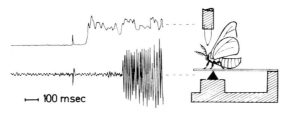

Fig. 55:
The male silkmoth flutters as soon as the attractant released by the female reaches him. By placing him on the pickup cartridge of a record player, one can record this response accurately. The fine wire above the moth is a thermistor, which measures the flow of scented air.

a glass tube containing a piece of filter paper impregnated with a tiny amount of attractant (bombykol). A paper loaded with only 10^{-4} μg of bombykol sets over half of the males tested into fluttering excitement. It must be an extraordinarily effective substance, for a ten-thousandth of a millionth of a gram to produce such a result!

Functional Principles of a Sense Organ

Such behavior must be based on a very high-performance sensory system, which immediately suggests to the biologist that all the components of the "apparatus" employed are nearly optimally constructed and matched to one another. Therefore such cases of peak performance offer particularly interesting opportunities for clarification of the underlying mechanisms. And that is what concerns us here; we want to find out how a sense organ functions. Fortunately, it is not necessary to treat all the many different sense organs individually. The principles, to the extent that they are of interest in our context, are so much the same everywhere that in studying a single example one can learn a great deal about receptors in general.

First, however, a few theoretical considerations before we turn to our exemplary case—the attractant receptor of the silkmoth, chosen because it has been so well investigated. Never mind that it has nothing directly to do with the pollination of flowers by insects. What it has to tell us will also inform us about essential aspects of what goes on in the pore plates of the bees and beetles, in the gustatory hairs and olfactory pits of flies, and in the visual cells of the compound eyes. All these receptors fit, in their own special ways, into the diagram of an eye shown in Fig. 56, with which we begin our digression into sensory physiology.

Animals, like people, are continuously bombarded by an abundance of the most diverse stimuli. The first important function of the sense organs is to filter out the biologically important stimuli that each particular type of sense organ is suited to detect. The eye is there for visual stimuli, the ear for acoustic stimuli, and the nose for chemical stimuli. The stimuli in each of these categories are characterized by a particular form of energy, the "adequate stimulus modality" in specialist terms. Stimuli of non-adequate modalities normally elicit no response. In many cases they do not even get to the sense cells—because there is no light-conducting apparatus with a lens, for example, because there is no mechanical structure by which tones can be converted to oscillation, or because tissues or other barriers prevent the passage of odors.

Moreover, the sense cells as a rule are not exposed directly even to their own adequate stimuli. Usually, on its way the stimulus is custom-tailored to the special requirements of the individual sense organ by means of accessory structures—a lens, in the case of Fig. 56. This process is called stimulus transport and, because the stimulus is altered, stimulus transformation. Here nature displays great richness of invention, a rainbow palette of physically ingenious structures, which amaze the technical expert as well as the biologist. High sensitivity, selectivity, and specificity are usually brought about even before the stimulus arrives at the heart of the organ, the sense cell itself. All the delicate complexity of the lens apparatus of our eyes, the brilliant micromechanics of our middle and inner ears, the filigree architecture of the pore plates, the mosaic of lenses in the insect eye—there are countless examples of nature's sorcery, puzzles that in the recent past have ever more rapidly been

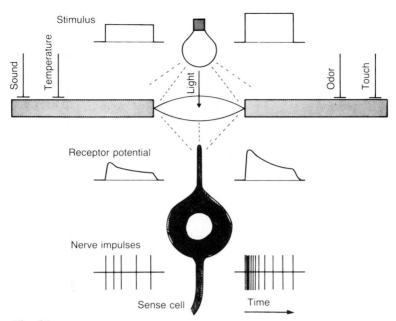

Fig. 56:
Diagram of a sense organ. In the middle is the sense cell. The thick horizontal bar symbolizes the filter through which can pass only the kind of stimulus for which the sense organ is specialized. The stimulus, the receptor potential, and the nerve impulses are diagrammed to show their amplitudes (vertical axis) and time courses (horizontal axis).

approaching a solution, thanks not least to the close collaboration of zoologists with physicists, chemists, and engineers.

Nevertheless, the sense cell is the heart of the matter. The reason: it is here that the stimulus, however different it may be in the various sense organs, is always translated into the same electrochemical language of the nervous system. Here, at the cell membrane, the form of energy in which the stimulus arrives is converted to the nervous signal.

The first event in this process that one can measure with electrophysiological methods is a change in the voltage across the cell membrane, which the specialist calls the receptor potential. The properties of this fluctuation depend on those of the stimulus; it is larger, the stronger the stimulus, and can also vary in duration according to the duration of the stimulus. However, this initial signal is not conducted to the brain, but dies out near the site of its production. What happens then? If the receptor potential is large enough, it sends a second kind of signal on its way before disappearing itself. Therefore it is also called the generator potential; it generates the actual nerve impulses—also called action potentials, for they show us that the nerve fiber is in action.

Action potentials are uniform signals, each as long and as large as the others. The nervous system uses them for the long-distance transport of information. Like a spark traveling along a fuse to the powder keg, the action potential is generated anew at each point on its way along the nerve fiber. It is conducted without loss of amplitude. In insects it moves at a speed of about 1 to 3 meters per second; in vertebrates the peak velocities are around 120 meters per second, which in racing terms amounts to no less than 270 miles per hour.

Alan Lloyd Hodgkin and Andrew Fielding Huxley, two British researchers, received the Nobel Prize in 1963 for their theory of the origin of the nerve impulse.

To cover all the details of the underlying physicochemical events would mean a long and exhausting march. Here we shall take the quickest short cut.

1. In the unstimulated state of the sense cell, there is a potential of seventy-thousandths of a volt (70 mV) across its wall.

2. These seventy millivolts arise because ions are not uniformly distributed between the interior and exterior of the cell and the cell wall is differentially permeable to the different kinds of ions.

3. The most important of these ions are the potassium ion (K^+), the sodium ion (Na^+), and the chloride ion (Cl^-). The resting potential is associated primarily with the K^+.

4. When the generator potential exceeds a certain threshold voltage, the delicately balanced ionic equilibrium across the cell wall breaks down temporarily. In particular, there is a great increase in the permeability of the cell wall to Na^+. More sodium ions flow into the cell, and more potassium ions flow out.

5. The nerve impulse is basically a manifestation of this transient collapse of the resting potential. It is about a tenth of a volt in amplitude and lasts only about a thousandth of a second, by which time the original resting equilibrium has been restored.

The crucial question: How can the brain, or simply the next station in the nervous system, read out the magnitude of the stimulus from such a digital signal? This information resides in the rate at which the impulses follow one another—in their frequency. The stronger the stimulus, the higher the frequency (Fig. 56). This is what an engineer would call analog frequency modulation. At first glance such a frequency code might seem to be a poor method. The receiver must always wait for the next signal before it can learn anything about stimulus amplitude. It must take an average over time, whereas an analog signal gives the precise information at each moment. But this disadvantage is compensated by an important advantage—digital signals are less vulnerable to disturbance. At the end of the line it amounts to a simple Yes or No: was there a signal or not? As in every technical type of signal transmission, distortion by external disturbances and by noise is also a problem in the case of conduction along nerves. When a digital code is used the information arrives safely even though the individual signals may be somewhat distorted. It is not easy to introduce errors into messages "telegraphed" in this way even though the distance may be long—from the toe of an elephant, say, up to its spinal cord.

The Antenna of the Silkmoth: A Sieve for Molecules

Now to the special case. We have the odor molecules of the female sexual attractant on the one hand and the response of the sense cells on the other. What happens in between, and what makes the animals so incredibly sensitive? A complete understanding of the underlying events is still only on the horizon. But we already have the answers to many important parts of the question.

The antenna of the male silkmoth is relatively enormous (Pl. 31). It amounts to a well-designed sieve for airborne molecules, which filters the female attractant substance out of the air. The trunk of the antenna sends out two side branches from each of its segments; these branches form a V shape and point "into the wind." Along each branch are rows of olfactory hairs, arranged so that they cover the space between the adjacent branches. Thanks to the work of Rudolf Alexander Steinbrecht[12,13] at the Max Planck Institute for Behavioral Physiology, we can cite several remarkable numbers for this structure. On each of the two male antennae are 1,700 olfactory hairs sensitive to attractant. They are about 0.1 mm long, and each is innervated by two sense cells (Fig. 52).

A single hair has a surface area of c. 550 μm², and the area of the entire antenna in projection is about 6 mm². For odor molecules to be effective, they must first be caught up on the antenna surface. The great effectiveness of the filter predicted from the geometry has been confirmed by direct measurements with radioactively labeled attractant. No less than 27 percent of all the molecules were fished out of an airstream (6 mm² in cross-sectional area) directed toward the antenna. When the scented air is allowed to flow over the antenna at a velocity of 60 cm/s for only one second, the odor concentration found on the hairs is a million times higher than that in the air itself.[5,6] The first reason for the great sensitivity, then, is the clever arrangement of the stimulus-conducting structures visible to the unaided eye.

Two Thousand Six Hundred Pores
per Olfactory Hair

Once lodged on the antenna, the odor molecule still has some distance to go before reaching the sense cell. The way leads through many submicroscopically small pores (Fig. 57). Each olfactory hair bears about 2,600 of these, around 32 in each thousandth of a millimeter of its length.[13] The molecules diffuse to the pores and through the little tubes beneath them, which extend close to the sensory cell processes. Each olfactory hair has around 13,000 of these fine pore tubules.

Diffusion is a passive process, and slow. It is of no importance

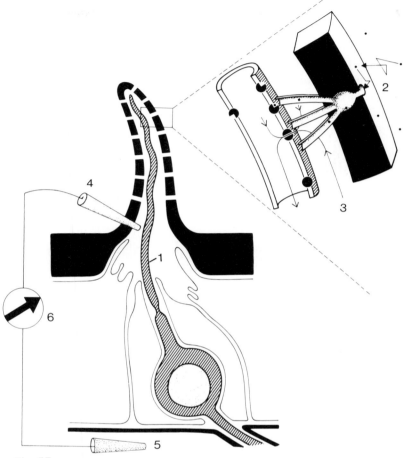

Fig. 57:
The lepidopteran olfactory hair. (1) The stimulus-receiving process of the sense cell; (2) one of the many pores in the hair wall, enlarged; (3) flow of current through the membrane after a scent molecule has struck it; (4) probe to measure the electrical response of the sense cell to the stimulus; (5) reference electrode in the blood within the branch; (6) measurement and display instrument (oscilloscope).

in biological situations involving the transport of substances over fairly large distances, a few millimeters or more. But it is very important in transport over short distances. A molecule of oxygen would take years to get from the lung to the tip of the toe if it

were not carried there by the bloodstream. Once it has arrived at
the place where it is needed, the molecule diffuses over the tiny
distance between the red blood corpuscle and the tissue in fractions of a second. The odor molecules on the silkmoth antenna
require only about five-thousandths of a second to diffuse from
the surface of the antenna to the sense-cell membrane, a distance
of the order of a thousandth of a millimeter.[13]

The Triggering of the Nerve Signal

Now the generator potential is produced. This process, unfortunately, is still rather mysterious. We can assume that the odor
substance is bound to certain molecules in or on the sense-cell
membrane and that as a result the permeability of the membrane
to certain ions (especially Na^+) increases.

The resting potential is changed by the binding of the odor
molecule to the cell membrane. If the change exceeds a critical
amount, a few thousandths of a volt, nerve impulses are dis-
charged. When the stimulus is intense they follow one another at
intervals of five-thousandths of a second or less, which corresponds to a frequency of 200 per second or more. Here, as in
other sense organs, the level of the generator potential controls
the frequency of the nerve impulses.

For a few years it has been known that in certain cases the sense
cells cannot be considered as isolated elements in the production
of a generator potential.[1,16] Rather, the sense-cell membrane (which
provides a voltage) can be thought of as one of the batteries in an
electrical circuit, with the auxiliary cells that envelope the sense
cell representing other batteries. In this situation the sense-cell
membrane at the point where it is affected by the stimulus should
be regarded not only as a battery but as an electrical resistance,
the magnitude of which is changed by the stimulus so that, like a
valve, it controls the flow of current in the overall system.

This notion of current control is very important in connection
with the conversion of the external stimulus into excitation of sense

cells in general. Why? It implies that the energy for this conversion does not come from the stimulus itself, but from the metabolism of the cell. The stimulus only turns the tap, so to speak, and does not itself drive the water out of the faucet. This concept also explains how the energy content of each nerve impulse can be considerably larger than that of the stimulus to which the sense organ is responding. An example: The energy conversion induced in a visual cell can exceed the amount of energy in the light stimulus a millionfold! Such an enormous energy amplification for minuscule stimuli is also the prerequisite for the great sensitivities that have been found, sensitivities approaching the limits of the physically conceivable—the response of a visual cell to a single light quantum, or that of an olfactory cell to a single odor molecule.

Visual Cells

This discussion of the primary processes in visual cells of invertebrates[15] will bring out some common features, and at the same time serves as an appendix to Chapter 13.

Visual cells count light quanta. In the part of the cell where the surface is greatly enlarged (Fig. 37) the light quanta are captured by means of the visual pigment rhodopsin. As the odor molecule alters a receptor molecule in the olfactory cell, so the light causes a chemical change in the rhodopsin molecule. The actual pigment-bearing component of the molecule, retinol, is initially bent at one end. The first change produced is a straightening at this site, as Fig. 58 shows. A number of other changes follow, eventually resulting in a receptor potential at the cell membrane. The interpretation at present is that the light stimulus opens "light channels" through which sodium ions, far more than other ions, can move down their concentration gradient from outside into the cell. As this happens, the electrical resistance of the membrane decreases, an effect that can be measured directly and demonstrated by the redistribution of radioactively labeled Na^+ (^{22}Na). As in many elementary processes, calcium ions (Ca^{++}) play a key role here

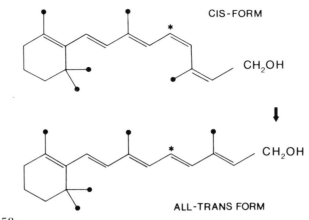

CIS-FORM

CH$_2$OH

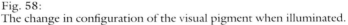

CH$_2$OH

ALL-TRANS FORM

Fig. 58:
The change in configuration of the visual pigment when illuminated.

(Fig. 59). Without Ca^{++} the visual cell is inexcitable. The hypothesis: in the visual-cell membrane is a gating substance, which controls the opening and closing of the light channel. Perhaps this substance is the visual pigment itself. In the dark it binds Ca^{++}, and the channel is closed; under illumination the Na$^+$ takes its turn in that position, and the gating substance is altered, and the channel opens.

Extreme Specialization

Let us return to the silkmoth one last time. The fluttering response of the male silkmoth is triggered quite specifically by the sexual attractant of the female moth. The sensors are unequivocally specialists—eminently suited to detect this one substance, but utterly unsuited to discriminate among a number of odor substances. Even slight changes in the form of the odor molecule bring about a drastic decrease in sensitivity. Cases are even known in which the mirror-image form of the actual key molecule can produce only a much reduced response of the sense cells.[4] Similar specificity has been discovered in various other insects, including the alarm-sub-

In darkness

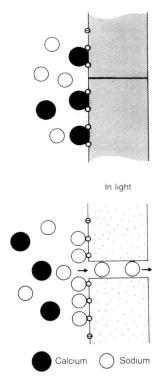

In light

Fig. 59:
Under illumination channels in the membrane of the visual cell open, allowing the passage of sodium ions. Calcium ions have an important control function in this reaction.

● Calcium   ○ Sodium

stance receptors of ants.[2] It is not clear to which of the successive steps in the reception process this specificity should be ascribed. It probably has nothing to do with the path the odor substance travels to the sense cell.

Currently the interest of sensory physiologists, in collaboration with chemists, is focused on the binding of the odor molecule to the receptor molecule in the sense-cell wall. The demonstrably great effects of small changes in molecular structure again and again bring us back to the notion that certain parts of the odor molecule must fit precisely with certain parts of the receptor molecule; the latter is like a lock that can be opened only by its own key.

The female silkmoth produces only a few millionths of a gram of attractant (164 nanogram[10]) in her scent gland, but this is in theory enough to set no less than 10^{13} males into a flurry of excitement. One reason for this extreme effectiveness we know already: the molecule-sieving antennae. Another lies in a really unsurpassable achievement: the olfactory cells of the male in the scent stream respond with a nerve impulse to a single attractant molecule.[7] There can be no greater sensitivity than that.

The female moth, so we must conclude, holds the male firmly in leash by her stream of fragrance. Indeed, the latest surprising news from the laboratory of Karl-Ernst Kaissling and his colleagues[8] is that it ought even to be possible for her to exert an inhibitory influence on the yearning male. A second substance is wafted into the air from the female's abdominal glands, and this one excites the second of the two sense cells in the olfactory hair. In the laboratory, when the male is stimulated by both substances at once, both sense cells are active simultaneously. Nevertheless, no fluttering response is seen. The inhibitory effect of the second substance is presumably produced by appropriate connections between the two sense cells and a higher-order element in the nervous system. It remains to be seen whether the female actually controls the male from afar, by carefully adjusted release of these odor substances. In any case, this example shows once again how important it is to know about the sense organs if one wants to understand behavior.

22 Tasting with the Feet

The notion that simple systems can perform only simple behavioral tasks dies hard.

Vincent G. Dethier, "A Surfeit of Stimuli: A Paucity of Receptors," 1971

"The Tarsal Taste Sense of Flies."

In 1961, as a fourth-semester biology student in the Animal Physiology course at the University of Munich, I performed this classical experiment. It is simple.

Experimental animal: *Calliphora erythrocephala* from the colony in the Zoological Institute; the animals have not been fed for at least two days, but have been given only pure water to drink.

Preparations: Anesthetize the fly briefly with ether (on cotton wadding). Then glue it by the back to the head of a pin. Stick the pin into a cork, and mount the cork on a stand.

Take a piece of paper twenty centimeters long and five millimeters wide, and glue it to form a ring. The fly holds this ring with the tips of its feet and turns it as it walks in place.

Procedure: With a carefully cleaned pipette put taste solutions at premarked positions on the ring: tap water, 0.1 percent quinine solution, 10 percent sugar solution. The foot tips of the walking fly touch the solutions. When does the fly extend its proboscis? Then take a new, clean paper ring and find the threshold concentration for the proboscis reaction, using sucrose solution.

In this experiment we found something interesting: the sucrose solution caused the fly to give a proboscis reaction at concentrations as low as 0.04 percent. At the same time we discovered that our own threshold for the sensation "sweet" was about ten times higher. Butterflies such as the peacock and the painted lady can be tested just like the fly. They respond to still lower concentrations, down to c. 0.00034 percent; that is, they are about a hundred times as sensitive as the fly. The flies do not respond to water as long as they have had enough to drink. But when they encounter the quinine, which to us tastes bitter, they not only fail to give the proboscis reaction but usually turn around, in a kind of avoidance behavior. Because in our experiment the flies are held by the back, these leg movements actually rotate the paper ring rather than turning the animal as they would on a fixed substrate. Two drops of quinine solution on the same ring often create a problem for the fly; it runs back and forth between them as though imprisoned.

One Thousand Six Hundred Gustatory Hairs

The ecological significance of this proboscis reaction is obvious. The sensory hairs on the feet apply a preliminary chemical test to things they encounter—puddles of water, the marmalade on the breakfast table, fatty substances in carrion and dung, and also potentially injurious substances—before the insect brain gives the command: stop and extend the proboscis. The animal does not actually begin to suck until the substance already classified as acceptable by the feet has passed a second test by sensory hairs at the end of the proboscis.

The fly's set of measuring instruments is quite respectable. Precise counts of the gustatory hairs by observation with a microscope have given the following results for the common blowfly species *Phormia regina*: foreleg 308, of which 32 are on the last tarsal segment; middle leg 208; hindleg 107 (Pl. 37). On the labellum of the proboscis are about 250 such hairs, together with 132 chemically sensitive papillae, which gives a total of approximately 1,600 taste sensors per fly.[2,8] Most of the hairs, as would be expected, are on the downward-facing half of the leg and near its end. The smallest of them are only 0.028 mm long and the largest reach a length of 0.5 mm, which is sizable on the biologist's scale.

In their fine structure they are all similar (Fig. 60). The stiff hair is hollow and open at the tip. Here the stimulus enters, striking the filamentous processes of four sense cells responsive to chemicals. Two of them are most sensitive to salty solutions (one to cations, the other to anions) and the others respond preferentially to water and sugar, respectively. There is a fifth cell but it has been left out of the picture, for it has nothing to do with the sense of taste. It ends at the base of the hair and detects the bending produced when the fly sets its foot down.

In view of the large number of gustatory bristles, it seems surprising at first that one hair alone can trigger the proboscis reaction if it is stimulated with sufficiently concentrated sugar solution. On the other hand, the proboscis reaction can be prevented by stimulating a salt receptor. The first control on the effectiveness

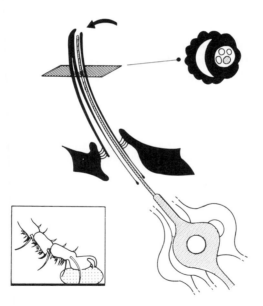

Fig. 60:
Fine structure of a taste hair. The arrow points at the pore in the hair wall through which the stimulus enters the hair to reach the processes of the sense cells. At lower left the terminal segments of a fly leg are shown, with taste hairs in a drop of liquid. At upper right is a cross section of the taste hair.

of a stimulus takes place at the level of the sense cell itself. That is, each of the four sense cells responds to several substances. If the classical stimuli are mixed, as is certainly the rule in nature, the responses to each are affected. For example, the response of a salt receptor is reduced when sugar is added to the salt solution, and as the sugar content increases the salt receptor responds progressively more weakly and the sugar receptor, more strongly.[1] The behavior of the fly toward a mixed solution such as it usually encounters in nature is ultimately the result of the interplay of excitatory and inhibitory influences on nerve cells, so-called interneurons, in the animal's central nervous system. Like the various taste bristles, the various steps of the reaction must be distinguished. The normal sequence is as follows:

1. Extension of the proboscis occurs when the hairs on the feet of a hungry or thirsty fly are stimulated with sugar solution or water, after the fly has stopped and turned toward the stimulus site.

2. Spreading of the large lobes of the proboscis occurs when hairs on the proboscis have made contact with the food[7] (Fig. 29).

3. Sucking up of the food occurs after it has been tested by the gustatory papillae on the outspread lobes.

4. Sucking is interrupted when the gustatory hairs and papillae are no longer stimulated, when they are exposed to useless or harmful substances that are rejected, or simply when the fly is full.

When Is the Fly Full?

This is a serious question. Flies, like people, must be notified of their own satiety as well as of their hunger. In fact, food intake is regulated not only by the gustatory hairs but also by receptors sensitive to mechanical stimuli, which detect the state of stretching of the foregut and the abdomen.[2,4,5]

The decision whether the fly will suck or not is made by summation, in the central nervous system, of the inputs from the sensory hairs with the inhibitory inputs from the stretch receptors.

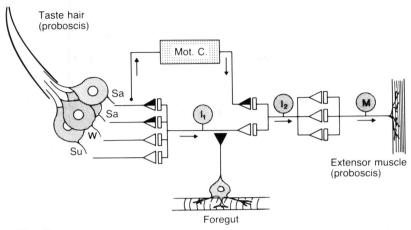

Fig. 61:
A simplified circuit diagram of the neurophysiological control of the fly's proboscis reaction. Sa, W, and Su stand for the salt-, water-, and sugar-sensitive sense cells. Mot. C. motor center in the central nervous system. I interposed nerve cells or interneurons. M motor neuron. The open triangles symbolize excitatory connections, and the black triangles, inhibitory connections.

The hungry fly sucks, because the excitatory influence from the gustatory hairs is large and the inhibitory influence from the stretch receptors, with the gut empty, small. The satiated fly stops sucking, because the inhibitory influence from the stretch receptors predominates once the gut is distended.[3,6] Figure 61 summarizes the most important points in a simplified diagram. In principle the sequence of events leading from the taste stimulus to extension of the proboscis is not at all complicated. We see that relatively simple connections among relatively few nerve cells can account for a substantial piece of behavior.

Fourteen Impulses in a Hundred Milliseconds

Vincent G. Dethier of Princeton University, who analyzed the sense of taste and feeding behavior of the fly for many years, showed that a difference of as little as three to four impulses in the response of a given sense cell can decide within a tenth of a second whether the proboscis will be extended or withdrawn.[1] He stimulated a single gustatory hair on the labellum of a thirsty fly with a 0.2 molar solution of table salt. The salt receptor responded with 14 impulses in 100 ms, and the fly extended its proboscis. Now if the same hair was stimulated with 0.5 molar salt solution, the salt receptor responded more strongly, with 14 impulses in only 70 ms, and the fly pulled the proboscis back again.

If one hair can accomplish so much, why have 1,600 of them? With a whole field of sensory hairs at various places on the body, the fly can also find out exactly where the food is and direct its body and the proboscis accurately to that position. It can also detect spatial gradients in the properties of the food by simultaneous multiple measurements. And finally, one must consider the implications of the fact that the sense cells are not pure specialists, but rather give responses of varying intensity to quite a number of substances. If the spectra of different sense cells partially overlap, the result is a vast increase in the amount of information that can be encoded and passed on to the central nervous system.

Even when the stimulus is a mixture of substances, each sense cell sends out only one message. Because the spectra of different cells vary, the message sent by each cell will vary in intensity. If the central nervous system were to "read off" the messages from a whole field of hairs, the complex mixture would be represented by a specific overall distribution of excitation, and a large number of different mixtures could be recognized by differences in the associated excitation patterns.

23 Perfume Collectors and the Tricks of the Orchids

> Rather, one must investigate the flowers in their natural habitat. . . . In brief, one must try to catch Nature in the act.
>
> *Christian Konrad Sprengel, "Das entdeckte Geheimnis der Natur," 1793*

In the New World tropics there lives a group of bees called "magnificent bees" in German because of their metallic blue, green, and golden coloration. They are the closest relatives of the bumblebees. Their "tongue" (Chapter 11), much longer than those of other bees, has given them the scientific name Euglossini, "those with the true tongue." Still another characteristic distinguishes them from all other groups of bees—the greatly enlarged hind tibiae of the males (Fig. 62). I still have vivid memories of my first meeting with these glorious insects. It was in Alta Verapaz, the mountainous central state of Guatemala in which there is very nearly eternal spring, the paradisiacal quetzal wings its way, and the famous highland coffee thrives. At the edge of the mountain rain forest the radiant colors of the bees flash in the bright sunlight. I caught two in a net and photographed them. Plate 35 shows the result.

Euglossine bees live in close association with orchids, those creatures of marvelous color and shape which, more than anything else, suggest the enchanted world of the tropics. Darwin knew of this association and described it in 1862, and in English the group is commonly known as the orchid bees. But the special nature and the details of this relationship became clear only in the last fifteen years. We owe this new knowledge mainly to the research of Calaway H. Dodson[6,8,10,17] of the University of Miami and Stefan Vogel[19,20] of the University of Mainz. Robert Dressler[11] of the Smithsonian Institute in Panama has recently summarized our present understanding of the biology of the orchid bees.

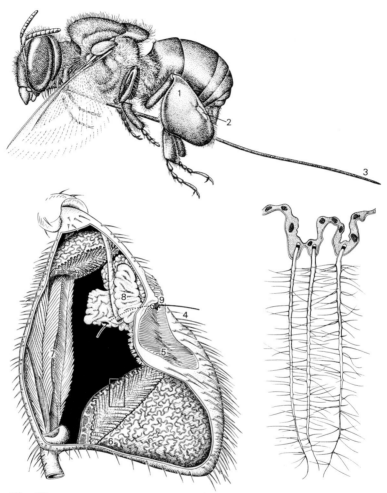

Fig. 62:
Orchid bees collect the odor substances of orchid blossoms. *Above*: A bee
in flight: (1) the swollen tibia of the hindleg with the opening (2) to the
scent container; (3) the typical long proboscis. *Below*: The interior of the
scent container exposed. The opening to the outside (bristle (4) inserted
for clarification) lies in the pan (5); part of the actual scent container (6),
with its dense hairs, has been removed here. (7) Leg musculature, (8)
glandular tissue, (9) scaly cup around the entrance. On the right, part of
the sponge (6) is enlarged.

Orchid bees are primarily solitary insects. Only a few of them can be called "semi-social," because in those species several females take care of a common nest. But even here there is no division of labor such as is found in the highly developed honeybee colonies. Female orchid bees gather the building material for the cells of the nest and construct them with no help from the males. Like other female bees, they collect pollen and nectar from all kinds of flowers and seal it up in nest cells for storage.

The male orchid bees are vagabonds. After emergence they never return to the nest of their birth. The supplies stored there are therefore of no use to them, and they forage for their own food. Like the females, they visit a variety of flowers. With the long sucking proboscis they feed preferentially on the nectar of flowers otherwise visited only by butterflies and moths, which have proboscises of similar length. Evidently the male orchid bees manage very well for themselves, for their life span—up to six months—is unusually long for a male bee.

Of the roughly two hundred species of orchid bees, those most commonly encountered on orchid flowers belong to the genera *Eulaema* (Pl. 35), *Euglossa*, and *Euplusia*. These account for about three-quarters of all euglossine species. The orchids they visit that are of particular interest here (especially members of the Catasetinae and Stanhopeinae) are ordinarily distinguished by a strong scent and by the fact that they offer no food of any kind to their insect guests. There is no pollen accessible for eating, and the nectaries are rudimentary. People looking for the customary pollinator's reward found a structure that they interpreted as a new kind of food tissue, but it has since turned out to be a special, highly active scent organ.[19,21] On the surface of this gland the odor escapes, and not only as an imperceptible gas; the substance is produced in such amounts that some remains as a liquid, in little droplets. This odor substance (terpenes) attracts the male orchid bees, and only the males.

Perfume Collection

The extraordinary thing is that the male bees collect the odor substance. While they do this, the long proboscis is folded back, for they are not feeding on the material. Instead, the forelegs are used to rub the surface of the scent gland vigorously. The tarsal segments have special mops of hair that absorb the odor substance while they are rubbing. Only the males have such finely branched hairs. About once a minute or more often the business of scrubbing is interrupted. Then the bees hover for a matter of seconds a few centimeters above the flower, kicking the legs rapidly in a manner reminiscent of the way honeybees pack pollen into the pollen basket. And in fact, they are packing the odor substance away. All the legs are used for this.[12,20] What is happening? First the bee scrapes the mop on each foreleg—which cannot, after all, absorb infinite amounts of odor substance—against the metatarsus of the middle leg on the same side (Fig. 63). For this purpose the middle-leg tarsus has a ridge equipped with rigid bristles that stand out like a rake. The droplets of odor substance remain hanging from the posterior side of these. From there the bee pushes the perfume into the swollen tibia of the hindleg. The hindleg is pulled forward and turned outward at the same time, so that the odor droplets touch the opening of the container. Fine, feathery hairs take it up and conduct it along a channel to the interior.

The whole transfer process involves about three to five repetitions of this sequence of movements, and lasts between two and six seconds, depending on the species of orchid bee. Then the bee again begins mopping up from the flower with the forelegs, and after five to sixty seconds what it has collected is transferred to the perfume flask.[12]

There is a major difference between the movements that store scent in the hindleg of the male orchid bee and those by which the female honeybee packs away its pollen (Chapter 9). The scent is brought into the container on each side entirely by the legs on that side, whereas when the honeybee packs pollen the right and left hindlegs work together.

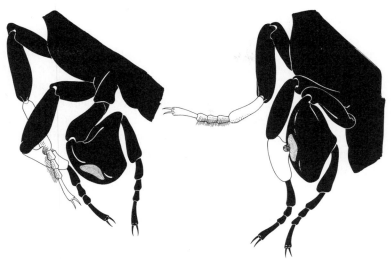

Fig. 63:
The orchid bee packing odor substance into the tibial container.

Anatomy of a Perfume Flask

The scent container itself has a fairly complicated structure.[18,20] As Fig. 62 shows, there is a "pan" on the outside of the leg, which first receives the odor substance; this leads to an interior space filled with tiny, feathery hairs. This space lies over the normal leg musculature, nearly filling the swelling of the hindleg that is so conspicuous externally. There are narrow ridges covering the wall of this container, on which the feathery hairs are seated. The capillary action of this hair-filled cavity makes it effectively a perfume sponge. The hindleg swellings of dead animals can be pressed out to see how much perfume they contain. The result is unexpected: in species of the genus *Eulaema*, about the size of a bumblebee, Vogel[20,21] found a volume of up to 30 mm^3, which means that a single animal can store as much as 60 mm^3 of odor substance.

The Odor Substance

Chromatographic analyses[20,22] show the orchid odor to be a mixture of several components, usually seven to ten. Both the nature of the components and their proportions in the mixture vary greatly from one orchid species to another. Eugenol and 1,8-cineole, which has a strong smell of eucalyptus and is also called eucalyptol, proved especially attractive to most male orchid bees (70 percent of the bees attracted by any substance) in field experiments. Therefore it is not surprising that they can be found in the odor mixtures produced by 60 percent of the bee-attracting orchids examined.[10] If a piece of filter paper is impregnated with these substances and set out in the right biotope, it is sometimes possible to catch several hundred male orchid bees with this lure in a few days. The attractiveness of an odor component may be diminished when a second component is added to it. The interesting implication is that the odors are not used as a general attractant but rather can serve as an isolating mechanism, in that certain orchids attract certain species of bees, thereby increasing the specificity of pollination (Chapter 30).

It is not quite clear how the scent container is emptied under natural circumstances. Probably the odor substance is released passively through a cuplike opening covered with scales, which pull it out like a wick (Fig. 62). The function of the sizable glands in the hindleg swellings is also still obscure. According to several observations, they could add oils to the odor substance, with the result that these lipid-soluble substances would become less volatile. This procedure is also used in the perfume industry as part of the process of concentrating odor substances. In any case, museum specimens of orchid bees often still contain odor substance in their hind tibiae after years of storage. It is also conceivable, of course, that the glands themselves produce odor, which is mixed with the collected substance to modify it.

What Is the Odor for?

Can it be that the male orchid bee perfumes himself to please the female? Unfortunately, the detailed significance of this scent in behavior is not yet quite clear. But certain observations already sketch a general picture of what we want to know.

First, female orchid bees are not attracted by the odor substances considered here. If they were, one would find them at the orchids, which is not the case. Therefore we are not dealing with a sexual attractant such as many insects produce (Chapter 20) to attract a reproductive partner. There are other orchids (*Ophrys*) that impersonate female bees with such substances, not only attracting the males but even seducing them into pseudocopulation with the flower. We shall come to these in the next chapter. As far as the euglossine bees are concerned, however, the old idea that their orchids produce a sexual attractant has proved erroneous. But even in the new view, the orchids are intimately involved in the reproduction of the bees.[10,20,23]

Again and again male orchid bees have been observed in a form of behavior similar to that of bumblebees,[4,13,14,15,16] flying along fixed routes in what is evidently a territorial patrol. Patrolling bumblebees deposit on plants odor substances they themselves produce, in a gland on the head. The swarming paths so labeled attract other males in mating condition and are also the sites at which the two sexes meet for copulation. In addition to the evidently territorial flights of the male orchid bees, another curious behavior has frequently been noted; the bees ventilate with fluttering wings while sitting at a favorite site, then fly up, circle in tight curves above the site, and return to ventilate again with stiffly outstretched hindlegs, on the original site or very close to it. It seems plausible that they are actively "blowing off" the orchid perfume.[20]

Often one or two additional males will fly up to the same site, whereupon the first chases them away. On top of all this, it has been observed that as many as five male orchid bees can fly along the same fixed route in the same direction and that the females copulate with the males here. Parallelism with the bumblebee behavior seems very likely. It is not established by the results so far available, however, and there is a large area for future research. In particular, the many interesting preliminary observations must be corroborated by behavioral studies made as quantitative as possible under experimental conditions. Perhaps the odor substance attracts only males, and the presence of several males at a given swarming site increases the probability of copulation with females passing by fortuitously or attracted visually by the shimmering males?

Intoxicated on a Slide

The orchid (and certain other plants such as *Gloxinia*, the Gesneriaceae, and the Araceae) not only attracts the bees with its odor but also allows the perfume to be taken away as a reward. What is it giving the reward for? For pollination, of course, which the male orchid bee performs unknowingly as it collects the odor substance. About 10 percent of all orchid species fall into this category.[17] Of special interest are the cases in which the orchid employs additional tricks as a means to this end. The narcotic action of the odor substance helps it to get away with these subterfuges.

It is almost too good to be true: "The immediate reaction of the male bees to the liquid can only be called intoxication. They lose motor control to a considerable degree and become clumsy and sluggish and are no longer wary. They apparently 'enjoy' the sensation for they return continually over long periods of time before tiring and flying away, only to return to other similar flowers which may or may not be of the same genus or species." So wrote Leendert van der Pihl and Calaway H. Dodson in their orchid book.[17] Other biologists have observed the same thing. It is certainly not mistaken, then, to conclude that the orchid could make pollination more likely with the intoxicating action of its odor substance, occasionally leading the male orchid bees into paths they would not otherwise voluntarily take.

In fact, the bees do slip on smooth surfaces and fall, or often slide into a position from which they can escape only by following one specific route. In a number of orchids such involuntary sliding is an essential part of the process of pollination, and is one more reason for the fantastic multiformity of their flowers. Two examples from a group of typical euglossine-attracting orchids (Stanhopeinae) give a good illustration of this magical world.

1. Figure 64 shows the blossom of the orchid *Gongora maculata*, which is visited by *Euglossa cordata*. Attracted by the strong scent, the bee flies up to the scent gland on the labellum, and, upside down, begins to soak up the odor substance with the mops on its forelegs. But the surface to which it clings is slippery; the bee loses its hold, falls onto a chutelike structure below, and slides down until its abdomen bumps against a sticky disk (viscidium) at the end from which the pollen packets (pollinia) are hanging. With this load attached to it, the bee flies to the next flower and repeats its slide. This time the pollen packets become attached to the stigma at the end of the chute. Pollination has been accomplished.[2,6] In orchids the male and female parts of the flower are more or less completely fused, forming a "gynostemium." The chute is this gyn-

Fig. 64:
An orchid bee collecting odor substance on the slippery underside of the labellum (1) of *Gongora maculata* falls into the chute below, loads itself involuntarily with the pollen packet (2), and pollinates the stigma of the next flower with it when it again slides down the chute (3).

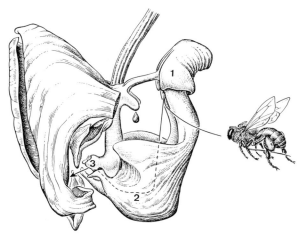

Fig. 65:
The orchid *Coryanthes speciosa* forces the visiting bee to pollinate it, for
when collecting odor substance at position (1) the bee slips and falls into
a liquid-filled trap (2) from which the only exit is a narrow opening (3).
In passing through it, the bee must crawl under the stigma and the pollinia.

ostemium, which explains the close proximity of pollen packet and
stigma at its end.

2. *Coryanthes speciosa* goes still further in manipulating the male
orchid bee. Here the chute dumps the bee into a barrel of water[1,7]
(Fig. 65). The barrel is part of the labellum, and draws its wet
contents from glands of the gynostemium (see above), which are
located directly above it and drip their watery product into the
container. In the upper part of the labellum is the scent gland. Its
odor attracts orchid bees of the genera *Euglossa*, *Euplusia*, and *Eulaema*. When they slip while scratching up the perfume, they fall
into the water barrel. They can leave it only by way of a narrow
tunnel, creeping under the stigma and the pollinia. The pollinia
become attached to the bee's abdomen. When it reaches the next
flower it splashes in again, and the pollinium is transferred to the
stigma as the bee crawls out. Again, pollination has been accomplished; the flower begins to wilt within hours, and its scent van-

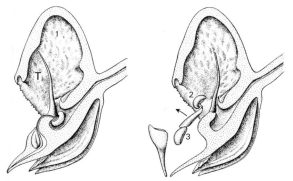

Fig. 66:
Orchids of the genus *Catasetum*—here partly cut away—fling the pollinia
against the visitor as soon as it steps on a trigger (T) in the labellum (1) in
its search for odor substances. The adhesive disk (2) flies toward the bee
and sticks to its abdomen. The actual pollen packet (3) is connected to the
adhesive disk by a stalk.

ishes. None of all this magnificence has really been a useless luxury. Everything is there to serve this single function.

In other orchids, the pollinium is thrown against the insect by
delicate mechanisms so that its adhesive disk sticks to parts of the
body characteristic of the different flowers (Fig. 66).

The Lady's Slipper, a Temperate-Zone Insect-Trapping Flower

It is not necessary to travel to the tropics to see orchids that so
guilefully exploit insect behavior to their own advantage. One of
the most lovely European orchids is the lady's slipper (*Cypripedium
calceolus*), which takes its name in all languages from its conspicuous yellow, bulbous lip (Pl. 7): *Frauenschuh, Herrgottsschüehli,
s-charpas u pantoflas, pantofella, Scarpa della Madonna*. The "slipper" is open at the top, with stamens and stigma projecting into
the opening. On either side is a fertile stamen, above them is a
sterile stamen, and below all is the stigma. Scent lures small species

of bees through the large opening into the slipper. But they cannot go out the same way, for they slide back down the inturned edges of the petal. There is only one way out. It leads through a much smaller opening, which forces the insect to push under the stigma and then past one of the anthers. This path and no other is not smooth but hairy, so that it offers good footing. Near its end it is flanked by translucent spots in the wall of the slipper. To what end? Many insects avoid darkness, and are driven away from it into the light. With the light that enters through these windows the lady's slipper guides its bewildered guests in the right direction. Incidentally, such windows are not a unique invention of the lady's slipper. The brightly translucent wall at the base of the deep funnel of the stemless gentian flower can be explained in the same way (Pl. 4).

When the insect crawls under the anthers the pollen of the lady's slipper sticks to its back. Leaving the next flower it visits, it must first pass the stigma before taking on another load of pollen on its way to freedom. Insects too large to fit into the one-way passage provided for exit from the lady's slipper are held prisoner and perish. Those so small that they do not touch the stigma as they leave fail to pollinate, but they also take no pollen with them.

The trap laid by the lady's slipper is not an infallible, invariably effective mechanism. Observation of one of its small visitors, of the genus *Andrena*, by Daumann[5] has shown that the trick works only about half the time with them. But in the effort to improve the chances of reproduction—which is always the end toward which evolution proceeds—even the slightest advantage counts, and 50 percent is certainly more than that.

In the classification system of pollination ecology, both the lady's slipper and its tropical relative *Coryanthes* are flowers of the "barrel-trap" type (*Kesselfallenblumen*). Having met the above examples, one can see that the defining characteristics of the group are evident in this well-chosen name.

24 The False Female

> I do not know what I seem to be to others, but to myself I
> seem to have been like a boy walking on the seashore, picking
> up another pebble more beautiful than the one before, while
> the great ocean of truth lay all undiscovered before me.
>
> *Isaac Newton, 1726*

That the orchids have developed the most adventurous pollination
mechanisms is shown by a further example. Here we have neither
slippery chutes nor perfume gathering, but again we are reminded
of the fact that the notion of mutual advantage of the participants
is a rule with glaring exceptions. Again there is no nectar or food
pollen for the insects. There is no question of mutualism: the orchid is a parasite on behavior patterns of the pollinator. In this
chapter we turn our attention to one of the best-investigated crime
stories in pollination ecology.

Flowers with Animal Names

Ophrys is a genus of orchids with around thirty species and a number of hybrids. *Ophrys* species are especially abundant in the late
spring in the Mediterranean countries, and for this reason alone it
is worth taking a walk away from the coast, into the inland coun-
tryside. Only four species have advanced as far as Central Europe.
There the fly orchid (*Ophrys insectifera*) is the most familiar. Its
northward march has gone the farthest, in Norway actually taking
it somewhat beyond the Arctic Circle.[7] With its "animal" name
the fly orchid is in good company. There are also "bumblebee,"
"bee," and "spider" orchids, names based on the visual similarity
to the animals concerned and bestowed at a time when people still
knew nothing about the true ecological relationships.

The most prominent morphological characteristic of the *Ophrys* blossoms is their lip (labellum), a structure that also has a major function in the lady's slipper and the other orchids in the preceding chapter. The *Ophrys* lip, one of the three petals, is thick and mechanically stable. It offers a convexly curved surface to the observer and to its insect visitors, a surface with a velvety texture. It is basically a dark purple, but on this background are various markings—sometimes of a surprising metallic blue (Pl. 38). Moreover, the labellum has a strong smell. The scent of the *Ophrys* originates exclusively in the labellum. Stefan Vogel[17] located the scent glands in a strip along the anterior edge, 1-2 mm wide, and noted that they are concentrated on the striking little appendage in the middle of this edge found, for example, in *Ophrys arachnites, Ophrys apifera*, and *Ophrys tenthredinifera* (Fig. 67).

Linnaeus wrote in his *Journey to Öland and Gotland,*[12] published in 1745, that the flowers of *Ophrys insectifera* so closely resemble a fly that the uninformed observer could not help but think that he was seeing two or three flies perched on the plant stalk, and that no artist could imitate flies so well as nature does it here. In the light of our present-day notions of a fly this claim seems greatly exaggerated. But there is truth at its core, which was recognized only later and generally accepted much later still. A milestone on this route is provided by the work of A. Pouyanne, who in 1917, after years of observation in Algeria, published his findings with

Fig. 67:
The thick appendage (A) of some *Ophrys* flowers (here *O. arachnites*) bears special scent glands. *Below*, the dense venation of this region is shown.

regard to pseudocopulation.[13] He writes that *Ophrys speculum* is regularly visited by only one insect, the wasp *Campsoscolia ciliata*, and that only the males show an interest in this flower even though the females, like the males, visit other flowers to obtain nectar. Soon after that M. J. Godfery wrote a confirmation of this finding, based on his observations in southern France,[5] and eventually studies done in Scandinavia[7,18] on *Ophrys insectifera*, in particular, considerably extended the picture. At present Bertil Kullenberg, of the Zoological Institute, University of Uppsala, is the acknowledged specialist in questions of the pollination biology of *Ophrys*. In 1961 he wrote a monumental paper on this subject, 340 pages long.

Pseudocopulation, Specificity, and an Exception to the Rule

The typical pollinators of *Ophrys insectifera* are not flies, but digger wasps (Sphecidae): *Gorytes mystaceus* and *Gorytes campestris*. In the search for a female willing to mate (the females emerge later than the males), they land on the flower with the head upward and remain there, sometimes for several minutes, fluttering the wings repeatedly and making movements very similar to those of copulation. The abdomen rubs against the labellum with the copulatory organs extended, and taps about on it as though in search of something (Fig. 68). Finally the animal tires, grooms itself, and flies away. Meanwhile the pollinia have become attached to its head. So far there is no evidence that sperm is released by the wasp. The sex drive is not extinguished by the activity on the flower, and the deception is repeated at the next flower. At the same time, the pollinia are transported to the stigma.

Other *Ophrys* species attract other insects. All of them are aculeate Hymenoptera, with the typical "wasp waist" of bees, ants, and wasps: wasps of the families Scoliidae and Sphecidae, and especially solitary bees (Apidae) of the genera *Andrena* (burrowing bees) and *Eucera* (long-horned bees) (Figs. 68, 69).

Although males of a species indiscriminately visit various *Ophrys*

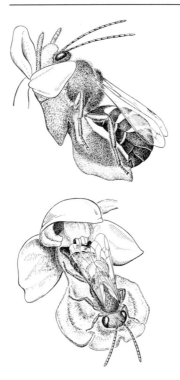

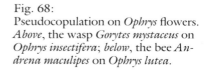

Fig. 68:
Pseudocopulation on *Ophrys* flowers. *Above*, the wasp *Gorytes mystaceus* on *Ophrys insectifera*; *below*, the bee *Andrena maculipes* on *Ophrys lutea*.

species, each *Ophrys* species is specialized for particular hymenopteran species—the fly orchid for the abovementioned burrowing wasps; *Ophrys speculum* for the scoliid wasp *Campsoscolia ciliata*; *Ophrys araneifera*, with its many spiderlike forms, for various andrenid bees; and the "bee-fly orchid" (*Ophrys bombyliflora*) for various bees of the genus *Eucera*.

Because of the close, specific relation between flower and insect, the distribution of the pollinators must set a limit to the range of the orchids. An exception proves the rule: *Ophrys apifera*, the bee orchid, is one of the typical Mediterranean species (Pl. 28). It lures long-horned bees (*Eucera*) to pseudocopulation. However, *Ophrys apifera* also lives in Central Europe, and it has made its way there

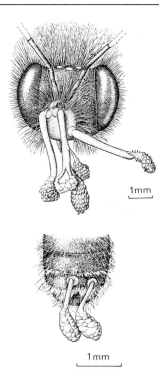

Fig. 69:
Above, the head of a longhorned bee
(*Eucera nigrilabrus*) with pollinia of
various *Ophrys* species; *below*, the abdomen of a bee (*Andrena maculipes*) with
the pollinia of *Ophrys lutea*.

only because it is capable of self-pollination, and hence no longer
depends on insect visits. In southern England self-pollination and
self-fertilization are evidently the rule of this species. One or two
days after the flowers have opened, the pollinia lean out of the
column (gynostemium), hang down, and become lightly attached
to the stigma of the same flower when the wind moves the flower
stem.[15]

The dependence of the orchids on passing insects is an enormous selection pressure. If the pollinator species become rare, the
self-pollination described for *Ophrys apifera* offers a way out. But
genetically this solution is not without its problems, at least in the
long term (cf. Chapters 4 and 30).

The Special Significance of Flower Scents

The cardinal question: What tricks does the *Ophrys* blossom use to disguise itself as an insect female? Kullenberg[8,9,10] in particular has done many field experiments in search of an answer. A number of features might serve—size and shape of the flower, its coloration, its mechanical characteristics, and its smell. To anticipate the most important result: the scent is the predominant factor, and not the visual similarity between the flower and a female insect, which seems most impressive to the human observer. Without the scent the male is neither attracted from afar nor sexually excited if he should come near. Kullenberg's field observations and experiments with flowers and scented models have shown the *Ophrys* odors to be species-group specific. Each of the six odor groups (*Ophrys* groups) that have been found attracts a particular species or species group of hymenopterans. One part of the experiments consisted in hanging a piece of velvet scented with labellum extract out in the open and studying the behavior of the insects with respect to this lure, classifying it according to the degree of attractant and excitant action. From the results were derived the six effectiveness groups: "*insectifera*-odor," "*speculum*-odor," "*scolopax*-odor," and so on.

In the search for the effective components in the natural compound odor, biologists scented such velvet lures with fractions of the natural odor or with synthetic substances that seemed likely candidates. And Kullenberg also extracted parts of the bodies of the hymenopteran females being imitated, and tested their effectiveness. Head extract of *Eucera grisea* excites not only the males of the same species but also those of *Eucera longicornis*. Both species are pollinators of *Ophrys bombyliflora*. Without doubt the orchid produces attractant substances that either correspond exactly to the female sexual attractant or have the same effect. But not all the findings fit so well into the picture. As often happens, there is much that becomes more complex when scrutinized more closely. For example, it has turned out that *Eucera* males also produce substances that stimulate male copulatory behavior. Going back to one of the topics in the last chapter, it should be noted that extracts of bumblebee heads (*Bombus, Psithyrus*) have the same effect as the marking substance from the head gland; when put on the velvet lure, they caused the animals to make territorial flights and to copulate, and in the experiment none of these actions was species-specific.[9,10]

Certainly the world of chemical signals experienced by the hymenopterans is very complicated. A multitude of questions remain to be answered. And the answers will derive in large part from the interdisciplinary collaboration of chemists and biologists.

Electroantennogram

In considering another elegant new approach, we again encounter electrophysiological techniques. The action of the odor substances on the olfactory sensilla of the insect antenna can be measured. When, as in the present case, the effectiveness of very many substances on very many species must be tested, it becomes too laborious to record the responses of single sense cells. Instead, one measures the summed responses of all the olfactory sensilla at the same time, obtaining an electroantennogram or EAG. To do this one need only insert a relatively large electrode into the tip of the antenna.

The EAG shows, first, whether the odor substances of interest have any excitatory action at all on attractant-sensitive sensilla. Moreover, it provides a much more rapid and precise description of their effectiveness than do behavioral observations. Ernst Priesner[14] of the Max Planck Institute for Behavioral Physiology, where the silkmoth is an important "domestic animal," tested the action of extracts from eighteen forms of eleven *Ophrys* species on fifty species of bees (*Andrena* and *Eucera*). The expected close relationships did in fact appear (Fig. 70). When the extracts are classified according to their effectiveness (as measured by the EAG amplitude), one finds a pattern very like the species-group specificity found in field experiments.[8]

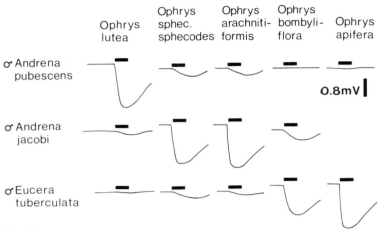

Fig. 70:
The electrical responses of the antennae of various *Ophrys* pollinators to
the scent of various *Ophrys* species. The 1-second stimulus is marked by
the horizontal bars.

The EAG tables also allow one to predict which *Ophrys* species
presumably contain the same effective components. And that brings
us to a more precise formulation of the question: Which substances are the crucial ones? The substances contained in the labella of some *Ophrys* species have been chemically identified.
Priesner[14] tested these chemicals in comparison with the flower
extracts. One with a specially strong action on *Eucera* species was
the terpene γ-cadinene: it is presumably the chief component in
the labellum extract of several *Ophrys* species. Other chemically
related substances were less effective, by a factor of a thousand or
more.

From the chemists we know[1,11,14] that in addition to γ-cadinene
the labella contain quite a number of other substances: alcohols,
aldehydes, ketones, esters, carbohydrates. It is mainly these that
give rise to the scents that seem typical of *Ophrys* species to our
noses. But they are not the reason for the high effectiveness of the
labellum on the nose of the pollinators. Even at the highest concentrations they do not trigger a large EAG. Such action as they
have is largely species-unspecific, and it is not at all comparable to

the action pattern of the *Ophrys* flowers. This is one more warning against a too anthropomorphic attitude, from which conclusions may be too hastily drawn. In the EAG test the species *Ophrys fusca*, which to us has a particularly strong scent, had little effect, whereas flowers almost odorless to us can be highly effective. For us, γ-cadinene is not a prominent odor substance. That it is also the effective component of the sexual pheromone of the *Eucera* females is suspected but has not yet been directly demonstrated.

Deception by Other Flower Features

Attracted by the odor, the pollinators locate the flowers by eye, and once they have landed their behavior is directed by tactile stimuli on the surface of the flower. The whole thing does not work without scent, but it is not only by the scent that the flower impersonates a female insect. Experiments employing primarily the fly orchid and sphecid wasps have shown that a number of features are influential.

First, the size of the flower is important. If the flower is too small the insect leaves immediately, having accomplished nothing. Too-large flowers are at a disadvantage in that the pollinator does not reach as far as the pollinia or the stigma. The labellum must be convex and mechanically stable, not yet beginning to wilt. Elongated flowers are more effective female impersonators than those more square in shape. As in the originals, models dark in color—even gray ones, but not green—are more attractive than light-colored models. Violet and purple hues come out best in comparative tests, even if they are lighter than green models. UV components increase the effectiveness, as does a high-contrast pattern on the labellum. The tactile sensations on the labellum are important in eliciting precopulatory movements. Velvety surfaces have a strong effect, whereas on smooth surfaces the animals do not even attempt to copulate. But the exact appearance of the hairs on the labellum is not important; what matters is their mechanical properties, their arrangement and the direction of the nap (Figs. 71 and 72).

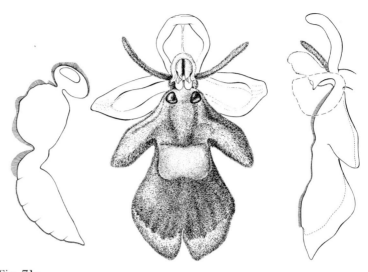

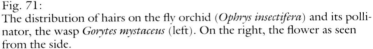

Fig. 71:
The distribution of hairs on the fly orchid (*Ophrys insectifera*) and its pollinator, the wasp *Gorytes mystaceus* (left). On the right, the flower as seen
from the side.

It goes without saying that the orchid flowers are very effective
with respect to the above features. Figure 71 shows the hairy covering of an *Ophrys* flower and that of the female insect, insofar as
it is relevant to the male in copulation. But it is possible to design
models that not only stimulate the males more effectively than real
flowers but even more effectively than real females. On the other
hand, such experiments show that the effectiveness of a model is
by no means dependent on perfect visual resemblance to the female. The similarity of *Ophrys insectifera* flowers to a fly, so highly
praised by Linnaeus, becomes very complex when one looks more
closely—quite apart from the fact that the pollinators are not flies
at all, but wasps. There are points of resemblance to the female
Gorytes; she has a black back and dark-purple wings, and when she
folds her wings together a shiny spot appears on her back, reminiscent of the "mirror" marking on the *Ophrys* flower. But there
is nothing on the flower corresponding to the white or yellow
cross-stripes on the abdomen of the female wasp, and it is ques-

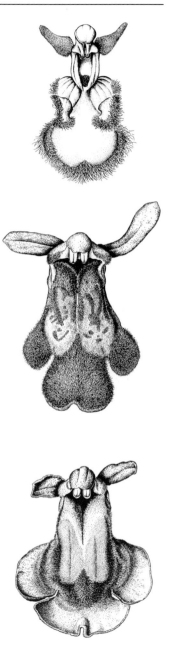

Fig. 72:
Three female-impersonating orchids:
Ophrys speculum, Ophrys fusca, and
Ophrys lutea (from top to bottom).

tionable, at least, whether the dark spots at the base of the labellum (once thought to be sham nectaries) serve as imitations of the eyes of the female *Gorytes*. The same is true of the two striking "antennae" of the floral female (Pl. 38).

Ophrys Pollinators and Orchid Bees

The chapters on color- and form-vision have surely left no doubt that difficult physiological questions are involved here. A glance back at the orchid bees reveals some important differences in the role of the odor substance the flower produces. For the euglossines it serves as a marking material and is collected, whereas for the *Ophrys* pollinators it is a sexual attractant that induces copulatory behavior. Among the orchid bees (as is also the case for the marking substances of bumblebees) the particular combination of substances is of special importance in pollinator selection. By contrast, the species-group specificity of the *Ophrys* attractant effect seems to be brought about more by the nature of individual substances than by a specific mixture of them.

The orchid bees are rewarded with perfume; the *Ophrys* pollinators leave empty-handed. As to their subjective sensations, nothing can be said. For the plant it would be fatal if the male insects were to notice the imposture and thenceforth avoid such flowers. "Flower constancy" associated with food collection, a characteristic of honeybees that manifests their highly developed capacity for learning (Chapter 25), is not a factor here. In this case the male is really deceived again and again by the same disguise—at least as long as the females have not yet emerged. The flower does not even offer any food; after all, the pollinator is supposed to do something quite different from eating.

At first it would seem that the probability of pollination would increase if as many insect species as possible were attracted. But this holds only if the attraction is associated with flower constancy. Each *Ophrys* flower imitates a number of characteristics of female insects, which considerably narrows the field of male insects attracted. That this selectivity is only partial is witnessed by the many naturally occurring *Ophrys* hybrids.

The *Ophrys* species are not the only known flowers with a sexual disguise. But all the other well-documented cases are also orchids.[2,4,6,16]

25 Learning and Forgetting

> The road is long and branching, distractions and obstacles are
> many, the goal is hazy and far away, pilgrims speak in many
> tongues. But we can look back and see progress, or look up
> and see some exciting peaks.
>
> *Theodore Holmes Bullock, "In Search of Principles in Neural
> Integration," 1976*

For the pollinators to flit unselectively back and forth among flowers of different species would be of little value to the plants. It is
an important prerequisite for cross-pollination that the insects carry
pollen from one flower to the stigma of another flower of the *same*
species. From the point of view of the insect, which can know
nothing about the needs of the plants, flower constancy is a matter
of making its behavior more economical (Chapter 29). The net
amount of energy in the food collected is that remaining after
subtraction of the energy investment required. The main expense
is fuel for the flight, but the energy needed, for example, to find
the best way to the nectary of a flower of complicated structure
must also be taken into account (Fig. 89). Economy requires that
the insect minimize the number of times such learning processes
must be repeated, just as it must minimize the distance over which
it flies to the flowers.

Where one flower is found, others of the same species will usually be nearby in fairly large numbers. Therefore an insect that
holds firm to a choice it has made shortens its travel distance;
accordingly, bees are known to exhibit not only flower constancy
but also site constancy.

Flower constancy is not a uniformly prominent feature of all
insect flower visitors. But it is present to a certain extent in considerably more insects than is generally realized.[19] This is true also
of the flies and lepidopterans, though the hymenopterans—the honeybee, in particular—clearly excel in flower constancy.

Even superficial observation gives one the entirely correct impression that a collecting bee on a single trip collects food only from flowers of a single species. More precise data can be obtained by analysis of the pollen packets the collectors bring home. In such counts 93.2 percent, or according to other authors as many as 98 percent, of the bees fly to only one kind of flower.[6,11] Honeybees visit as many as 500 flowers on one trip. Their ability to choose, then, is very accurate and reliable. In the case of bumblebees, around 55 percent of all pollen packets contain pollen from a single flower species, and 32 percent contain only two kinds of pollen.[12]

This selectivity is based on achievements of learning and memory that enable the bee to identify flower characteristics, associate them with food, and remember this relationship for long periods. It is such adaptive abilities that concern us in this chapter. Which characteristics does the bee learn particularly well or poorly, how quickly does it learn, and how long does it remember what it has learned? Finally, one would like to know how the bee extends and revises what it has learned, for the food sources do not always remain unchanged for the whole four to six weeks of a bee's life, and it is clearly of elemental importance to adjust to a new situation. The research of the last ten years has made astonishing additions to what was known previously. We owe these new results in particular to Martin Lindauer and a number of his former students who have themselves become highly regarded professionals—chief among them Randolf Menzel and his coworkers at the Free University in Berlin.

The Learning of Spectral Colors

The principle of this experiment is an elegant modification of the "color-vision test" designed by Karl von Frisch in 1910. One must understand it in order to comprehend the learning curves that result.[24,27,28,30]

First, bees are allowed to find sugar-water in a small dish in the center of a large gray table, about thirty to fifty meters away from the hive. This reward encourages them to return to the table repeatedly and to notify others in the hive. Two similar but empty dishes are positioned at equal distances from the center of the table. All three dishes can be illuminated from below with light of various colors. During this first part of the experiment none of them is lighted, and the bees have access only to the center one.

In the actual test only the two peripheral dishes are lighted, one with the color for which the learning curve is to be found (the test color) and the other with its complementary color. There is no food on the table. The arriving bee chooses one of the two dishes spontaneously. Then the intensity of the other light is changed until the two colors are equally attractive. In four minutes the bee flies to the two colors as many as forty times, twenty times to one and twenty to the other. Then the test color is associated with a reward, by illuminating the dish in the middle with the test color and allowing the bee to collect sugar-water there, after which it returns to the hive. From now on each time the same bee comes back to the table, it is again first presented with the test color and its complementary color in the peripheral positions, to see whether the previous association of the test color with food has increased its attractiveness. After the bee has decided upon one or the other color its response is recorded, and it is rewarded in the center as before. The consecutive percentages of correct choices in several repetitions of this procedure constitute the learning curve. After how many rewards does the bee choose the test color reliably? The learning curve (Fig. 73) tells us.

The bee learns any color that it perceives as such (cf. Chapters 12 to 14), but the rate at which it forms the association with food varies. The color most rapidly learned is violet (413 and 428 nm). After only a single reward the bees choose this color with a probability of 85 percent! With blue-green (494 nm) learning takes longest, but even here 59 percent of the choices are correct after only one reward. Blue (444 nm) is learned more rapidly than yellow or orange, but after more than six rewards all the learning curves reach a level between 89 percent and 93 percent.

The speed of learning is independent of the intensity (luminous flux) of the training color over a wide range, as long as it is above the threshold for detection.

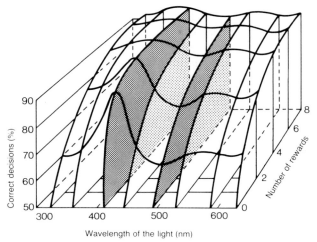

Fig. 73:
How rapidly do honeybees learn colors? They learn most quickly when the color is violet (c. 410 nm; the third curve from left rises most steeply) and most slowly when it is blue-green (c. 490 nm; the fifth curve from left rises least steeply).

Color Vision Depends on Behavior

When the bees' ability to learn colors is compared with their actual color vision (Chapters 12 to 14), it turns out that the sensory mechanisms alone by no means explain the learning process. The brain evaluates signals to be learned in a manner independent of their effectiveness as stimuli and of the mechanisms in the visual cells. In "bee-subjective" terms ultraviolet is the brightest and most saturated color, and as such is particularly attractive. But color-discrimination ability is especially great in the violet (400 nm) and even more so in the blue-green (500 nm)—bee-subjectively the darkest color, with the least stimulus value (see p. 96). On the other hand, blue-green is learned most slowly, and violet most rapidly. The curves for ultraviolet (c. 340 nm) and green (c. 530 nm) are between these extremes (after one reward about 65 percent of the choices are correct).

These and similar experiments show us that the color world of the insects is subdivided into various functional categories. Colors are evaluated differently in different behavioral contexts; color vision is not employed in the same way for all visually controlled behavior patterns. According to very recent experiments, it is no longer correct to speak of *the* spectral sensitivity of an insect, for it depends heavily on the kind of behavior being studied.

Ultraviolet, which for the bee is primarily the color of the sky, is important for navigation by sky light. Accordingly, the ultraviolet receptors are especially numerous in the dorsal part of the eye.[1] Bees can use the pattern of polarization of the sky for navigation, and the polarization of the light is very pronounced in the ultraviolet region (Chapter 27). Pure UV, although it is the most effective stimulus color, is ordinarily associated with the sky rather than with food, and therefore the bee has greater difficulty in learning the food association than was at first expected. Remember, too, that the way to the nectar is commonly indicated by UV-free guide marks on the flowers (see Chapter 15). Green and blue receptors are especially important in direct orientation by the position of the sun, whereas the UV receptors are not.[4] Green receptors are the most numerous in the bee eye. In a protracted series of experiments carried out with exemplary precision, the Darmstadt zoologist Walter Kaiser and his coworkers succeeded in demonstrating that the visual control of movements in so-called optomotor behavior (a turning of head or body found in many animals, by which the animal attempts to prevent shifting of the picture seen by the eye—that is, to keep a moving environment visually constant) is dominated by green receptors and that color vision is not involved in this behavior.[13,14,15] Interestingly, the situation is quite different in phototaxis, a similar reaction in which the animal moves toward a light source or away from it. Here color-specific effects can be clearly demonstrated, although the contribution of the UV receptors is weighted especially strongly.[16]

The good color discrimination in the blue-green is presumably of particular use to the bees in orienting to their collecting sites by landmarks, such as trees and meadows. This background color is not primarily associated with food in their normal life. Finally, most flowers—in temperate latitudes, at least—are violet, blue, or bee-purple (a mixture of UV and yellow, see Chapter 14).[3] It would seem, then, that the rapid learning of colors in the violet region when they are associated with food in an experiment is explicable on the basis of the common occurrence of these as flower colors.

For a color to become established as a food label, the time when it is presented is a critical factor.[25,30] The bee must see it during the last phase of its approach flight. Colors first seen while sucking or while the bee is flying away are not learned. To be precise, the color signal must be presented within the time span from about two seconds before to about half a second after the onset of feeding; otherwise it is not associated with the reward. Once a bee has inserted its proboscis and is sucking, in many flowers the colors will no longer be visible to it. To appreciate what the numbers are telling us, consider the following: the bees need only three short seconds in a collecting flight that can easily last an hour, in order to identify and memorize the flower color! This can be demonstrated experimentally by presenting different colors during the approach, the feeding, and the departure, and then presenting all three at once when the bee next approaches. It will choose the approach color.

Learning of Scents and Shapes

Of the various signals bees associate with flowers, scent is more rapidly learned than color or shape. Flowery odors are chosen correctly 97-100 percent of the time after only a single exposure[17] (see also Chapter 15), whereas colors on the average are identified reliably (over 90 percent) only after three to five visits,[24] and shapes only after twenty visits; indeed, in some experiments shapes were never learned as well as odor or color, with a maximum of 85 percent correct choices for shape discrimination.[33] Nevertheless, in experiments in which all three modalities are presented simultaneously, this ostensible hierarchy can break down—for example, in cases where a color label is higher in its relative effectiveness than a scent label.[18] More about this later. First let us consider the results of pure scent training in greater detail.[17,18] The bee's speed of learning varies with the odor involved. After only one act of sucking, a bee can distinguish a food source labeled with a flowery odor such as rosemary, thyme, or geraniol from odorless sources or those having a different odor with 93-100 percent certainty.[17] With nonflowery odors, the 90 percent level is reached only after two or three sucking acts (bromostyrene, methylheptenone, caprylic acid, caproic acid, isobornyl acetate) or may not be reached even after ten or twenty sucking acts. For example, the maxima for valeric acid and butyric acid even after so many trials were only 86 percent and 87 percent, respectively.[18]

This greater expertise where flowery scents are concerned seems to make sense biologically. The more rapid learning of such odors as compared with color and shape signals has long been thought to be associated with communication among the bees in the hive. This explanation seems plausible at first, but it does not suffice. It is true that information about the way the food source smells is passed on by the scent clinging to the pelt of the collecting bee, whereas information about shape and color is not. The bee learns the odor so perfectly by communication within the hive alone that the increase in choice accuracy produced by an actual visit to the site is so slight as not to be statistically significant. This is nothing less than prospective learning, not simply trial and error. An amazing achievement for an invertebrate animal, and an impressive documentation of the effectiveness of communication in the bee society! But here is the crucial point: the bee can also learn the odor without information from another bee, by its own experience alone.[17]

The more rapid learning of flowery than of nonflowery odors

◊

The antenna of *Hoplia farinosa*, a beetle that frequently visits flowers (see Pl. 11). The three enlarged terminal segments can be spread out; on their inner surfaces they bear a large number of olfactory organs (pore plates). Magnification 22 ×.

Plate 33   257

The "devil's claw," *Stapelia*, a cactuslike plant of tropical Africa, attracts insects with a penetrating carrion odor, the action of which is presumably reinforced by the meat color of the flower and its woolly hairs. Flies gather in large numbers on what they evidently take for carrion and lay their eggs, preferring the middle of the flower.

Plate 34   259

The spreading bellflower (*Campanula patula*) belongs to the common
type of flower in which the intensity of the scent increases toward the base
of the flower. There the nectar is secreted. From the standpoint of the bee
the spreading bellflower is "bee-violet." Because of its open structure it is
visited and pollinated by a great variety of insects.

Plate 35   261

Orchid bees from the Guatemalan highlands. The iridescent green species, above right, is *Exaerete smaragdina*; the enlarged photo on the facing page shows its hindleg with the swollen tibia, which has been converted to a container for odor substance. The other species, above left, is *Eulaema* sp.

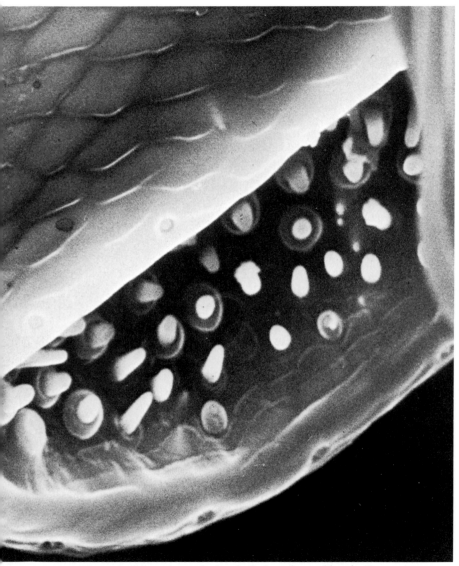

The end of the palp on the head of a long-horned beetle (*Leptura*) commonly found on umbelliferous flowers in the summer. A battery of conical sense organs is clearly revealed. Magnification 2,350 × .

Plate 37 263

The tip of a tarsus of the blowfly *Calliphora erythrocephala*, with various hairlike gustatory and tactile bristles. Two claws are also clearly visible; these, together with the filigreed adhesive pad below them, enable the fly to walk on smooth and overhanging surfaces. Magnification 315 ×.

The fly orchid (*Ophrys insectifera*), the best-known case of a flower parasitic on the courtship behavior of an insect. It gives such a good imper-
sonation of a female digger wasp that the male is deceived into pseudocopulation with it, during which pollen is transferred between insect and
flower. In addition to the odor of the flower, its form and surface structure play a role in the deception.

Plate 39   265

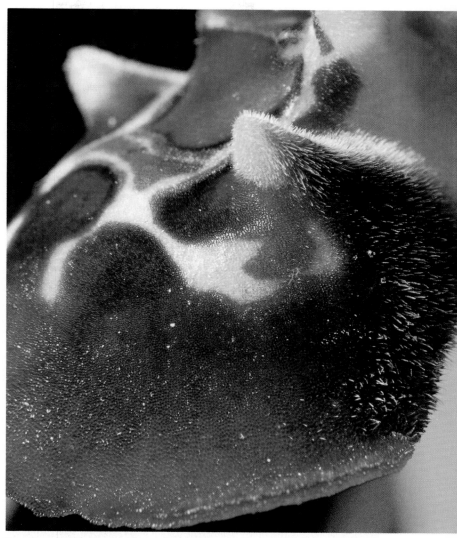

The flower of the late spider orchid (*Ophrys fuciflora*) in the enlarged photo shows the bulbous lip typical of *Ophrys* species. Its velvety coat and its stability are a prerequisite for pseudocopulation by male insects. The green pollen container (not shown) above the lip contains two pollen packets, each of which is joined by a stalk to adhesive disks. This orchid takes many forms, and its many subspecies are difficult to identify.

Plate 40

◊
The water lily *Nymphaea* demonstrates a phylogenetically primitive type of flower, like the magnolia. It contains no nectar but an abundance of pollen, and it is regularly visited by beetles.

Herb Paris (*Paris quadrifolia*), justly respected because of its poisonous fruit, has a remarkable flower. Only the eight slender yellow stamens are colored, unless one counts the brownish-purple ovary with the four threadlike stigmas. The perianth, which in most insect flowers is clearly set off from the green background by its color (see Pl. 1), can hardly be distinguished from the leaves here. The mechanism of pollination is not quite clear. It has been claimed that the ovary resembles rotting meat and hence attracts flies, but evidently pollination by insects has never been observed directly. All the more interesting that the possibility of wind pollination has since been demonstrated experimentally. Has herb Paris converted secondarily to wind pollination? Its pollen is only slightly sticky, it has no nectar, and the inconspicuous coloration of the flower is like that of grasses and conifers, which are wind-pollinated. Only the pollen is yellow; it was so in the primitive plants and still is in the wind-pollinated plants. Attraction is not a primary function of its color.

is very probably innate, a predisposition fixed in the central nervous system. In any case, there is no clear evidence that the receptors are responsible, for there is certainly no tendency for them to respond less strongly in general to nonfloral odors (cf. Chapters 15 and 16).

The concentration of an odor substance, like the intensity of a color, has no effect on the animal's success in learning, as long as it is above the threshold for detection. This, again, seems biologically sensible. In nature large fluctuations in the intensity of the scent of a flower can be expected, not only because of external conditions such as wind and temperature. Scent emission, like nectar secretion and the exposure of pollen, can also exhibit a strict diurnal rhythm (Chapter 26).

Shapes and Patterns

Bees learn shapes and patterns relatively slowly. Large and small disks (55 mm and 20 mm in diameter) are chosen correctly 90

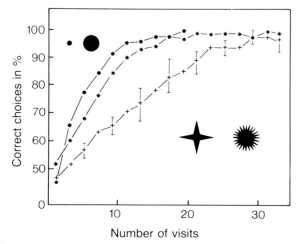

Fig. 74:
Learning curves for the discrimination of various shapes by the honeybee.
Upper curve: discrimination between large and small round disks. Middle
and lower curves: discrimination between four- and twenty-four-pointed
stars; the training pattern was either the twenty-four-pointed star (middle
curve) or the four-pointed star (lower curve).

percent of the time after ten rewards, and in tests of discrimination
between four-pointed and twenty-four-pointed star figures a score
of 92 percent correct was achieved after about thirty visits. Although the final score was independent of which of the two stars
was associated with the reward, the shape of the learning curve
was markedly affected; the bee learns more rapidly when the training shape is the highly subdivided twenty-four-pointed star (Fig.
74).[21]

Actually it is not quite right to speak of learning by *the* bee
(honeybee) in this section. There are genetically fixed predisposi-
tions for learning which are race-specific, so that differences are
found, for example, between *Apis mellifera carnica* and *Apis mellifera ligustica*. Josta Lauer and Martin Lindauer commented on
this as follows in 1971: "The sky compass leads both races into
the immediate vicinity of the site. The carnica bees are additionally
aided in orientation by characteristic guidelines in the terrain. The

ligustica are not, or only to a lesser extent. Different learning pre-
dispositions also play a role subsequently, in close-range orientation. After the first learning acts both races are brought to the
target by the shape of the site itself. For the carnica race the site
shape then rapidly loses attractiveness, for it learns the spatial relationship of the site to the surrounding landmarks, especially when
the features of this relationship are obvious. The ligustica bees do
not have this ability to such a degree and must rely longer on the
appearance of the site itself; but eventually they learn to find the
target by its position in the constellation of landmarks just as the
carnica bees do. The difference between the two races, then, is as
follows: the carnica bees encode less conspicuous visual markers
in the surroundings than the ligustica bees do. As a result they are
more easily able to construct a map containing the site and store
it as an engram."

Flexible Learning: An Ecological Adaptation

The pollinators would not be very well off if one learning act were
to form an inalterable, permanent association with a particular odor
substance. Flower constancy reaches its limit when the food supply changes and, in the course of time, other flowers with other
scent and color labels offer something better. The pollinators must
add to and change what they have learned, if they are to be optimally adapted to a changing situation. Doesn't the ability to remember a color for at least two weeks after only three rewards
make such flexibility more difficult?[24]

It is indeed harder for the honeybee to change an already learned
response than to learn for the first time.[8,26] Changing to a new
color is easier than changing to a new scent. But this difficulty is
really only relative; having learned the first odor on a single trial,
the bee learns to choose the second with a probability of 86 percent after ten trials.[17] During training to a pure spectral color the
bee learns to respond positively to similar colors (Chapter 14);
that is, it is not necessary to undergo a new learning process for

each nuance or to change what has been learned.[26] This is entirely reasonable, for within a population of flowers such variations in hue are common.

Experiments are ordinarily made more clear-cut by working with only the color, or the odor, or a visual pattern. But flowers have all of these at once. Moreover, the flowers open and secrete nectar and scent at different times, not only during the year but also during the day. It will come as no surprise, then, that honeybees adapt to this situation by associating several simultaneously presented features with one another in complex experimental situations. This is evident in the fact that they learn best when the configuration of these features is undisturbed; when one of two signs evidently learned as a unit is altered, it is difficult or impossible for them to continue using the other for orientation. This is especially true of the sign pair "time" and "color" and the pair "color" and "scent," and less so for the configuration "time" and "scent." A flower that changed its color and its time of nectar secretion each day would be nonsense to a bee—even if the odor, for instance, were to remain unchanged.

The ecological interpretation springs immediately to mind. The collecting activity of the worker bee is initiated by a time signal. The bee leaves the hive at a certain time and looks for flowers. In this research, color is particularly important for long-range orientation and scent, for short-range orientation (Chapter 18). In a sense, then, color is closer to the time signal than scent is. In the immediate vicinity or on the flower itself, the close coupling of color and scent ensures continuity of orientation.[2]

Short-Term and Long-Term Memory

All this is astonishing enough, when we recollect that it is being done by insects. It may well seem even more exciting that even in the mechanism of information storage and the establishment of memories there are evident similarities to the vertebrates.

Beekeepers have always known that bees have retentive memories. After periods of bad weather they resume flying to the old food site, and when the hive is moved the collecting bees continue to return first to the old position for almost two weeks. A record has been claimed by the famous bee researcher Martin Lindauer.[2] He observed bees emerging from a 173-day hibernation and flying to the feeding site they had last visited in the autumn.

In the vertebrates two kinds of memory are known, short-term and long-term. We experience both of them daily. Having heard a new telephone number just once, we forget it by the time we have finished dialing, or at most a few minutes later. But one's own name or telephone number or the way home has been repeated so often that it seems quite unforgettable. Such things are permanently stored in memory. The transfer from short-term to long-term storage requires a certain amount of time. Transfer can be hampered by hypothermia, electroshock, carbon dioxide narcosis, and exposure to violent mechanical forces. Therefore accident patients with concussion cannot remember the moments before the accident or the accident itself, although information already in long-term storage is affected far less or not at all. The fixation of information in the long-term memory in turn can be disturbed by drugs that interfere with protein synthesis. Antibiotics such as puromycin are substances of this kind.

Experiments have been done in which puromycin is injected into the brains of mice; afterward they can no longer learn anything new, although what they had learned previously is unaffected.

The interesting thing here is the similarity to the bee brain. In the bee, too, a long-term and a short-term memory have been found. The persistence of memory is tested in the bee by observing the frequency of correct choices at various times following the last reward. During the first hours the effectiveness of the memory increases, and then performance declines slowly but steadily. The same thing happens in vertebrates; in both cases the result is thought to reflect the consolidation phase of the memory and the transfer from short-term to long-term memory. In the bees, too, this phase is very susceptible to electroshock, carbon dioxide anesthesia, and cooling of the brain; all of these block the ability to recall what has been learned.[27]

But such blocking agents are effective only if they act shortly after the last reward; as early as seven minutes afterward they have no effect in the bee.

There is now good experimental evidence to suggest that the two "mushroom bodies" in the insect brain have something to do with memory (Fig. 75). These mushroom-shaped regions of the brain are thought to be associated with the higher, "intelligent" functions of insects. They are particularly well developed in the "intelligent" social insects such as bees, ants, and bumblebees. A microprobe can be used to produce localized cooling, to 0°C, of selected parts of the mushroom bodies, the so-called α-lobes. The proboscis-extension reaction (see Chapter 15), which before this interference could be elicited by odor alone after only one learning trial in which odor and reward were combined, falls from about 75 percent responses to the odor to only 23 percent when the α-lobes have been cooled to 0°C for about a minute, one minute after the reward is given. If the cooling is done six minutes after the reward, the proboscis-extension reaction is triggered as readily as if no cooling had occurred.[23,27]

The short-term memory is not just an unavoidable stage on the way to the long-term memory. Biologically it also makes sense because it makes possible the adaptive management of new information and the alteration of previously stored information as required. This ability is especially important for that highly organized social being, the honeybee. The coordinated cooperation of tens of thousands of individuals ensures a considerable degree of independence of external factors. Food stores and a constant high hive temperature even in frosty weather permit a steady succession of new worker bees to be raised throughout the collecting season. During this long period, several months, the menu changes continually. It would be extremely inconvenient if the bees were unalterably bound to one or a few species of flower by their genetic predisposition. They must be able to adjust as new opportunities become available.

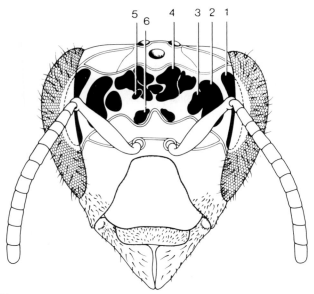

Fig. 75:
The brain of the honeybee contains about 850,000 nerve cells and has a volume of one cubic millimeter. Here it is shown in black. Behind each eye are three regions (1, lamina; 2, medulla; 3, lobula) that process mainly visual information. In the middle are the so-called mushroom bodies (4), of which the α-lobe is one section (5). The signals coming from the sense organs on the antennae are first processed in the antennal lobes (6).

Of the roughly twenty thousand species of bees, most are solitary. Here the situation is different. Their brief adult life, in which they must rely on themselves alone, occurs in an accurately "predictable" season with just as "predictable" a food supply. In this case the species becomes spatially and temporally bound to a few or only one flower species. This rigid but precise limitation is evidently the better way, under such circumstances, to obtain the energy required to provide for the young in the short time available.[5,12,22] In any case, the learning capacity of the honeybee is in a class of its own, excelling everything of which other insects, such as flies,[29,31] are known to be capable. More than two thousand years ago Aristotle wrote in his *Historia animalium*: "On each expedition the bee does not fly from a flower of one kind to a flower of another, but flies from one violet, say, to another violet and never meddles with another flower until it has got back to the hive." How long it has taken for us to develop the ability to study the physiological mechanisms that underlie this flower constancy!

26 Keeping Track of Time— Punctuality Is a Key to Success

The bees' work is marvelously mapped out on the following plan: a guard is posted at the gates, after the manner of a camp; they sleep till dawn, until one bee wakes them up with a double or triple buzz as a sort of bugle-call; then they all fly forth in a body, if the day is going to be fine—for they forecast winds and rain, in case of which they keep indoors.

Pliny the Elder (23-79), "Naturalis historiae libri"

The Flower Clock of Carl von Linné

Many flowers open and close at specific times of day. Over two centuries ago Linnaeus (Carl von Linné, 1707-1778), the Swedish physician and botanist who, as the leading systematist of his time, invented an orderly scientific nomenclature for plants and animals, concluded from this behavior of the flowers that there must be a flower clock. In opening their flowers one after another, like a clock, the various species tell us the time.

There are decidedly early risers, but also slugabeds and notorious nightowls. Linnaeus found that, for instance, the goatsbeard (*Tragopogon pratensis*, also called "Jack-go-to-bed-at-noon") opens its blossoms in the earliest morning hours, between three and five o'clock; around ten o'clock they close again. The turn of the common dandelion (*Taraxacum officinale*) comes between eight and ten o'clock, and among the very late risers are the cranesbill *Geranium triste* and the appropriately named night-scented catchfly (*Silene noctiflora*). When the cranesbill opens it is the eighteenth hour of the day, and when the catchfly begins to perfume the air, the twenty-first. The most famous nocturnal species, though, comes from Central America—the queen of the night (*Selenicereus gran-diflorus*), a slender climbing cactus. Its magnificent calyces are as much as twenty centimeters in diameter. They are fully open at midnight; but the glory of the night is followed by a rapid wilting after daybreak.

Later researchers confirmed Linnaeus's idea of a flower clock. About a hundred years ago the Austrian botany professor Anton Kerner, Ritter von Marilaun, discovered that the clock in Innsbruck is two hours ahead of that described by Linnaeus for the same species in Uppsala. Why? In Innsbruck the sun rises two hours earlier; for the flowers it is an important timing signal.

The flower visitors are not unaffected by this phenomenon. We must take it for granted that their behavior is adjusted to the environmental conditions for their own advantage—to maximize economy. With the astonishing performance of their sensory equipment and their ability to learn, we can expect them to find ways of flying to their food stores when they are open, most of the time at least. In fact, bees are trained to remember these hours of business by the flowers. But even without actual learning, the collecting activity of the pollinators is often synchronized by a special signal: the flowers not only display their wares but also send out an attractive scent only at certain times of day. The infatuating, intense fragrance of the queen of the night is an example; it shows the night-flying moths the way. Some European flowers behave similarly; the Turk's-cap lily (*Lilium martagon*) (Pl. 19), the evening primrose (*Oenothera biennis*), the lesser butterfly orchid (*Platanthera bifolia*), the Nottingham catchfly (*Silene nutans*), and many others smell only—or at least most strongly—in the evening. Others release their scent at other times.

And it is still more interesting that the food itself is frequently made available with a diurnal periodicity. Both the amount—as a rule of thumb, one to five milligrams are produced per flower per day—and the quality (sugar content) of the nectar can fluctuate considerably in the course of a day.[4,8] In some cases, when the nectar is most abundant it is also sweetest. In others the quality is constant throughout the day but the amount passes through one or more maxima, and in still others the amount can be constant while the quality varies. Usually the best nectar is presented at midday, even by flowers that secrete nectar mostly in the morning and evening. In general the nectar is sweeter when the sun is shining, the temperature increasing, and the humidity decreasing. Under these circumstances, after it has been secreted the nectar thickens. But in its details the interplay between nectar production and the alteration of the nectar by environmental factors is neither entirely simple nor uniform. It is certain that external factors not only affect the nectar after it is secreted but influence the process of secretion itself.[6] For our purposes it suffices to note that these fluctuations exist and are very often distributed in a regular manner through the day. The same is true of the pollen,[8] which is often present in abundance early in the morning whereas later there is none at all. This is the case, for example, in the corn poppy (*Papaver rhoeas*) (Pl. 2) and the mullein (*Verbascum thapsiforme*).

The Honeybee's Sense of Time

The honeybee has a true sense of time. Ingeborg Beling, the pioneer of research on this subject, wrote an essay in honor of the eightieth birthday of her teacher Karl von Frisch,[18] in which she recalled the exciting experiments she had done thirty-seven years previously:[3] "I had been feeding my bees every day, at an outdoor feeding table, from four to six o'clock in the afternoon. After three weeks I left the feeding dish empty, but observed the table from early in the morning to late in the evening. It was hardly to be believed: my marked collector bees investigated the table only at the time to which they had been trained; they must have noticed when the feeding was done, and knew exactly what time of day it was. No matter what time of day the training period was scheduled, the result was always the same. It was even possible to train them to two feeding times." Later three-time and five-time training proved successful, and the experiment worked even in an indoor flight room with constant external conditions—and, if there was no alternative, even at night.

Soon after this discovery an answer was found to the question whether bees can also learn the time when the nectar quality is highest.[19] They can, and they can also appear at the right time at various places, when the training procedure demands this achievement.

The bee, then, can do what it must do to take advantage of its food supply most economically. Indeed, even under natural conditions it saves itself unprofitable flights. An adjustment to the daily fluctuations in nectar and pollen availability is evident in the fact that the bee activity at different flowers is maximal at different times of day.[8] The collectors spend their "time off" in a quiet corner of the hive, from which they emerge only when their flowers have opened,[11] even though the weather may already have been good for flying for some time.

A remarkable limitation is placed on the time sense of the bees by its coupling to the twenty-four-hour rhythm. Even after weeks of training it is not possible to cause the bees to visit a food source every eight, nineteen, or forty-eight hours, for instance. No allowance has been made for such an unnatural rhythm; but this is normally no problem, because the flower clock also runs in a twenty-four-hour rhythm.

From Paris to New York and from Long Island to Davis

As yet we understand hardly anything about the mechanism of the clock that underlies this sense of time. But a few details of its performance that recent research has revealed are worth our attention.

At the outset, much time was devoted to the question whether the "internal clock," despite being linked to the twenty-four-hour rhythm, is independent of external factors—that is, really endogenous, controlled from within the organism. Key experiments on this point were those of Maximilian Renner at the Zoological Institute of the University of Munich, another former student of

Karl von Frisch.[14,15,17] The basic idea is a simple one: externally controlled periodicities are associated with the rotation of the earth, with factors shifted in time at different geographical longitudes so that they always occur at the same local time. If bees are trained in Paris to feed between 8:15 and 10:15 in the morning, and are then flown across the Atlantic overnight and tested the next morning in New York, they come to the feeding dish at 3 p.m. Eastern time. This is exactly twenty-four hours after the last feeding in Paris. Because this experiment was done in closed rooms where the temperature and lighting conditions were kept constant, the result is unequivocal. The internal clock functions without being influenced by external factors that change in the diurnal rhythm, such as the alternation between light and dark and a number of geophysical factors. But under natural conditions would it not be possible for the position of the sun and the day-night alternation to affect the bee clock?

Examined more closely, the situation is indeed more complicated than it seemed at first. In 1955 Maximilian Renner carried out a second "displacement" experiment. This time he trained bees in the open, on a large field of grain on Long Island, eighty kilometers northeast of New York City. They were then displaced by exactly 48° of longitude by a nighttime flight over the continent, and tested on a plowed field in the Sacramento Valley near Davis, eighty kilometers northeast of San Francisco. Now the foraging activity of the bees at the feeding site exhibited two clear maxima, the first forty-five minutes before the expected twenty-four-hour recurrence of the trained time (this amount of deviation is normal, and can occur without displacement), and the second an hour and a half after the first. After only three days the second maximum had caught up with the three-and-one-quarter-hour difference in local time between the training site on the East Coast and the test site in California. Therefore exogenous factors are also involved in the bees' time sense; such factors are normally synchronized with the endogenous factors, but can become important aids when it is necessary for the bees to make an adjustment to the local time of the flower clock. In laboratory experiments this ability to adjust was demonstrated still more precisely. Bees need three days to adjust to an artificial shift of the day-night cycle by three and one-half hours.[1,2] Analogously, the dissociation of the internal clock by carbon-dioxide anesthesia can be understood in terms of endogenous control of part of the mechanism with exogenous influence on another part.[12] Time-trained bees tested after deep carbon-dioxide anesthesia come to the feeding site both at the trained time and at a time shifted by the duration of the anesthesia.

The Social Entraining Agents in the Bee Colony and Time-Coupled Learning

And there is still more to the story. In addition to endogenous rhythmicity, extremely widespread throughout the plant and animal kingdoms, and the similarly widespread possibility of entrainment of the endogenous rhythm by exogenous signals (especially the day-night alternation), the time sense of the honeybee is characterized by a special third aspect—social entrainment.[13] The rest of the colony becomes entrained to the time when the collector bees are most active, and it is capable in turn of signaling this time to the collectors. If time-trained collector bees are anesthetized and transferred to a strange colony with another collecting time, on the very next day their collecting activity passes through three maxima: the time to which they were trained, a time shifted by the duration of the anesthesia, and the collecting time of the host colony.

When the honeybee always visits a certain species of flower at the same time of day, a time when it is offering food in particularly large amounts or of particularly high quality, the bee demonstrates time-coupled learning. This time-coupling has now turned out to be a fundamental element in honeybee learning and remembering. Its biological significance is immediately apparent. It is nonetheless surprising to see how accurate this coupling can be. In an experiment, bees were presented with a number of scents at nine times during a day, and each time a different scent was associated with a reward, for three collecting flights only. On the next day, the bees picked out the right scent at each of the nine times. They can do this even if the times are only twenty minutes apart. Performance like this is found not only for scents but for colors as well,[9] which emphasizes the general significance of time-coupled learning.

Auguste Forel, the great Swiss psychiatrist and entomologist (1843-1931) and a professor in Zurich, enjoyed experiments like this. In his book *The Senses of Insects* (1910) he describes in great detail meals taken outdoors in summer: "For several years we have taken our meals [in Chigny, where he lived until 1907] during the summer in the open air on the terrace. In the morning, from 7:30 to 9:30 or 10:00, preserves are provided, which remain upon the table, for, the children going to school at an early hour and the elders rising late, breakfast is a movable feast." It provided the ever-curious mind of Forel many opportunities for important observations. One day the bees discovered the preserves, and thenceforth they arrived in swarms at breakfast time, even when the professor had given instructions "to put the table as usual on the terrace next day, but not put any preserves thereon." On the 18th of July, 1906, at eight o'clock, Auguste Forel discovered and documented the time sense of the bees while breakfasting outdoors. His experiment ended in a rather unscientific way: "My wife, from sympathy with the bees, beginning to give them sweetened water and jam, after several days they ceased to come only at the times of certain meals, and in this regard the experiment was spoiled."

Sequential Blooming

In conclusion, let us examine the story once again from the viewpoint of the plants. When different species share a given habitat, they compete for pollinators. In addition to all the differences in shape, color, and fragrance, this competition has often led to the development of characteristic sequences of blooming times—with differences not only in the time of day at which the flowers open and offer food, but also in the time of year when the plant is in bloom. In this way competitors for a given pollinator keep out of one another's way.

Still more: If what the flowers can offer the insects is in limited supply, sequential blooming can mean that pollinators are available for a longer time because the supply of food is maintained, and it may be only under these conditions—as in the case of the bumblebees—that the pollinators themselves have time to form colonies and reach sexual maturity. Viewed in this light, these plants would be not only competing with one another but also helping one another to feed their mutual pollinators.[20]

27 The Language of the Bees and Its Sensory Armamentarium

> There is no form of communication in the whole animal kingdom that could even approximately be equated to the dance of the bee.
>
> *Martin Lindauer, "Verständigung im Bienenstaat," 1975*

If one places a little dish filled with sugar-water in front of a bee-hive, it may take hours for it to be discovered. But once one of the foragers has found it, a fascinating performance follows. Almost immediately a horde of collectors descends on the food. It seems clear that the rumor has gone the rounds. And it does so by the "language" of the bees.

Hardly any other human ability contributes so greatly to the special position of mankind among all organisms as the ability to articulate speech and understand the speech of others. "In the beginning was the Word, and the Word was with God, and the Word was God." For John the Evangelist language is divine, and consequently it is precisely because of their language that humans are human in the most fundamental, special sense of the word. For many linguists, "human" and "having the gift of speech" still remain essentially synonymous concepts. And indeed there is nothing in the animal world to equal this ability. Nowhere else is there such a wealth of signals, so completely detached from the requirements of the moment. Human language is unimaginably productive because it allows an exceedingly free employment of words, the creation of new ones, and the adaptation of old ones to a new function; it is an open system of symbols. Merely the position of a word in a sentence, or its intonation alone, can change its meaning. Even the chimpanzees, our closest relatives, are far from having such abilities.

Are we to believe, then, that invertebrate animals really have something that deserves the name "language"? Today the dance language of the bees, almost forty years after it was first decoded, is a biological classic. And even though from the very beginning no one wanted to call the special position of human speech into question, it was clear from the beginning that the bees have a system of communication with certain traits unusual in the animal kingdom, especially among the invertebrates. It is a language of coded gestures; its elements are signals that indicate not only the existence of food but also how good the food is and the direction and distance of its location. These are signals, the employment of which is independent in space and time from the object being signaled, and which can refer to various objects other than food.

Round Dance and Waggle Dance

When a bee that has discovered a food source returns to the hive, it distributes the nectar it has brought to its waiting comrades. Many of these are young workers, which process the nectar to form honey but do not yet go foraging themselves. The older bees, however, not only accept samples of the nectar but eagerly follow the dance of the successful collector. Yes, the returned bee dances!

If the feeding dish or field of flowers was only ten or fifteen meters away, the messenger performs a round dance on the comb. It runs in tight circles, changing direction occasionally by sudden reversals (Fig. 76). Other bees follow immediately after the dancer, keeping close contact with their antennae. They are aroused by the food scent the dancer has brought in as well as the move-ment of the dance itself, felt at such close quarters.

Now, there are two ways of interpreting the bee's dance. If the bees attending to it are experienced collectors, the flower scent that clings so well to the furry coat of the dancer tells them that their old food source is still worth another visit. A dancer with a different scent is not interesting to them. When one of the attend-ant bees goes out to the food source, upon its return it also dances.

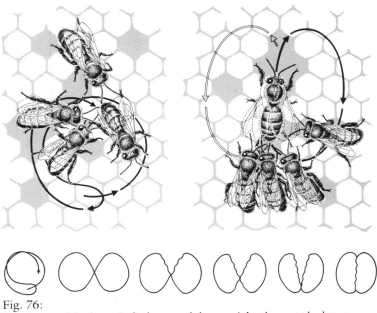

Fig. 76:
The dance of the bees. *Left*, the round dance; *right*, the waggle dance.
Some transitional forms are diagrammed at the bottom.

Often it takes only minutes before the crowd of bees appearing at the feeding site has grown like an avalanche.

And the second possibility: The attendant bees may be novices, which have never visited the feeding site from which the dancing bee has come. They, too, are aroused, fly out, and search in the vicinity of the hive in all directions for the scent brought back by the dancer from its flower visit (cf. Chapter 18). Again, the old group of foragers is soon considerably enlarged. The more food is found and the better it is, the longer and more vigorous are the dances, and the more effective the recruitment of the collector bees. And when the supply deteriorates, the bees advertise it less enthusiastically and eventually cease altogether. The newly recruited bees give up first, and finally the original foragers also stop collecting.

The waggle dances are still more ingenious. They are performed when the food is farther away from the hive. For the race of honeybee most common in Germany (*Apis mellifera carnica*) the critical distance is about eighty-five meters. Again, the successful collectors dance on the vertical comb in the darkness of the hive. But this time they run not in circles, but in horizontal figure-eights (Fig. 76). The waggling occurs in the straight part between two loops; the body is swung rhythmically from side to side as though it were rotating about an axis a short distance in front of the head. They waggle about fifteen times per second. Unlike the round dance, the waggle dance informs the followers not only about the existence of a rewarding food source and its richness (apart from the odor of the food source), but also its direction and how far they must fly to reach it.

First the direction. The angle between the vertical and the straight, waggling part of the dance is equal to the angle between the sun (its azimuth, not its elevation above the horizon; Fig. 77) and the flight direction from hive to food source. For example, when the dancer has flown to the food in a direction at an angle of 60° from the sun, with the sun on its right, the waggle run performed on the vertical comb after its return will be at an angle of 60° to the left of the vertical. Other angles have corresponding significance. If the dancer runs directly upward while waggling, that means "look for food in the direction of the sun," and a waggle run directly downward means "fly away from the sun; the hive is between the sun and the food" (Fig. 77). Novices, which have never before visited the site so described, understand the message. With no guidance by other bees, they reach the goal. They have received their directions and arrive even if they must fly for kilometers.

Very recently there has been a lively controversy about the significance of the bee dance. For the specialist these discussions provided great insight.[10,11] But since the upshot was that all the essential concepts remained as before, we need not go into the arguments here.

Karl von Frisch, who has been mentioned often in this book, in 1965 published a comprehensive work on *The Dance Language and Orientation of the Bees*. This is a summary of the life work of

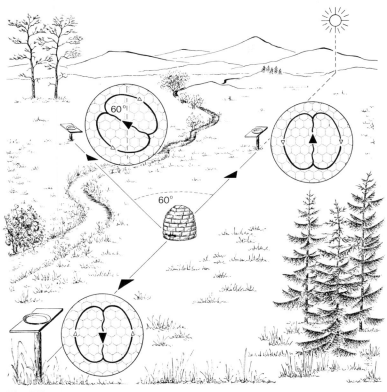

Fig. 77:
The indication of direction in the waggle dance. The angle between the beehive, sun, and food source is represented in the dance on the vertical comb in the dark hive as a deviation from the vertical direction. If the beehive is between the sun and the food, the dancer performs the waggle run downward, and if the food is between the hive and the sun the waggle run goes upward.

a giant among scientists, who could meet the strict demands of science and still be capable of describing the most complicated things in simple words. And it is the end result of all the contributions added to the original discoveries, bit by bit in the course of about forty years, by nearly fifty doctoral students and coworkers—some of whom have themselves become widely known. His book is an inexhaustible mine of information, a vivid compendium of countless masterly experimental findings, patiently assembled. Here we can report on only a small fraction of them.

The Sun Compass

Viewed more closely, the dance language of the bees proves to be a complicated interplay of many closely linked single achievements.

Is the sun, despite its apparent traveling across the sky, a reliable guidepost?

If the directional information in the waggle dance is to function for more than a brief time each day, the bee must know at all times where the sun is. For short distances the sun may be a reliable reference point, but if the food source is several kilometers from the hive—Martin Lindauer[16] cites a record of twelve kilometers—then the position of the sun will have changed considerably in the time between the outward flight and the dance performed on returning. The round trip of a collector bee can very well last an hour. A further complication lies in the fact that the speed with which the sun's azimuth changes depends on the time of day, being greater at noon than in the morning or evening. In other words: the bee must know not only what hour of the day it is, but also how the sun's position changes at this time of day. And it does know. We are already familiar with the internal clock from the preceding chapter. That it allows for the apparent movement of the sun is evident in the fact that the direction indicated by the waggle run is correct not for the time when the dancer flew out, but—amazingly enough—for the time of the dance.[2] Moreover, dances have on several occasions been observed to last for hours,[14] and even though the sun is not visible in the hive, the direction of the waggle run changes, following the position of the sun. As a result, the dance always indicates the same magnetic-compass direction—the actual direction of the food source.

We already know that the internal clock functions at night as well as by day. The sun-position indicator also continues to operate then, even though the bees have certainly never seen the sun at night. Occasionally nocturnal dancers have been observed, and they show the direction of the feeding site visited the preceding evening with reference to the position of the sun at that time of night. Again their dance gives approximately the true compass direction. Martin Lindauer, the closest collaborator of Karl von Frisch, who has himself long been a world-renowned bee researcher, did the following ingenious experiment in 1959. Bees raised without sight of the sun were trained outdoors in the afternoon but otherwise kept in darkness. The first time they were allowed outdoors in the morning sunshine they looked for food in the correct compass direction, despite the unfamiliar position of the sun. That is, they need to see only a small part of the sun's apparent path in order to extrapolate the entire daytime (or nighttime) path. This ability explains the remarkable performance of the nocturnal dancers—remarkable even though they do not indicate the direction quite as accurately as the bees that dance by day.

This curious ability is not inborn, but learned. Only after five afternoons of training do the bees fly on the right course.

What does a bee do when it is cloudy?

In temperate latitudes an overcast sky is quite common. Clouds cover the sun only too often. Do the bees wait until the sun again emerges from behind the clouds to serve as a reference point for their orientation? Or can they, perhaps, discern the position of the sun even under conditions such that it is invisible to us? They can indeed. The bee dance has often been observed to show the right direction even when the sun, to our eyes, had long ago vanished behind the clouds.

The bee sees that the clouds in front of the sun radiate differently from the rest of the overcast sky. That is, the position of the sun appears to the bee in a color that contrasts with the rest of the cloud cover. At first the experiments seemed to show unambiguously that the proportion of ultraviolet, about 5 percent higher here, was the essential factor.[9] But the most recent findings indicate that the longer-wavelength components of the light are the more probable cue.

A Bit of Blue Sky

We come to an entirely new sensory quality when we consider the following situation. Suppose that the sky is so thickly overcast that the sun's position is not betrayed by a difference in the appearance of the clouds, but at one place a bit of blue sky is showing. The bee can use that little hole in the cloud cover for sun-compass orientation.

In the darkness of a wooden box, bees on a horizontal comb dance in a disoriented way. But if they can see a patch of blue sky through a small opening in the box, they become oriented immediately.

"This does not have to be a broad blue area of the sky. An opening 10 cm wide in the fiberboard hut is sufficient. In other experiments a stovepipe, 40 cm long and 15 cm in diameter, was set into the north wall of the hut, so that from the dance floor the bees could see a circular piece of blue sky whose diameter subtended a visual angle of 10-15°. That was enough for them to orient by; they pointed toward the west, where the feeding station was. If I set a mirror in front of the stovepipe, so that on the comb the reflection of a portion of the southern sky was seen instead of the northern, the dances were inhibited to a noticeable degree but were oriented uniformly toward the opposite direction, the east." So wrote Karl von Frisch, in 1965.

Bees, like many other insects, spiders, and crustaceans, perceive the direction of oscillation of polarized sky light and use it for long-distance orientation. What does that mean?

Natural light, coming directly from the sun, oscillates in all possible directions—it is unpolarized. Light coming through the earth's atmosphere from the blue sky is partially polarized; that is, it has a preferred direction of oscillation. The direction of polarization of the blue sky light varies over the sky, in a pattern depending on the position of the sun. Therefore, like the sun's position, this pattern changes predictably in the course of the day (Fig. 78). Unlike us, insects see this pattern, and bees know as much about the way it changes during the day as they do about the sun itself. If they are trained to a certain direction in the afternoon, in the shadow of a mountain so that they can see blue sky but not the sun, and then they are moved to an unfamiliar region, on the next morning they continue to fly in the direction to which they were trained![8] They infer the position of the sun from the pattern of polarization of the sky. Therefore even when the sun is entirely concealed behind a thick cloud cover, it can be used for navigation as long as only a small patch of blue sky is visible.

We also know now that the ability of the arthropod eye to

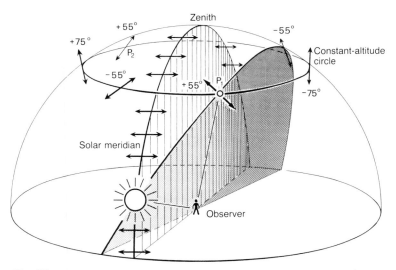

Fig. 78:
Diagram of the polarization of sky light. The direction of oscillation of the linearly polarized light is perpendicular to each great circle through the sun (shown for the solar meridian and the great circle through the observed point P_1 in the sky). Along a circle at constant altitude the direction of oscillation systematically rotates through 360°, with the consequence that an observer on the ground sees a given direction of oscillation at two points in the sky (e.g., P_1 and P_2).

detect the direction of polarization of light is closely related to the organization of the molecules of visual pigment. They tend to be arranged in a particular direction in fine tubules, the fringe of protrusions perpendicular to the ommatidial axis described and illustrated in Chapter 13 (Fig. 37). In the vertebrate eye, by contrast, these molecules lie in all directions, none being preferred. The effect of the arrangement in a preferred direction is that polarized light is absorbed more strongly, the more closely its direction of oscillation matches the direction of the "tubules" and their pigment molecules. However, a single polarization-sensitive receptor would suffice to determine the direction of polarization of light only if the animal were to rotate it systematically under a precisely maintained point in the sky, and if the brain were to process appropriately the successive items of information so obtained. Why must it be so complicated? Because the degree to which a polarization-sensitive visual cell is excited depends not only on the direction of polarization of the light but also on its degree of polarization and its overall intensity. But there is another, more appealing solution to this problem of ambiguity. With at least two polarization-sensitive receptors aimed at the same spot in the sky but having different preferred directions, plus a non-polarization-sensitive receptor, the bee's brain could extract the desired information by comparing the different levels of excitation in these receptors.

Moreover, we know that the honeybee's polarization sensitivity is a property of visual cells that respond especially strongly to ultraviolet. Not all three such cells, but only the short cell numbered 9. The two long UV cells (numbers 1 and 5 in Fig. 37) are so tightly twisted that the little tubules containing the visual pigment have no preferred direction over the entire length of the cell. This coupling of polarization detection to ultraviolet seems to make good sense, because the proportion of UV is especially high in the scattered light from the blue sky.[3,18] The association is still another indication of the great biological significance of insect UV vision.

If we go one step further we see immediately that an animal

cannot orient simply by detecting the oscillation direction of the polarized light from one spot of sky, because various other parts of the sky also emit light with that direction of polarization. If the bee in an experiment is allowed to see only a single direction of oscillation, its waggle dance is ambiguous, indicating two directions. The bee can eliminate such ambiguity by processing information from several regions of the sky—and this is presumably what it normally does. But even if this is the case, further questions remain. Does the bee carry around with it a complete, and therefore quite complicated, map of sky-light polarization in order to determine the precise compass direction? Or does it carry out simpler calculations in steps, a process that would require only a rough knowledge of the pattern? Just what the bee does is at present the subject of absorbing, complicated research, from which we can expect still more fascinating results.[20,23]

The Sunstones of the Vikings

This world of polarization patterns is beyond our own experience. But by looking through a polarization filter, which passes only a certain direction of oscillation of the light, we can easily see how the direction of polarization of the light from the blue sky varies. Turn the filter while looking at a single spot, and whenever it lets the most light through, the direction of polarization of the filter is the same as that of the light from that part of the sky (Fig. 79). Vikings very probably made use of this phenomenon a millennium ago to navigate on their long sea voyages to Greenland and Newfoundland.[19] There is good reason to suppose that they used a small patch of blue sky and a sunstone—the existence of which is documented by ancient legends—to find the position of the sun even when the sun itself could not be seen, at twilight or when it was very cloudy. Sunstones are polarization-sensitive crystals that in principle behave just like a man-made polarization filter (Fig. 79), with which one can analyze the direction of polarization of light very simply, by turning them. Among the polarization-sen-

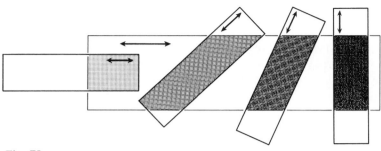

Fig. 79:
Two superimposed polarization filters transmit the most light when their directions of polarization (arrows) are the same, and the least when they are perpendicular to one another.

sitive crystals theoretically available to the Vikings (including andalusite, calcite, and tourmaline), cordierite has attracted particular attention. It is a common constituent of gneiss and is found in Norway, for example, near Kragerø and other places on the coast of the Oslo fiord. Its color closely resembles the blue of sapphire. Chemically, cordierite is a magnesium-aluminum silicate. If we hold one of these saga-hallowed stones against the zenith and rotate it in the horizontal plane, we soon find a position in which it appears brightest, where it transmits the most light. Now the direction of orientation within the crystal (the analyzer direction) corresponds to the direction of oscillation of light from the part of the sky being viewed. But where is the sun? In the perpendicular direction! Why? Because—Figure 78 illustrates it—the direction of oscillation of light from the sky is perpendicular to the plane defined by the observer, the sun, and the observed point in the sky (the zenith, in our example). In practice a cordierite crystal can be used to find the position of the sun to within 5°. For the slow ships of the Vikings this was certainly accurate enough.

Let us assume that the bees find the solar meridian by the same principle as the Vikings did. Now, how do they know whether the sun is in front of them or behind them? Theoretically, various items of additional information are available: the color of the sky light, the degree of polarization, the amount of ultraviolet.

In the so-called sky compass, the ancient principle of the Vikings was put to use as late as the mid-1970s. The sky compass was a portable device that Lufthansa navigators took with them into the cockpits of their Boeing 707's when they expected to have difficulties in obtaining a fix on astronomical reference points while flying in the polar regions. Trouble was especially likely in the autumn and spring, the times of long twilight, when at latitudes near the pole (where the magnetic compass also becomes unreliable) it is neither day nor night for six to eight hours, and neither the sun nor the stars are available to establish direction. With the sky compass, the basic element of which is a polarization filter, the direction of the sun could be determined even when the sun itself was as much as 7° below the horizon—as long as the zenith was not obscured.

After 1974 inertial navigation rendered the sky compass and other such accessory devices superfluous—around a thousand years after the Vikings, about three hundred years after the discovery of sky-light polarization by the Danish scholar Erasmus Bartholinus, and only about twenty-five years after an American physicist at Johns Hopkins University developed the instrument for the Navy.

Distance Information and the Special Significance of Vibratory Signals

How troublesome it would be—and how much time and fuel would be consumed—to take an automobile trip in which we knew that the highway was going south but, because we had no information as to the distance involved, we had to drive slowly past every exit while trying to decide whether it might be the one we wanted. Directional information alone is not enough to determine a target unequivocally. We cannot expect the collecting bee to test every flower it encounters on its "correct" route, just in case it might have the same scent as that brought home by the dancing bee. Bees aroused by their hivemates, even if they have not collected before at the site, begin to search at the right distance with remarkable accuracy. Where do they get the information they need? There are several features of the waggle dance that change with distance: the number of circles, the time it takes to return to the starting point, the number of waggling movements, the duration of the waggle run, and the distance it covers. Which is the decisive factor?

Again, as in the communication of direction, the waggle part of the dance is particularly important. Its duration changes especially systematically and precisely with the distance of the food source. In the case of the Krainer bee (*Apis mellifera carnica*) it increases from around 0.5 seconds at 200 meters to 4 s at 4,500 m.[7] But the signal is conveyed not only by the duration of waggling; an acoustic marker associated with waggling also contributes (Fig. 80). The bee produces this sound with its flight musculature, which causes the wings to vibrate slightly during waggling. The frequency generated is about 250 Hz. We can easily hear it at close range.[4,5,25] The duration of this sound signal is the same as that of the waggle run. Why, then, is it so important that the waggling be acoustically labeled? Sometimes—for instance, when the food is of very poor quality—collector bees dance silently. Harald Esch of the University of Notre Dame in Indiana has observed 15,000 such dances. Not a single one of these caused the bees following the dancer to fly to the food source.

Unlike grasshoppers, crickets, and many lepidopterans, for example, the bee has no organ that we would call an auditory organ in the human sense, no organ specifically suitable for detecting airborne sound at a long distance. Nevertheless, at least two bee sense organs could serve to detect the sound associated with waggling. One of them is the Johnston's organ at the base of each antenna, which responds to the most minute oscillations of the antenna. The other possibility is organs in the legs that are sensitive to vibrations of the substrate. It is still unclear how the signal that is actually detected looks physically. Is it oscillations caused by direct contact with the abdomen of the dancer? Is the antenna moved by the rhythmic currents of air that surround the dancing animal, without contacting the animal itself? Or is the comb set into oscillation, passing the information to the attendant bees indirectly as substrate-conducted sound? Whatever the details of this masterpiece of communications, the message is understood and the attendant bees take off on the route we would predict theoretically. They arrive with an accuracy greater than the accuracy of the dancer. Evidently the newly recruited bees take an average of several dances. As a rule, they do not fly out until they have attentively followed six dances. In fact, they plan ahead so well that for the flight to the food, often kilometers long, they take on only the exact amount of fuel (nectar) that they will need.

Energy Expenditure and Head Winds

How can a bee possibly measure the distance to the feeding site so as to communicate it by dancing? With no devices to count kilometers or wingbeats, no magnetic compass or map, no clock, and no signposts! A lone hiker without all these aids would find himself in great difficulty. If he wanted to know how many kilometers he had covered he would presumably first have to estimate how long he had been walking by the change in the position of the sun, and then multiply that time by his average speed in kilometers per hour. If he really always walked at the same speed, the

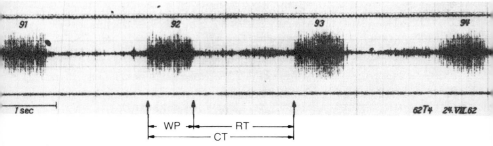

Fig. 80:
Sound production in the waggle dance. Recording of four circuits (91-94). WP waggle phase, RT return time, CT circuit time.

elapsed time would be a good measure of the distance covered. Perhaps he would also know exactly how far he could normally walk without getting tired, and so could estimate the distance by how tired he felt. But a calculation of this kind is very much affected by the terrain, and he would have to know the right correction factors for "forest trail," "hill country," and so on.

Bees measure distance not by time, and also not by visual landmarks, but by the amount of energy they consume. That is, what they measure and signal to the others is not distance as such, but rather the energy that must be expended to reach the feeding site from the hive. If the bee has been flying upwind, the distance expressed in its dance language is "extended," and if the flight has been downwind, it is "shortened." One can stick small weights onto the bees, or flags to increase the air resistance they must overcome in flight. Both have the same effect as a head wind.[21]

The outward flight is the critical one, not the flight back. In a particularly interesting experiment, collector bees were made to walk to the food, through a narrow passage. These bees, too, began to dance when they returned to the hive, indicating a nearby site with round dances and a more distant one with waggle dances. But the transition from the round to the waggle dance, which occurs at 50-80 meters in the case of flight, came much sooner when the bees had to walk, at only 3-4 meters. To walk 3-4 meters the bee needs around forty seconds. In the same time it could fly 330 meters. Therefore time cannot be the critical measure of distance. It is fuel consumption. To march 3 meters on foot a bee must burn up as much sugar as for a flight of 55 meters![1,22]

We have no idea how the bee measures its fuel consumption. Perhaps by how full the fuel tank is?

I can still vividly remember the occasion when I first encountered the language of the bees. I was fortunate enough to be given a close look into this magical world on the roof of the Munich Observatory, as a student assistant of Martin Lindauer. The question at issue then was what cues the bees use to orient when the sky is overcast. The fascination still remains, and it is hard to say what is the most admirable feature of the bees' language.

First of all, perhaps, are the astonishing sensory abilities involved—especially those we do not have ourselves: the perception of ultraviolet and of the plane of polarization of light, the sun compass, corrected by the internal clock, and the measurement of effort expended. And there is another thing I have not yet mentioned: bees can perceive the magnetic field of the earth.[17]

Interplay and Flexibility

The waggle dance of the collector bees is normally slightly in error. The direction of the food it indicates is not quite right; the error may amount to as much as ten degrees and, surprisingly, it changes systematically during the course of the day. People tried in vain for years to interpret this remarkable phenomenon, until the earth's magnetic field gave the unequivocal answer. The deviation from the correct direction is reduced to $\pm 1.5°$ in experiments in which the earth's magnetic field and its changes are compensated!

Still more fascinating than all these abilities themselves is their interplay in orientation and communication, the close coupling among them, their synthesis to create perfect biological order. This order is much less rigid than one might expect of the behavior of an invertebrate animal. The bee's dance is by no means always a routine, fully automatic performance. The food must be abundant and attractive (high sugar content), it must not be overcrowded with other bees, and the collector must have made several successful collecting trips before it begins to dance. The sugar concentration sufficient to motivate dancing varies with the season as the availability of food changes,[12] with the scent (a stronger tendency to dance if the scent is flowery), and with the demand in the hive. If the combs are full the bees do not dance even for food of such high quality that in harder times it would have made the colony wildly excited.

The most convincing evidence of the flexibility of communication, however, is that the dances are used to send other bees not only to food sources—to nectar and pollen—but also to water and sometimes to plant resins, and even to something quite different, a new nesting site.[13,16]

Once the swarm has moved out of the nest and is hanging clustered in the open, so-called scout bees fly off to look for a new nesting site. When they return they signal their find with the familiar waggle dance, the same that is used by the collector bees to advertise a food source. Again the value of the find is indicated by the vigor and duration of the dance. This is also the basis of the process by which the bees reach an agreement when they have a choice among several nesting sites—which is usually the case. They must agree, because they have only one queen, and a subgroup without a queen could not survive. They arrive at a consensus in a most interesting way. The scout bees that have found only moderately good sites let themselves be won over by colleagues campaigning more vigorously for the quality of the site they have discovered. They follow the latter scouts to the better site, examine it themselves, and when they return, convinced, to the swarm they also dance vigorously for it. When all the scout bees are united, the move is made. The decision process can take several days. The queen has no part in it; the negotiations are entirely the responsibility of the scout bees.

28 On the Evolution of the Bee Dance

> They seek food as much as sixty paces away from their hives, and when they have sucked dry the flowers nearby they send out certain scouts to reconnoiter and find other more distant food for them.
>
> *Pliny the Elder (23-79), "Naturalis historiae libri"*

Fascinated by the complexity and precision of a form of behavior, biologists will always look beyond the analysis of the situation as they find it, and inquire about its evolution. From a biological viewpoint, our understanding of what exists does not become complete until we can satisfactorily explain how it came into existence. To be sure, this is often extraordinarily difficult. Behavior leaves no fossil footprints behind, and in all too many cases we dare not hope that the detailed history of its development will be worked out in the foreseeable future, if ever. It is often said that evolution has had plenty of time to bring about complicated things by many small steps, but this is not much more than an expression of our ignorance about particular cases.

What has been going on in the seventy million or more years since bees appeared on earth?[18]

Well, comparison of the communication behavior of various bee species has produced some plausible suggestions as to trends that may have been important in the evolution of the bee dance.[5,6,8,14,17]

The Four Species of Honeybee

About 3,500 species of bees have been described,[20] but as far as we know at present only four inform their hivemates about the direction and distance of a food source by dancing. All of these species belong to the genus *Apis*, the honeybees in the restricted sense, and these are the only species in the genus:

1. *Apis mellifera*, our western honeybee; within its extensive range, which includes the Near East, Africa, and Europe, there are many geographical races.

2. *Apis cerana*, the Indian honeybee, a native of eastern Asia.

3. *Apis dorsata*, the Southeast Asian giant honeybee. It is feared because of its sting and eagerness to attack; when aroused by alarm substances, within a few seconds thousands of bees hurl themselves upon an intruder.

4. Finally *Apis florea*, the dwarf honeybee, also native to Southeast Asia.

What differences are there in their communication about food sources?

The "nest" of the dwarf honeybee consists of nothing but one comb, only a little larger than the palm of one's hand, which all year long hangs in the open from the branch of a shrub or tree. At the top, the comb spreads out to form a horizontal platform. This is the dance floor. Bees returning from flowers walk up onto it to communicate, by dancing, with other worker bees. Because the dwarf honeybee, without exception, dances in the open and not—like the European honeybee and its close relative, the Indian honeybee—in the darkness of a hive, it need not convert the angle between the sun and the outward flight to an angle with respect to gravity (cf. Fig. 76). Its dance points directly toward the food. The European honeybee also does this occasionally, when it dances outside the hive on a horizontal landing platform (Fig. 81). But as we know, it does not require a horizontal dance floor. With the dwarf honeybee it is different, as Martin Lindauer demonstrated in 1956, in an admirably simple way. As he described it:[17] "We cut off the little branch to which the comb is attached and turn the comb about its horizontal axis, so that the dance surface, previously horizontal, is now vertical. Instantly all the dancers stop dancing, race to the edge of the platform that is now uppermost, run excitedly about until they have trampled down a miniature platform, and resume dancing as before." Another experiment

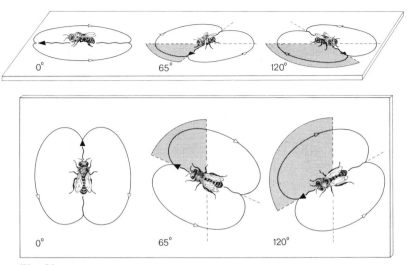

Fig. 81:
The waggle dance of the honeybees. *Above*: on a horizontal surface outdoors the waggle part points directly toward the food (the sun is considered to be on the left of the picture). *Below*: the same directions being indicated on a vertical comb in the darkness of the hive.

consisted in depriving the animals of all horizontal surfaces. Lindauer covered the comb with a glass roof-ridge, causing utter confusion among the dancers.

The giant honeybee, as it seems, occupies a position intermediate between the dwarf honeybee and our western honeybee. Its
comb also hangs in the open, but it has no horizontal dance surface. The giant honeybee dances vertically and, as would be expected, like our honeybee transposes the sun angle into a gravity
angle. But it dances only on the parts of the comb with a view of
the sky. It may be that this makes it easier for the attendant bees
to switch back from the gravity angle to the sun angle when they
start out for the food.

The Indian honeybee is so similar to our own that we need no
special description of it.

Comparison of these four dancing bee species suggests that the evolution of dancing to show direction may have taken place in the following steps:[17]

1. Dance in the open on a horizontal surface, in which the direction of the food is the same as that of the dance.

2. Dance in the open on a vertical surface, with the food direction represented by transposition from visual to gravitational cues—a transposition of which many other insects are also capable.

3. Dance in the darkness of an enclosed chamber on a vertical surface, in which case the direction must necessarily be represented by transposition.

This last step is a critical requirement for life in enclosed nests, which in turn is a prerequisite for overwintering and survival in our sometimes harsh climate. Very recently the discussion about the phylogeny of the four bee species has been reopened.[13] In particular, some objections have been raised to the idea that the earliest form was a florealike species that lived in the open air.

A Side Glance at Flies and Moths

But how did dancing arise in the first place? This question is hard to answer. Perhaps blowflies (*Phormia regina*) represent an important forerunner of the bees' dance. Vincent G. Dethier, then at Johns Hopkins University, in 1957 reported in the journal *Science*[3] that after flies have sucked up a small drop of sugar-water they run in circles on a horizontal surface, repeatedly turning clockwise and then counterclockwise. In these dances the fly is evidently searching for more food. The more concentrated the food and the hungrier the fly, the more tightly the fly turns and the longer it continues to do so (Fig. 82). In the dark they have no preferred direction. But there is an immediate change when the surface is illuminated from the side; then the flies walk parallel to the direction of the incident light (Fig. 83). Having established this, Dethier then tipped the surface up vertically and turned the light off, whereupon the flies ran mostly up and down. That is, constant stimuli such as light or gravity can impose a preferred direction

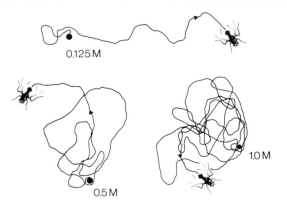

Fig. 82:
The walking behavior of the blowfly *Phormia regina* after it has consumed
sugar-water at increasing concentrations (0.125 to 1.0 molar).

on what would otherwise be undirected behavior. When a fly that
has just been fed is placed among a group of other flies, it almost
always regurgitates a little food. Flies from the group follow its
circular runs, trying to lick sugar-water from its mouthparts, and
after a while actually begin to run in circles themselves. The par-
allels with the honeybee are striking. But note that the fly does
not show the way to the drop of food. Although their dancing
can become aligned with the direction of light or gravity, flies
cannot be induced to dance at a particular angle to either of these
stimuli. Moreover, the excited flies following the dance do not fly
anywhere, to say nothing of flying in a particular direction. Nevertheless, it may be that the flies are demonstrating something that
could resemble the primitive form of the round dance.

The search for a possible precursor of the waggle dance leads
us to the Lepidoptera. In 1960 D. Blest published an article in
the British journal *Behaviour* with the long title: "The Evolution,
Ontogeny and Quantitative Control of the Settling Movements of
some New World Saturniid Moths, with Some Comments on Distance Communication by Honey-Bees."[1] In brief, he found that
New World moths of the family Saturniidae make sideways shak-

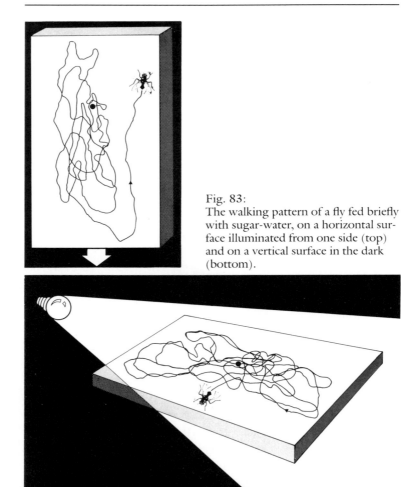

Fig. 83:
The walking pattern of a fly fed briefly
with sugar-water, on a horizontal surface illuminated from one side (top)
and on a vertical surface in the dark
(bottom).

ing movements after landing, and that the duration of this behavior, like the waggling of bees, increases with the duration of the
preceding flight and therefore with distance. An example: flight
duration two minutes, four movements; flight duration thirty
minutes, twenty-five movements. The cause and adaptive value of

this remarkable shaking are unknown. But in our context it is tempting to speculate that the original form of distance communication by the honeybee may have looked like this.

Scent Marks and Pilot Bees

Let us return to the bees themselves. In the tropics and subtropics of the world, in particularly large numbers on the American continent, live the stingless bees (Meliponinae). There are about three hundred species of them. Their distinctive characteristic is the great reduction of their sting, which is no longer of use in defense. In compensation, the bites of many stingless bees are formidable. Some species produce a caustic secretion from a large gland in the head that makes their bites exceedingly unpleasant. The stingless bees need some kind of weapon; they are social animals and their massive food stores must be defended.

In the nests of the various species of stingless bees from about 300 to 80,000 individuals live together. The collector bees of all the species so far studied have found a way to notify their nestmates of a rewarding food source—as would be expected of a social creature. But it soon became evident that their communication is simpler than that of the honeybee, although it is not always less successful in recruitment.

Again it was Martin Lindauer who did a crucial pioneering study. Together with Warwick Kerr[15,16] at the University of São Paolo he took a close look at the Brazilian species of stingless bees. Their finding: all of them have a communication system, with which foragers call a rewarding collection site to the attention of bees that have not yet been there. Their success in doing this differs in the different species. But in four species of the genus *Trigona* as many (or even more) newcomers were brought to the feeding site in a given time as would be the case for honeybees in the same situation. In these experiments the feeding site was located 50 to 150 meters away from the hive (Fig. 84). The *Trigona* species that communicate relatively unsuccessfully simply encourage the bees

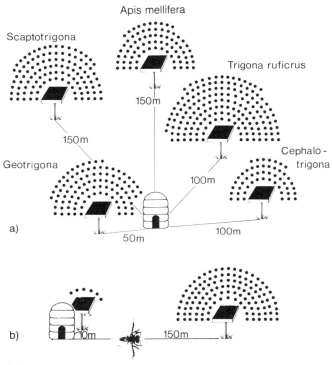

Fig. 84:
(a) Various stingless bees with very effective arousal signals, in comparison to the honeybee (*Apis mellifera*). The dots around the feeding table
correspond to the number of new bees recruited. (b) The new recruits of
Scaptotrigona, one of these successful species, direct their flight toward a
distant goal even after a control table with food has been set up close to
the hive.

in the nest to forage in general, whereupon the new recruits first
search in all directions and at different distances from the hive for
the scent the collector has brought back (Fig. 85).[12] The more
successful species give the new recruits precise instructions as to
direction and distance. Lindauer and Kerr observed that they fly
to the feeding site to which they have been trained even if there
is a competing food table quite near the hive (Fig. 84).

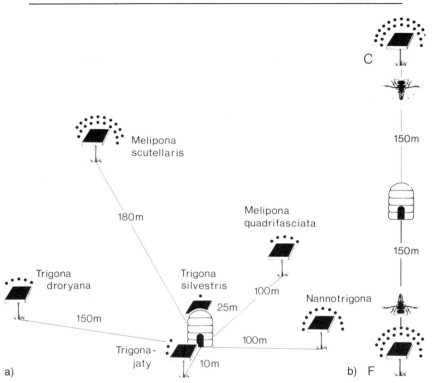

Fig. 85:
(a) Examples of stingless bees that recruit less successfully (cf. Fig. 84).
(b) illustrates the lack of directionality in the flights of recruits in one of these species (*Trigona droyana*); even more new recruits arrived at the control table C in the north than came to the feeding table F.

How is the information conveyed? Stingless bees do it quite differently from honeybees.

The details were first revealed by *Trigona postica*. This is one of the aggressive species, which makes things very awkward for an intruder by attacking his eyes, ears, and mouth and crawling into his hair.[18] Biological field work is not always as much fun as it looks in television documentaries!

A forager trained to collect at a distance of thirty-five meters flew quite normally eleven times between the feeding table and the hive. Its twelfth return flight followed a zigzag path, interrupted thirty-two times so that the bee could wipe the secretion of its mandibular gland off on stones and blades of grass, holding its mouthparts wide open (Fig. 86). Surprisingly, the bee turned around when it was nine meters from the hive and, after two minutes, like a pilot boat guiding a fleet, came back to the feeding site with nine newcomers. In another case there were fifty-seven recruits! This process was then repeated. The scent marks last for a good ten minutes, but no longer; then they must be renewed or replaced by others.[11] This is important: they are renewed only if the food at the site is still abundant. When the food supply begins to run out the scent marks soon vanish, so that pointless flights by the nestmates soon cease. This behavior is reminiscent of the bumblebee males that mark their surroundings with scent on their courtship flights (see Chapter 23) and, of course, of ants that leave chemical marks to show the way to food.

In *Trigona postica*, then, the new recruits are guided personally to the food. This aspect makes even the advanced *Trigona* species seem more primitive than the honeybee, which finds its goal independently and by memory, from information acquired before the flight.

Sound Signals

Before they leave the hive the new *Trigona* recruits are aroused by foragers on the comb. The forager runs around in a zigzag, roughly jostling the inactive workers. The latter then follow, touching the forager with their antennae so as to learn, from the scent clinging to the hairy pelt and in the nectar, the kind of flower from which the forager has come—but not its location. All the *Trigona* species that have been studied have an additional arousing signal, a distinctly audible buzzing. Lindauer and Kerr[15] write that it is produced in irregular bursts like Morse code, and that the nestmates detect it by way of the vibration of the comb.

Once aroused, the bees run to the exit from the nest and wait

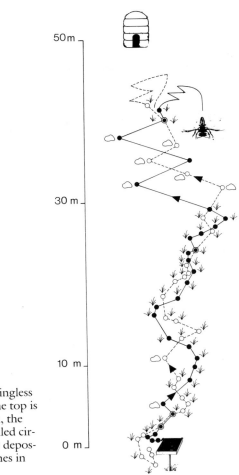

Fig. 86:
The marking flights of a stingless
bee (*Trigona postica*). At the top is
the hive and at the bottom, the
feeding table. Open and filled circles symbolize scent marks deposited on grass tufts and stones in
two flights.

just outside, in a loose swarm, for their pilot.[2,15] On the way to
the food they swarm around the scent marks, which serve as guideposts even though they are not sufficient in themselves; without
personal guidance by the pilot bee, the recruitment is unsuccessful.
On the other hand, some *Trigona* species can presumably do without the scent marks. This brings us to another genus, *Melipona*.

There is so far no evidence that it leaves scent marks.[18] But its sound signal is unusually differentiated.

Like all other stingless bees, *Melipona* gives no sign of direction when it arouses its mates. But distance is another matter! Harald Esch, now Professor of Zoology at Notre Dame University in Indiana, in 1967 made an exciting discovery in São Paolo, where he was studying two Brazilian species of this genus (*Melipona quadrifasciata* and *Melipona merillae*). Unlike the *Trigona* species, these make good use of their buzzing signal on the comb as a distance indicator. For the first few seconds a continual buzz is produced, which then gives way to pulses. The duration of the pulses increases systematically with the distance of the food from the hive. For example, Esch observed one-second pulses for a distance of 200 meters, and only half a second for 50 meters. The relation of pulse duration to distance is remarkably like that of the waggle noise produced by the honeybee (*Apis mellifera*) (Fig. 87). Several other facts support the idea that the sound signal can be used to indicate distance:

1. *Melipona* is not known to leave scent marks in this behavioral context.[18]

2. The sound is produced only when the food is at least of a

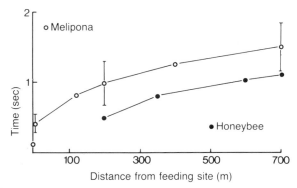

Fig. 87:
Sound signals indicate distance. Their duration changes systematically with the distance of the feeding site from the nest, in the same way for both the honeybee and the stingless bee *Melipona quadrifasciata*.

certain minimal quality, corresponding to a sugar concentration of 10-20 percent.

3. Esch[5] observed that new recruits arrive at the feeding site *alone*.

There are also certain peculiarities in the way these bees indicate direction. The experienced forager shows the aroused new recruit the direction by making a zigzag flight together with it in the vicinity of the hive. Farther away, the flight path straightens out and the contact with the recruit is lost. After twenty to thirty flights with this initial guidance, the recruit no longer waits at the nest for the pilot, but flies out alone and arouses other bees when it returns.

The Shortened Zigzag Flight

Now let us imagine that the initial guided flight were to be gradually shortened (a shortening to 10-20 meters is actually found in *Melipona seminigra*), and eventually we would arrive at something very like the honeybee behavior. The direction and distance information would then coincide, with the zigzag flight of the pilot bee becoming a waggle dance; now scent marks and guide bees have simultaneously lost their significance.[5,6] Can we say, then, that the waggling of the honeybee in the waggle dance is a flight-intention movement? There is evidence for this view in the fact that the sound signal that accompanies waggling not only is produced by the flight muscles but has a frequency, 250 Hz, that corresponds to the wingbeat frequency, although the wings do not actually beat.[4]

We do not know whether this is really what happened in evolution. But it is the best-founded idea we have.

Nicolaus Unhoch and the Bee Ballet

Karl von Frisch always used the word "language" metaphorically when referring to the bees. He knew, of course, that bees cannot give names to things, that they cannot form concepts in the human sense, and that their tiny brain, with a volume of no more than 1 mm³, can be of no use for thinking in the anthromorphic sense but rather serves to organize behavior controlled by instinct. When he spoke of "dance language" he was not thinking of sound production, at least not at the beginning. Since then we have learned that sound signals do play an especially important role in the communication systems of the collector bees of all the species that have been studied.

By the way: in bumblebees there is so far no sign of communication about the position of nectar and pollen sources.[5,10] The scent brought back from the flowers may play a certain role.[7] This finding must come as a surprise, at first, for in other respects the social organization of the bumblebees rivals that of many stingless bees. But their colonies do not survive the winter, and as far as food stores go they live more or less from hand to mouth. In bumblebee colonies individual initiative is considerably more important than it is among bees, particularly honeybees.

"On reaching the hive they throw off their load, and each bee on its return is followed by three or four others. One cannot well tell what is the substance these gather, nor the exact process of their work. Their mode of gathering wax has been observed on olive trees, as owing to the thickness of the leaves the bees remain stationary for a considerable while." Aristotle, in his famous *Historia animalium*, set down many details of bee biology. Some of them seem ludicrous today, but many are correct. As the above quotation implies, he very probably knew about the waggle dance, more than 2,300 years ago. Quite an accurate description of the round dance comes from an *Introduction to the True Knowledge and Most Appropriate Handling of Bees after Thirty-Three Years of Close Observation and Experience* published early in the last century. It was written in 1823 by Nicolaus Unhoch, the prebendary of Oberammergau. In Chapter 6 of the first section he writes about the bee ballet: "Many will find it laughable, even incredible, when I claim that the bees, when the hive in general is in good condition, actually have their own amusements and pleasures, that they occasionally engage in their own kind of dance." A little later on we find a more detailed description of this entertainment, which Unhoch often watched in a glass observation hive—though only, as he quite rightly says, on fine sunny days: "A single bee all of a sudden pushes itself in among a quietly standing group of three or four other bees, lowers its head to the floor, stretches its wings apart and trembles with its upraised abdomen for a little while; the nearest bees do the same thing, lowering their heads to the floor, and finally they turn together in something more than a semicircle, now right and now left, five or six times back and forth, in a ceremonious round dance. All at once the dance mistress goes away from them to another place to join another group of quiet bees and does the same as before, and the nearest bees dance with her." The author acknowledges that friends to whom he showed this marveled at the "fun" the bees were having and laughed heartily, and he wonders whether it is indeed a matter of "enjoyment and high spirits" among the bees. But he adds the critical comment that he cannot explain the real meaning of the dance, and leaves for the future the interpretation of its actual purpose.

This future would presumably have made the author even more enthusiastic. All the details we now know about what is really behind the bee ballet—however accustomed we may be to the wonders of modern technology—must fill anyone who takes the trouble to learn about them with admiration.

29 The Temperature-Controlled Bumblebee and Economy in Behavior

Nature has neither core
Nor shell;
She is everything at once.

Johann Wolfgang von Goethe, "Zur Morphologie," 1820

"Being adapted" in the biological sense is an indivisible state. The relationship between the properties of an organism and its surroundings must be comprehensively appropriate. The more of such a relationship we can bring into our field of view at once, the more clearly is the harmony of the biological order revealed. Particularly conspicuous adaptations, of course, command our attention most forcefully, and in this book, too, they have been portrayed separately. But this individual treatment is necessary only because our brains have too much trouble focusing on many single aspects of a complex system with the same sharpness at the same time, and appreciating the interplay among them.

In addition to the sensory and neurobiological adaptations of insects for visiting flowers, one of the most interesting viewpoints from which modern biology considers this encounter is that of energy balance. How large are the receipts, and how large the expenditure? Does the behavior of insects show a profit? Is it economical? Do the accounts balance?

Food from flowers is the energy source from which the next generation is ultimately produced. Because the system obviously functions, it must be operating with balanced books. Seen from a distance, the situation is clear. But we want to know more about what is actually going on.

The energy taken in follows tortuous paths before the end product appears as "grams of progeny." The list of investments the insect is required to make is long. The net income is very much smaller than the gross receipts.

As always in the natural sciences we need measurements, numbers, if we are to understand things better. Here we encounter several difficulties. It is simplest to determine the energy content of the starting material; the sugar content of nectar can be found quickly even in the field. Considerably more effort is needed to find out how much nectar a flower secretes at different times of day, at different temperatures, and with variations in insect visitation; how the composition of the nectar changes during the day and the following season; how nectar intake by the insect depends on the supplies remaining "at home," on the time of day and year, and on the degree of competition; how fuel consumption changes with the temperature, the distribution of the flowers, their accessibility, and many other factors. No shortage of questions! And we do not know all the answers to any one of them. So here we shall do the next-best thing—take an example that demonstrates the problems at issue particularly well.

This chapter focuses on the bumblebees. Along with other zoologists, Bernd Heinrich of the University of California at Berkeley has recently studied them very thoroughly, and in 1979 he published many of his measurements and ideas in a highly recommended book with the title *Bumblebee Economics*.[8]

Receipts and Expenditures

Bumblebees, like the honeybee, live in social groups. But a bumblebee colony, at least in temperate latitudes, is a summer society. Its activities must be directed toward producing as many young queens as possible before the winter comes. Only these queens survive, and in the next spring some of them succeed in establishing a new bumblebee colony. Then they can be seen on all sides, and we notice them because the spring bumblebees are especially large.

What happens to the energy brought into the bumblebee nest? Figure 88 gives a diagrammatic summary.

In June of 1977 a group of American zoologists[1] observed a sizable bumblebee (*Bombus vosnesenskii*) nest near San Francisco, housing about 400 adult bees, of which 261 were workers. Between five o'clock in the morning and nine in the evening they saw 1,932 foraging flights. At the time of greatest activity there were 200 takeoffs and landings per hour at the nest entrance. On 938 of the returns, the workers brought pollen with them, in an average amount of 0.021 g. The average weight of the sugar each carried was 0.027 g. At the time they were observed, the total daily intake of this bumblebee colony was 20 g pollen and 45 g sugar.

This harvest is stored in communal pollen and honey pots. These stores are then distributed to the consumer. Nectar (sugar) is there chiefly to fuel the bees' operating metabolism, whereas pollen (proteins) is especially important for raising the young (see Chapters 10 and 8).

The first fraction of the sugar harvest, then, leaves the nest with the collector bees. They take it along as fuel for the flight, an average of 0.0021 g per animal per flight. Subtracting this amount from the 0.027 g brought back, we find that the yield of the thirty- to ninety-minute foraging flight is about 0.025 g of sugar. A worker bee making eight to ten flights daily provides the colony with 0.2 g sugar per day (0.3 ml honey) and, if it collects pollen, 0.2 g pollen.

The honeybee is traditionally held up as the prime example of industry—a view we began to put into perspective in Chapter 6. Bumblebees are far more industrious. This is immediately evident if one imagines a bumblebee colony the size of a honeybee colony, with, say, 60,000 workers. Sixty thousand bumblebees each day would bring back enough nectar for 18 liters of honey! In fact, for a honeybee colony to produce 1 kg of honey per day is a respectable success, achieved only at times when nectar is most abundant.

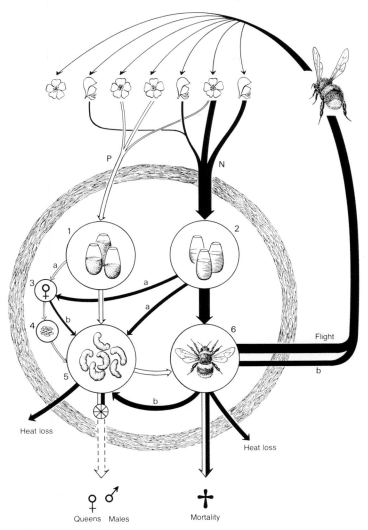

Fig. 88:
The flow of energy and materials through a bumblebee colony. P pollen
and N nectar are the inputs to the system. They are stored in pollen pots
(1) and honey pots (2). (a) Use as food for the queen (3), which lays the
eggs (4), and for the larvae (5). (b) Use in thermoregulation; queen and
workers (6) warm the brood and heat the nest. The outputs of the system: energy expenditure for flight and thermoregulation by the collectors,
heat loss, losses by the departure of queens and males from the colony,
and losses by the death of the animals in autumn.

Most of the supplies delivered daily by the 261 workers in our bumblebee colony was used as food by the workers themselves, the 136 new queens, and the 239 larvae. The observed nest did contain some reserves: 195 ml (260 g) honey and 5.7 g pollen. But this can be regarded as a longer-term store for periods of bad weather, which has little to do with the day-by-day events.

Calculations involving the end product of the entire bumblebee economy, the young queens, seem simple at first. A queen weighs about 0.4 g. Assuming food conversion at a rate of one to one—that is, 1 g pollen must be fed to produce 1 g bumblebee mass (this is a reasonable assumption)—it follows that a pollen collector needs two days to accumulate the 0.4 g necessary for the production of a queen. If this is the case, shouldn't queens be produced more rapidly and in much greater numbers? The reality is more complicated.

The energy supplied by the collectors is not used only for raising the larvae and feeding the queens. In fact, this use accounts for only a small fraction. According to the findings of Bernd Heinrich,[4,7] much more is expended on the regulation of temperature, both within the nest and outside. This is most surprising, for the bumblebee is a poikilothermic animal, and one would ordinarily expect it always to be about as cold or as warm as its surroundings. Not at all. The temperatures of the bees, the larvae, and the nest are controlled with great effort.

Eight Hundred and Eighty Kilometers South of the North Pole

Bumblebees (genus *Bombus*) are typical inhabitants of the north. Their home is the temperate zone, and they are especially common in its colder regions. Bumblebees are the only members of the major group of bees to have advanced into the arctic. The most northerly part of their range recorded so far is in Ellesmere Island, the northernmost tip of Canada, only 880 km from the North Pole.[16] Accordingly, it is unusual to encounter them in deserts.

Even along the Mediterranean they are relatively rare, as in the tropics.[12] Bumblebees, then, have managed to make themselves at home in the cold, and even in warmer regions they fly at temperatures so low that no honeybee would venture forth from its hive. On cold days bumblebees can be seen busily collecting very early and late in the evening, even at 10°C or less, regardless of rain. No wonder that they are masters of temperature regulation—they must be. If they cannot warm their flight motor up to 30-37°C, they cannot even take off.

A Warm Nest and the Warmed Brood

The choice of the new nest site by the founder of the colony is an important first step in the direction of saving heat. In temperate latitudes abandoned mouse burrows, with their insulating lining, are favorite sites, as are birds' nests. Wax coatings, coverings of moss, and the like protect from cold and dampness (Fig. 11). The insulation of the nest is repaired by the bumblebees, improved and altered to suit their requirements, depending on the outside temperature. Arctic species avoid the permafrost by positioning their nests on the soil surface, where they can also take advantage of the heat of the sun. If the interior of the nest nevertheless becomes too cold, the bumblebees heat it by "trembling" with their flight musculature. This trembling is not externally visible, because the wings are mechanically uncoupled. On the other hand, it can become too warm in the nest; then the bumblebees, like honeybees, fan fresh air in. The result of this behavior, in the case of the European bumblebees, is a nest temperature held constant at 30°C, at least when the bumblebee colony is fully developed and enough workers are available.[3]

Taking a closer look at the individual animal, we find that temperature regulation goes considerably further than this.

Bernd Heinrich inserted minute electrical thermometers into the thorax and abdomen of bumblebees and recorded their temperatures.[7,9] The heat-producing "uncoupled" flight does not only serve to maintain the general nest temperature. The brood in particular needs warmth in order to develop without delay. It has been postulated for over 150 years that real brooding goes on in the bumblebee nest, and now there is clear confirmation.[4,9] Bernd Heinrich tells of a queen that pressed herself against her brood, a clump of larvae and eggs in the early stage of colony development, by day and night, whenever she was not out foraging. She stretched out her legs and curved her abdomen around the brood clump in such a way that she could reach a container of stored honey with her proboscis. In cold nights a brood-nurse can drink an entire honey pot to the dregs. It is practical that, whereas most of the body is hairy, the underside of the abdomen, which touches the brood clump, bears few hairs and is thus relatively poorly insulated; the heat she produces is released at the right place. It almost seems appropriate to speak of a "brood spot" like the bald, specially warmed place in the skin of the underside that birds develop in the brooding season. The temperature measurements have shown clearly that as long as the bumblebee is not brooding, the temperature of the brood is approximately the same as the ambient temperature. As soon as the bee presses herself against the brood, its temperature jumps upward. In an experiment the difference from the external temperature was as much as 25°C!

The brooding bumblebee heats her thorax up to a constant temperature between 34.5° and 37.5°C. She can do this in ambient temperatures from 3° to 33°C. The temperature of the abdomen is only about 2°C lower. That is, heat flows from the thorax (flight musculature) into the abdomen; the colder it is, the more heat is transferred. In a cold night the brooding bumblebee uses up as much energy for heating as she has collected during the day. To keep her thorax at 30°C when the ambient temperature is 5°C, she must expend about half a calorie per minute. This is almost exactly the fuel consumption during flight. In the race against time, the effort to speed up the development of eggs, larvae, and pupae by raising their temperatures, a great deal of energy is needed (Fig. 88). On warmer days the fuel is much reduced.[9]

Fuel for Flight

The energy consumption during flight, including the warmup before takeoff, is just as imposing.

The bumblebee thorax is packed full of flight musculature, which must have a temperature of at least 30°C to contract rapidly and powerfully enough to lift the animal into the air. In some species the thoracic temperature is a constant 37°C, very close to our own body temperature. But what happens in cold weather? Many insects are then grounded, unable to make their foraging flights. Bumblebees have freed themselves from this restriction by active thermoregulation, and this is precisely the reason why they have been able to spread so far north. Bernd Heinrich's measurements have brought physiological masterpieces to light.[5,7]

The temperature in the thorax of a bumblebee that looks as though it is quietly sleeping can suddenly rise, from 24°C to 37°C in only one minute (Fig. 89). It takes seventeen minutes to heat up from 6°C to 37°C, and during this time not even a tremor of the wings can be seen. Again, however, the heat source is the flight musculature. The bumblebee shivers inside its thorax, with the wings uncoupled. When the right temperature has been reached, it takes off on its foraging flight. Now the thoracic temperature still remains between 35°C and 45°C, even when the reverse problem is encountered. That is, the thoracic muscles of course continue to produce heat when they are being used for flight, so that when the ambient temperature is high there is danger of overheating. A thoracic temperature above 45°C is lethal. The bumblebees overcome this problem by transferring heat out of the thorax into the abdomen. This transfer allows the flight system to function at ambient temperatures between 2°C (for queens; 10°C for workers) and 30°C (Fig. 90).

How high is the energy expenditure for flight? To heat the musculature before takeoff to a final level of 35°C requires (in units of heat) 2.9 calories at an ambient temperature of 24°C, 7.5 calories at 13.5°C, and 15.7 calories at 6.5°C.[5] Converted to sugar

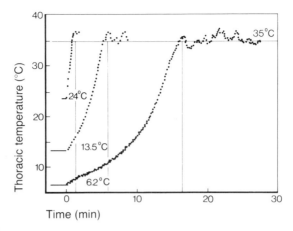

Fig. 89:
A bumblebee queen warms herself up. The graph shows the rapid increase
in thoracic temperature to 37°C, starting from various ambient temperatures (24°C, 13.5°C, and 6.2°C).

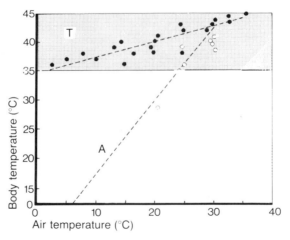

Fig. 90:
The temperature in the thorax (T) and abdomen (A) of queens of the
bumblebee species *Bombus vosnesenskii* during flight. Whereas the temperature in the thorax remains relatively constant despite the large changes in
air temperature, there are marked changes in the temperature of the abdomen. If the ambient temperature rises above 30°C, the bumblebees find it
difficult to keep even the thoracic temperature below the lethal limit of
45°C.

(1 mg sugar corresponds to about 4 calories), these figures amount to 0.7 mg, 2 mg, and 4 mg. The flight itself—not including the cost of thermoregulation—costs about 0.3 calories per minute, or about 0.07 mg sugar per minute. In absolute terms this expenditure may not seem like much, but remember that a bumblebee weighs only about 0.2 g. Calculating their metabolic rate relative to their weight, one finds that they exceed even those enormously metabolically active animals, the hummingbirds. Now consider a bumblebee colony with a collecting team of 300 bees, each of which flies for only five hours; the daily expenditure of the colony is 6.3 g, almost one-third of the total daily harvest of nectar.

Heat Flow through the Wasp Waist

Evidently the bumblebee can do two things with the temperature of its abdomen: keep it constant when brooding, even when the weather is very cold, and not regulate it during flight, in which case it changes in parallel with the air temperature, with the abdomen always 5°-10°C above the air (Fig. 90). How is the heat retained in the thorax in the second case, and released to the abdomen in the first?

The answer lies in the "wasp waist," the stalklike section connecting the abdomen and the thorax. The technical term for this constriction is "petiole," and to be precise it is located between the first and the second abdominal segment. If we cut a vertical section lengthwise through the bumblebee, we can see the structures that allow regulation of heat transfer[6] (Fig. 91).

The insect heart is a tubular structure just under the upper surface of the abdomen. The vessel running forward from it, the aorta, carries blood through the flight musculature to the head. There the blood leaves the vessel and pours into the body cavity, through which it slowly flows back to the heart, reentering it through holes along the sides. As the returning blood flows through the stalk to the abdomen, it passes under a diaphragm which forms a sheet over the entire lower section of the abdomen. Because there are

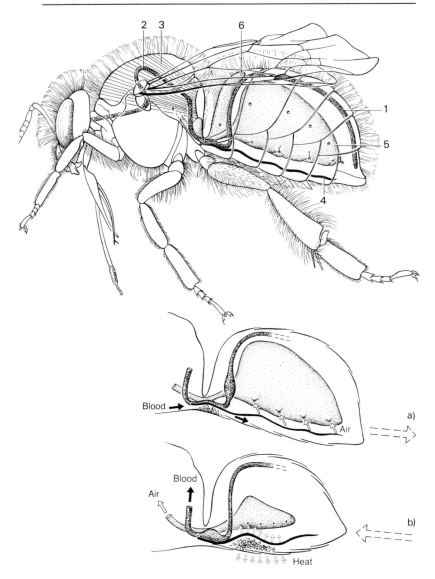

◊
Fig. 91:
A "transparent" bumblebee displays its apparatus for thermoregulation. *Above*: The thorax and the upper surface of the abdomen are covered by a thick pelt of long hairs, which acts as thermal insulation. The lower surface of the abdomen is relatively bare, and acts as a thermal window. The narrow connection between thorax and abdomen and the air sacs (6) in the anterior part of the abdomen counteract the flow of heat from the thorax into the abdomen. Finally, the countercurrent principle: The heart (1) pumps relatively cold blood forward from the abdomen (2, aorta; 3, thoracic musculature). The loop of the vessel passing through the waist brings this blood into close contact with the warmer blood from the thorax, which is propelled toward the hind end by the diaphragm (4). The cooler blood warms up, and the heat is retained in the thorax. *Below*: If heat conservation by the countercurrent is to be reduced, perhaps in order to avoid overheating of the thorax or to warm the abdomen for brooding, the two opposed blood currents presumably do not flow simultaneously through the bumblebee waist, but rather one after the other. Phase a: the abdomen expands and air flows into the air sac (5) from outside. At the same time the diaphragm is elevated and blood flows out of the thorax. Phase b: the abdomen contracts, air flows out of the large air sac of the abdomen into the thorax. The diaphragm has been depressed, so that although the abdominal blood can be pumped into the thorax by the heart, no room is left for flow of blood in the opposite direction. The blood that enters the abdomen releases its heat there (small arrows).

neither veins nor capillaries, the zoologist calls this an open circulatory system. In the bumblebee the aorta makes a "hairpin turn" to pass through the stalk.

In insects gas transport is the function not of the blood, but of a system of much-branched air tubules, the tracheae. Their delicate arborizations penetrate the tissue of all the organs. Particularly in the abdomen the tracheae of many insects—including the bumblebees—are greatly distended, forming tracheal sacs. Two large tracheae pass through the bumblebee waist. Pumping movements of the abdomen drive air through the system.

A large number of different measurements regarding the thoracic temperature have been done, and it looks as though what happens is as follows.[6]

1. First consider the case in which heat is retained in the thorax. The shape of the narrow abdominal stalk and the animal's dense

hairy coat in themselves act to prevent heat loss. In addition, some of the heat in the blood flowing back to the heart is transferred to the blood in the aorta. This involves a simple trick known as the countercurrent principle. The current of cold blood from the abdomen flowing through the aorta and the current of warm thoracic blood in the opposite direction are separated from one another by only a very thin layer of cells. As the two currents pass one another, heat is transferred into the cooler aortic blood and is therefore retained in the thorax. The same principle operates in many other situations in the animal kingdom: in gas exchange in the fish gill, for instance, in urine production by the mammalian kidney, in ducks that stand on the ice in winter with bare legs and must limit the loss of heat from their bodies; finally, many mammals keep their heads cool in this way.

2. How can the same apparatus be used to achieve the opposite—release of heat to the abdomen? Probably by means of a clever "switch" that causes the two opposed currents to flow not simultaneously but in alternation, so that the countercurrent system no longer functions. Figure 91 shows in detail how this would work.

Incidentally, one must be very cautious in applying such findings to other animals. Even in one of the bumblebee's closest relatives, the honeybee, there is no such switch. That is, the countercurrent heat exchange is always in operation, so that the abdomen cannot be used as a receptacle for surplus heat from the overheated thorax. Nevertheless, the bee can fly even in the extremely high ambient temperature 46°C without becoming too hot—a record among the insects studied so far! The trick: the bee regurgitates a droplet from its honey stomach and holds it on the proboscis, where it evaporates and causes cooling. Not only the head is cooled—the thoracic temperature is also lowered by about 10°C. In ambient temperatures below 30°C the flying honeybee does not regulate the temperature of either head or thorax.[9]

The Best Way to the Food

When we talk about economical behavior, what we mean basically is the profitable management of three things: energy (the currency of our biological economic system), time, and risk. The three factors must be mutually adjusted in such a way that the production of offspring is ensured. In evolution, the fittest will turn out to be those whose net profit per unit time is greatest, with a tolerable amount of risk.

With regard to energy: we have seen the paths it follows and can construct for ourselves a concrete picture of what it means for a bumblebee to manage energy economically.

With regard to time: there are quite a few temporal factors of which the bumblebee must take account in its behavior. Above all, there are seasonal and daily periodicities. The production of new queens must be completed before winter. In collecting food good timing with respect to the flowering period of the plants, the daily fluctuation in temperature, and the hours of maximal nectar secretion (Chapter 26) is important. Time plays a role in the flight from flower to flower; here, as elsewhere, "time is money." The amount of nectar that can be obtained must be in reasonable proportion to the duration of flights from the hive and back again; the bee must not fly indiscriminately about among the flowers in an inflorescence. Finally, the entrance to the flower must be found quickly; a bee visiting a complexly built flower for the first time must spend quite a while probing various places before it is successful (Fig. 92).

With regard to risk: a risk always arises when the time or energy accounts do not balance—for example, when periods of bad weather find the bees with inadequate food stores, or when the young queens mature too late.

Let us return briefly to the starting point. How does the bumblebee behave when actually collecting?

In recent years there have been quite a few experiments designed to raise the explanation of bee behavior—especially the bumblebee, taken here as an example of the many flower-visiting

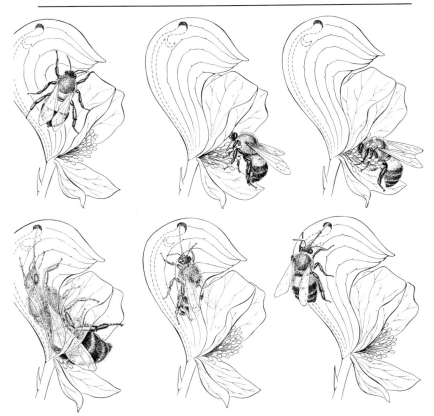

Fig. 92:
Bumblebees on monkshood flowers. *Above*: On the left an inexperienced
animal tries to get into the flower from the top; in the middle a bumblebee is searching in vain for nectar among the anthers; on the right a bumblebee is shaking the anthers to gather the pollen. *Below*: Large (left) and
small (middle) bumblebees reach the nectar in various ways; nectar
thieves (right) bite a hole in the "hood" and suck up the nectar from outside, without entering the flower and assisting pollination.

insects—above the level of simple plausibility, by supplying numerical measurements.[2] As yet, though, there is no single, unified
theory of the optimal strategy of food collecting. Presumably there
never will be one, for the ecological conditions in which collecting
is done are too varied. But the many measurements available allow

us to make a concrete analysis of the problem for our concrete case.

Graham Pyke of the University of Utah in Salt Lake City made detailed observations of the North American bumblebee species *Bombus appositus* as it sucked nectar from a typical bumblebee flower, the monkshood *Aconitum columbianum*; he found that the bee proceeds quite systematically.[14,15]

The bumblebees almost always begin their visits at one of the lowest flowers of the inflorescence. Of all starts, 84.6 percent occur at the three lowest flowers. From there the bee proceeds upward, usually to flowers it has not recently chosen. It is rare for a bee to make a downward "detour." In 90 percent of all cases the bumblebees fly from the flower just visited to the nearest or next nearest flower. If one were to give a rule for the bee's flight, it would be something like this: "Always fly to the nearest flower you have not just visited, unless you have just moved downward. If you have just arrived at the inflorescence, then fly to the nearest flower above you." This command would also prevent the occurrence of two downward movements in succession.

Surprisingly, the bumblebees usually do not leave the inflorescence at the top, but in 67 cases out of 100 stop collecting at one of the lower flowers. Why? Within an inflorescence the amount of nectar in the flowers decreases from bottom to top. It seems sensible, therefore, to begin at the bottom and stop before one has gone so high that the net profit becomes questionable. One might suppose this to be a disadvantage to the plant, but it is not. In the monkshood, as in other typical bumblebee plants with similar inflorescences (for example, the foxglove and the rosebay willow herb), the age of the flowers decreases from bottom to top. Flowers with receptive stigmas are lower down, and flowers with ripe pollen are above them. When the bumblebee flies from one flower spike to the next, it does just what the plant needs—it carries the pollen from the upper flowers of the inflorescence it has just left to the stigmas of the lower flowers of the new inflorescence. Cross-pollination is assisted, and pollen is saved, for as much as possible reaches stigmas ready to receive it and is not wasted upon flowers

Fig. 93:
The goldenrod *Solidago canadensis* and two bumblebees, which arrange
their simultaneous collecting in such a way that the larger species (*Bombus
terricola*) exploits the inner flowers, while the smaller (*Bombus ternarius*)
visits the outer flowers.

that are too young.[14] On the other hand, the bumblebee does not
carry enough pollen around with it to pollinate an infinite number
of flowers. Does the spiral arrangement of the monkshood flowers
on their spike have anything to do with this? Because of it, as the
bee moves upward it always leaves some flowers out. Perhaps the

result is that it visits just as many flowers in a single inflorescence as it can actually pollinate, before flying to the next plant. By having a spiral flower spike the plant would also have increased the value of its pollen investment. It is a plausible idea, but not yet proven.

In any case, here we have yet another clear demonstration that many features of the structure and behavior of the two partners make biological sense only in the light of their mutual relationships.

Avoiding Competition

Foraging behavior can change when there is competition, in the bumblebee as in other insects. *Solidago canadensis*, a relative of the asters, is called goldenrod because of its long rows of yellow flowers. Along the coast of Maine, goldenrod is an important source of energy for bumblebees. Often several species can be seen sucking nectar from it simultaneously. The small species *Bombus ternarius* and the larger species *Bombus terricola* have arrived at an interesting arrangement (Fig. 93). The small bumblebees retreat to the outermost flowers as soon as the large bees appear, allowing the latter to exploit the flowers nearer the axis of the plant. The large bumblebees stay away from the flowers further out because the tapering stem cannot bear their weight near its tip. Their small cousins can suck everywhere, and they do so whenever the bulky competitors are not there. But when they come, the best strategy for the small bees is to get out of their way and not waste time and energy in an unequal confrontation.[13]

A similarly peaceful division of resources among different bumblebee species is observed when it is a matter of food-plant selection. *Bombus appositus* and *Bombus flavifrons* were first found to be collecting from different plants, each with flowers just as deep as the bees' proboscises were long. When the experimenter removed one species of bee from the area, there was an immediate increase in the frequency with which the other visited the flowers preferred by the first species.[10] Flexibility is the crucial prerequisite for their success. The bees do well not to persist stubbornly in visiting a particular kind of flower, but rather to look at the situation in the neighboring flowers from time to time. If the bumblebee with the long proboscis (*B. appositus*) is absent, it suddenly becomes worthwhile for the one with the shorter proboscis (*B. flavifrons*) to visit the delphinium (*Delphinium barbeyi*) preferred by the other. Why? Because the level of the nectar in the flowers has risen so high that the shorter proboscis can reach it.

It is questionable whether all bumblebees in all external conditions compete so peacefully with one another for food. Some of the stingless bees of the tropics (Chapter 6) are definitely aggressive (for example, *Trigona silvestriana* and *T. corvina*) (Pl. 9). Sometimes disputes about food are lethal for the loser; the bees can bite one another for an hour or more, when the battle is most intense wrestling belly to belly and excreting a sticky substance, and the victor often finishes off the opponent by biting its head to pieces. The more concentrated the nectar and the more abundant the pollen supply, the longer and more intense are the fights among competitors. Although such behavior means an initial loss of time and fuel, it is evidently worthwhile. The less aggressive species is denied the food source. Usually the larger species wins, as one might expect. It is this species that must expend more energy in flying around and therefore sooner reaches the limit at which the collection of nectar and pollen becomes unprofitable, because the yield from the flowers is too low.[11]

30 Coupled Evolution in the Competition for Limited Resources

> ... for in his work I must admire the first serious scientific
> attempt to explain all the phenomena of organic nature from
> one grand, uniform point of view, and to replace the
> incomprehensible miracle with the comprehensible natural
> law.
>
> *Ernst Haeckel on Charles Darwin, 1862*

As we marvel at the precision and orderliness that attention to
biological phenomena reveals, we are repeatedly faced with the
question: How did this come to be? None of the biological problems we have explored so far can be entirely solved without an
answer to this question. The more delicately insect and plant are
adjusted to one another, the more urgently we would like to know
the history of this partnership. Think back to the first chapter; one
can hardly imagine a better example than the gall wasp and its
figs. The balance of mutual advantage and mutual dependence is
especially apparent in such spectacular cases of coevolution. The
close matching between the sensory performance of insects and
the special characteristics of the signals sent out by the flowers is
no less remarkable—including the example of the fly orchid, which
insinuates itself so subtly into the sex life of the male wasp. But
we are not concerned here with listing the wondrous feats of nature—especially because at every turn we have found that even
"simple" things reveal exquisite perfection if one takes a close enough
look. This final chapter is devoted to the process of evolution in
the context of the relationship between insects and flowers.

"During the summer of 1787, as I was attentively examining

the flower of the wood cranesbill (*Geranium sylvaticum*), I found
that its petals were covered with fine, soft hairs near their bases,
on the inner surface and the two edges. Convinced that the wise
Creator has not produced a single hair without specific intent, I
reflected upon the purpose these hairs might serve." So wrote
Christian Konrad Sprengel in 1793, in the introduction to his
classic book on flower ecology. For him, undoubtedly, to occupy
oneself with nature was to occupy oneself with the will and wisdom of its creator. The question as to how all the things he ad-
mired might have developed in the course of time did not arise.
For us, however, it is a central question.

One Hundred Thirty-Five Million Years of Flowering Plants

About 135 million years ago, before the dinosaurs and ammonites
vanished from the earth, the plant kingdom began to develop vas-
cular plants with enclosed seeds, the angiosperms. On the geolog-
ical time scale, the angiosperms spread rapidly. By the early Cretaceous, about eighty million years ago, they were already beginning
to crowd out the ginkgo trees, tree ferns, palm ferns, and Bennet-
titales that had dominated the plant communities until then. The
age of angiosperms initiated at that time has lasted to the present.
With about 250,000 living species, they are by far the largest present-day plant group. They have conquered all the continents and
are absent only from the sand deserts and the arctic regions. They
are the ruling group of land plants. Their variability and adapta-
bility are unrivaled. They have had a decisive influence in the evolution of continental animals, because all such animals live—at
first or second hand—from the energy made available to them by
the photosynthetic activity of the angiosperms and other plants.
Man and animal, in this sense, are parasites of the plants.

The typical adaptations of angiosperms are adaptations of the
reproductive organs to pollination by insects. The egg cells develop in the shelter of the ovary. The display apparatus of the

flower attracts insects searching for pollen and nectar, and the seed primordia must be protected from being eaten by the same insects—which originally were probably mainly the unspecialized beetles—by enclosure in the base of the pistil. This situation is expressed in the name "angiosperm," from the Greek *angeion*, container, and *sperma*, seed. The stigma is a further development in the same direction. It not only receives the pollen and stimulates the male gametes the pollen contains, but also sorts out and rejects undesirable pollen, and promotes cross-pollination, to the genetic advantage of the plant.[9]

That such packaging of the seeds of land plants also provides an important protection against desiccation goes without saying.

The flower made a fundamental contribution to the extraordinary success of angiosperms. As a reproductive organ, it is more accessible than all other plant organs to natural selection. No wonder that the genetic diversity of angiosperms is manifest above all in the great diversity of their flowers.

How did the evolution of the flowers proceed?

A magnolia flower from the Cretaceous, very like the present-day magnolias, must have been close to the starting point from which all the variety we see today developed. It was typical of such flowers to have large numbers of stamens, pistils, and petals arranged in a spiral. In the course of time the numbers decreased and the spiral condensed to a circle. The transition to regular radial symmetry and then to bilateral symmetry is a further trend in the evolution of the flowering plants. As these occurred, parts of the flower fused with one another. Eventually the flower became progressively "three-dimensional"; corolla tubes, nectar spurs, and the like developed[5] (Fig. 94). The bilateral symmetry of complex types of flowers such as the lady's slipper, snapdragon, or monkshood is a late step in evolution. Even present-day flora can be arranged in morphological series that correspond to these general trends in the evolution of flower shape.[5]

This general scheme may seem to offer a fairly complete picture. But in many individual cases the process of evolution was more complicated. A given result has often been achieved by different

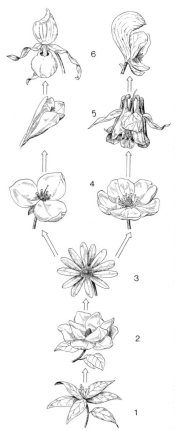

Fig. 94:
Important trends in the evolution of
flower shape over a span of 100 million
years. (1) Most primitive amorphous
flower without clearly discernible shape
or symmetry. (2) Flower of open hemi-
spherical shape with no clear symmetry
(like the magnolia flower). (3) Typical
open radially symmetrical flower (like
that of the yellow adonis). Subsequent
divergence into different lines of development, such as flowers of the monocoty-
ledonous plants shown here on the left,
and those of the buttercup family
(right). (4) Flowers with reduced but
fixed number of petals (like those of the
spiderwort, left, and buttercup, right).
(5) Flowers of increasingly three-dimensional shape with hidden nectar and often bilateral symmetry (like those of the
freesia, left, and columbine, right). (6)
Complex flower shapes at the highest
level of development (like those of the
lady's slipper, left, and monkshood,
right).

parallel routes. In many cases the flower is shaped mainly by adaptation to certain pollinators, and these may change. Once a flower
form has developed, it may become the point of departure for an
array of special ecological adaptations; the phlox family is a prime
example of this kind of history (Fig. 95).[3,8]

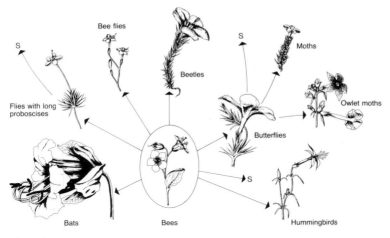

Fig. 95:
The phlox family illustrates well how flower shapes diverge within a family under the selection pressure of different pollinators, for better adaptation. The hypothetical starting point was flowers pollinated by bees. Self-pollination (S) presumably evolved secondarily several times from insect pollination.

Insects: The History of a Unique Success

The insects are no less successful than the flowering plants. Among the animals, they are the dominant group. This leadership is evident, for example, in the number of species: of the c. 1.2 million known animal species, no less than c. 900,000 are arthropods, the most important groups of which are the crustaceans, spiders, and insects. And within the arthropods, the insects are by far the largest group, with c. 800,000 species (Fig. 96). Among the groups of insects that visit flowers, the largest is the beetles, with c. 345,000 species (fossil and living), followed by the Lepidoptera (c. 165,000), Hymenoptera (c. 105,000), and Diptera (flies and mosquitoes, c. 90,000).

Insects have invaded nearly all habitats—the tiniest crevices in the soil, the water, and as the first true terrestrial animals in evolution not only the land but the air as well. The number of indi-

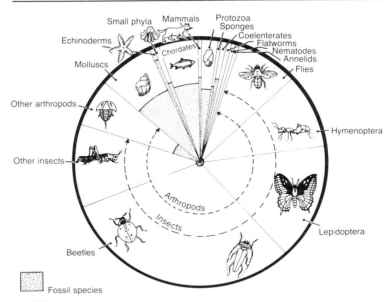

Fig. 96:
The phyla of the animal kingdom (see text).

viduals is astronomical. It has been estimated that for every human there are almost a billion insects. Just as the botanists regard us as living in the age of the angiosperms, from a zoological viewpoint we live in a world of insects.

Their history goes back considerably further than that of the flowering plants. It begins in the darkness of the Paleozoic. The oldest insect known so far is a springtail from the Middle Devonian in Scotland;[4] it is about 350 million years old. The first insects known to have existed in large numbers, as documented by their fossil remains, lived about 300 million years ago in the gigantic forests of tree ferns and lycopsids such as *Lepidodendron* and *Sigillaria*, the remains of which have formed our present-day anthracite coal. This was the time when the reptiles were beginning to replace the amphibians as the ruling animal group—long before the first birds and mammals evolved. By then the insects were highly developed, and had wings. The most important steps in their evolution were already behind them. Some of those ancient insects could fold up their wings and undergo a complete metamorphosis during their development, passing through a pupal stage. The giant dragonfly *Meganeura monyi* from the coal deposits at Commentry in France is one of the earliest fossil finds. It does justice to its name, with a body length of thirty centimeters and a wingspan of as much as sixty centimeters. Cockroaches are also among the first demonstrable insects (Fig. 97). About 30 million years ago (perhaps even more, as is now thought) in the Tertiary, when the horde of Mesozoic reptiles had been extinct for many million years and the evolution of the mammals was far advanced, the insect fauna was so similar to what we know today that it is sometimes difficult to distinguish the species of those days, meticulously preserved in amber, from modern species. The long, uninterrupted success of the insects, founded on their adaptation to terrestrial life and their mobility, is without parallel.

Among the present-day flower pollinators, the beetles are a particularly old group. The most ancient beetle fossils come from the earth's antiquity, the Permian, and are around 280 million years old. Bees, flies, and lepidopterans are considerably younger (Fig. 97). Hymenoptera first appear as fossils in the Mesozoic (Triassic, about 200 million years ago). But the history of the bees and bumblebees, hymenopterans so remarkably adapted for visiting flowers, is inseparable from that of the angiosperms, and these did not become the dominant plant group until 100 million years more had passed. There is as yet no reliable demonstration that Lepidoptera existed at any time during the entire Mesozoic, which ended about 70 million years ago.

Coevolution and Specialization

The highest degree of specialization for flower-visiting is found in the insects that have evolved entirely or mainly in the epoch of the angiosperms. This specialization is particularly clear in the shapes of the mouthparts (Chapter 11). As the flowers acquired special-

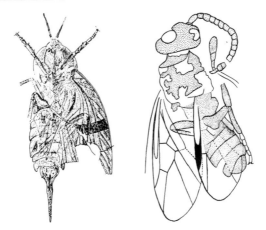

Fig. 97:
Fossil insects. At the left a species of cockroach that presumably lived
more than 200 million years ago, in the Paleozoic (*Kunguroblattina mi-
crodictya*, Blattopteroidea, from the lower Permian of the Urals); to the
right, a hymenopteran at least 140 million years old, from the Mesozoic
(*Mesohelorus muchini*, Hymenoptera, from the upper Jurassic of Kazakh-
stan).

ized shapes, selection among the specialized visitors came into play.
A source of nectar at the bottom of a long corolla tube immediately becomes inaccessible to a bee; its proboscis is too short and
its body too thick to penetrate the tube. Even if the tube is no
longer than the proboscis, bumblebees and bees may be unable to
visit unless a landing platform is provided. Lepidoptera have no
problems here. Their proboscises are long enough, and many of
them need not land because they can suck while hovering. But
butterflies and moths themselves are so highly specialized—and
that always means limited in their behavioral repertoire—that they
can use only the nectar, not the pollen. They have no jaws with
which to chew pollen.

Considerations of this sort have led to the categories beetle
flowers, fly flowers, bee flowers, lepidopteran flowers, and so on
(Chapter 3); but these must not be relied on too heavily. Such a
classification is certainly useful for the extremely specialized flow-

ers. It becomes more problematic when we consider the many flowers of simple structure, which attract many different insects.

As insects become more specialized, they must depend on an ever-diminishing selection of flowers. Among the flowers from which they can choose, they favor those that offer food most abundantly and that have the most attractive shape and smell. Variants in a flower population that stand out from the crowd in this sense have an increased chance of being pollinated. In this way, the insects exert selection pressure on the flowering plants. The result is the same as that of the selection practiced by animal and plant breeders, and it necessarily follows that the sensory and learning capacities of the insects are closely related to the signals sent out by the flowers. The bee is a prime example of this effect (Chapters 12 to 22).

It would be nice to know whether the sensory abilities of the evolutionarily more primitive insects can be understood by reference to simpler flower forms and are thus "more primitive" in this sense. In the course of evolution the recognition of flower forms and patterns must have become increasingly important. Eventually the insects had to learn to deal with the spatial configurations that the most highly developed flower forms presented to those seeking their nectar.[5] The insects must have learned to learn, for in these complicated flowers the food is not directly available; only the association of various signals with the presence of a reward shows the insects the path to the hidden nectar.

The bee is unique among insects in the amount of study that has been devoted to it. What we need now is a large-scale investigation of the other groups of pollinators. Such research is difficult, because there are so many characteristics that may be explained by aspects of the animals' history that are unknown to us, and that need not have anything to do with a current species-preserving function. Many special adaptations are certain to be only indirectly related to the evolutionary association between insects and flowers. The complex performance of the honeybee nervous system, for example, is surely superior to that of the phylogenetically younger Lepidoptera, even though the bees visit many simple, open flowers of primitive shape, which are not accessible to the specialized lepidopterans. The advanced position of the bees is much more appropriately understood in relation to their social organization and—closely associated with it—their care of the young (Chapters 6 and 7).

Directed Evolution

Why does evolution have a direction at all? Are not evolutionary events unintentional and unprogrammed? Is not one of evolution's firmest foundations the random alteration of the hereditary material, the mutations that occur with no foreknowledge of their eventual adaptive value? These questions invite some discussion. Darwin's own views about the bases of inheritance were entirely inadequate. The correctness of his theory—which, by the way, was paralleled by the insightful reasoning of Alfred Russel Wallace, developed simultaneously and independently, and yet bafflingly consistent with Darwin's theory—is all the more intriguing. Darwin's theory did require the spontaneous, undirected alteration of the hereditary material. But it was not until much later that the modern science of genetics showed the ways in which regularities could become established in the course of millions of years of evolution, and gave us an idea of how the harmonious interplay of the parts of an organism was and is maintained, despite continual genetic variation.[6]

The great majority of mutations are small steps. Evolution is not—as was thought in the first decades of this century—explicable in terms of drastic changes, jumps that create new species at a stroke. Just the opposite. It is a matter of minute differences in the genetic equipment of the individuals of a population. Evolution depends not on mutation alone, but also on sexual reproduction, the essential biological function of which is the creation of genetic variability. In the process of fertilization, two separate sets of genes unite, one from the male and one from the female, to produce a new organism. But when this organism itself becomes a parent, it does not pass on this combined mass of genetic material without alteration. As the germ cells of the next generation are formed, the mixed genetic material separates again, and before it does so it is recombined—put together in a new way. The new set of genes in each germ cell is a mixture of the genes of the two parents (the special situation in the bees is described in Chapter 7). The genetic diversity of a population is enormous; hardly any two individuals are genetically identical. The sameness of such rare pairs of identical twins (formed from a single egg) is indeed striking. By contrast, fraternal twins (from two eggs) provide a good illustration of genetic variability. The separate components of genetic information from the parents can be handed on to the progeny in random, free combination. This is one of the basic rules of heredity. Gregor Mendel worked it out long ago; but the subdivision of the genetic material into individual genes, which for him was at first merely an intellectual concept, was incomprehensible to his contemporaries and had to be discovered anew around the turn of the century. In Mendel's time—which was also Darwin's— the notion that the blood was the carrier of the hereditary material was widespread and generally accepted. It survives today in terms such as "full-blooded" and "half-blooded," with which horse breeders characterize the hereditary makeup of various breeds. According to the blood theory, children were always a simple mixture of the components from the parents, and it would follow that the individuals of a population should grow steadily more similar from one generation to the next, eventually becoming genetically identical. The contradiction was clear to Darwin, even though he could not resolve it: if evolution is to occur at all, there must be variability within a population.

Genetic variability, which is based on mutation and recombination, is not the process of evolution itself but a prerequisite for it. For evolution as we understand it to occur, there must be natural selection. Selection acts not on the genes themselves but rather on the structures and functions produced by the genes in the prevailing environmental conditions—the so-called phenotype.

Even in this century it was long thought that the chromosomes of an organism were made up of components more or less independent from and unrelated to one another. The quite logical conclusion was that any change in the hereditary material would be very likely to disrupt the obvious harmony of the organism. It has since been discovered that each characteristic derives from the action of dozens or hundreds of genes, and that the gene actions are intimately interlaced. Only a few of these genes are "structural" genes; many others are "regulatory" genes, which supervise these interactions. A harmonious genetic interplay of this sort can continue to be harmonious in the long term only because selection acts on the phenotype, which the genetic interplay brings forth as a unit, a coherent system.

The directedness in evolution—the trends that one finds again and again, at least when considering long sections of the phylogenetic history leading to the present day—arises from the fact that the environmental conditions select among the species-preserving abilities of all organs and behavior patterns, in the direction of improved species preservation.

Therefore although mutation and recombination occur randomly, natural selection is neither random nor undirected. The term "selection pressure" is very appropriate, for it is like a force pushing the genetic composition of the population in a certain direction. The measure of selection is "fitness," the degree to which an organism can cope with life. Only in certain conditions has fitness anything to do with a long life span, and it is not necessarily true that the brawny beach boy is fitter than the frail scholar. Fit in evolution biology means successful in passing on one's chromosomal material to the next generation, to achieve reproduction and thereby generate many well-adapted offspring. Only the successful reproducer contributes to evolution. Nevertheless, it would be incorrect to classify organisms as "fit" and "unfit." Natural selection does not separate the wheat from the chaff. It ensures that from a palette of individual genetic variation with many subtle gradations, the better gradually crowds out the good. Alteration in the common genetic pool of a population—in the frequency of occurrence of certain gene combinations—is the pacemaker of species modification and hence of evolution itself.

The Colorful Summer Meadow: Environment and Reflection of the Insects

The relationship between flowers and insects is particularly close to this process of natural selection. Ultimately it is a matter of pollination, which depends directly on the species-maintaining ability of the flower. The evolution of all the characteristics mentioned in this book that make a flower more attractive to the insects is based on the fact that the "better" genotypes have a greater chance of being pollinated, and therefore slowly crowd out the less attractive plants. Because the insects perform this selection, it is they that to a large extent determine how the summer meadow will look. The greater the number of plants existing side by side and even blooming at the same time, all of which depend on cross-pollination, the stronger is the selection pressure on each to be unique, to look different from the competitors and have an unmistakable scent. Insects—at first attracted by the abundant pollen offerings—were involved in this process from the very beginning of flower evolution. Even the primitive flower type of the magnolias is pollinated by insects (the present-day magnolias are specialized for beetles[10]). The diversity of the devices employed by the flowers reflects the diversity of ways to be more attractive, so that the insects will help them reproduce under the pressure of severe competition. Conversely, the plants also help to shape the insects, which are exposed to equally strong pressure of competition. The insect with the best chance of harvesting the food is the one with mouthparts best suited to exploit a certain flower economically, and with the most suitable sensory abilities and behavior. In a population of pollinating insects, the one of the many variations that will be most successful in passing on its genes is the one that goes about acquiring food in the most effective manner. In this sense the plants and their pollinators are environment and reflection of one another.

Supply and Demand

In the competition for limited resources, whether for pollinators or for food, selection pressure is directed toward increasing the excellence of the match between flower and pollinator. The term "coevolution" applies here because it is a process of mutual adjustments of flower and pollinator. In this coupled evolution by reciprocal selection, one partner is always leading by a nose, with the other close behind. Changes in one of the partners demand the selection of variants of the other that are capable of restoring the close match between the two. The sucking proboscis, evolved in intimate relation to the appearance of nectar, changes in parallel with the flower tube containing the nectar. This process could also be characterized in terms of supply and demand. Its result is the adaptations produced, not only in organ structure but also in physiology—flowering time, composition of the nectar and the time of day when it is secreted, the self-sterility of many plants, the time sense of the honeybee and its ability to learn, skill in penetrating complicated flowers, or behavior patterns like those of the orchid bees and the *Ophrys* pollinators. This book is full of examples.

Coadaptations of plants and pollinators are never the final result of a successful interaction. In an environment that changes continually and unpredictably, only continual modifications of structure and function can guarantee the continuing success of the cooperation. In this sense, adaptation is limited by the flexibility of the organism, its ability to produce a new generation with new gene combinations. In the context of evolution biology, this requirement not only explains the special value of sexual reproduction, it also makes comprehensible the fact that the life of an individual, without exception, eventually comes to an end. The death of the individual is to the advantage of the species. It makes room for the new generation with its novel characteristics, keeps evolution going, and ensures that the species as a whole always has a large number of different gene combinations available—enough to survive in a future changed environment.

Female impersonators and nectar thieves show us that, in the partnership of plants and animals, giving and taking are not always in balance. They remind us that in the random history of evolution one's own advantage comes first, that the process of evolution is opportunistic.

Adaptation is specialization, and specialization narrows the range of possibilities; it makes one dependent. The primitive, nonspecialized insects such as beetles became less important pollinators in the course of time, whereas the highly specialized bees, flies, butterflies, and moths gained steadily in importance to the flowers. The long proboscis of the butterfly is adapted to the sucking of nectar, but makes pollen-eating impossible. The long corolla tube of the typical butterfly flower is adapted to the butterfly, but constitutes a barrier to the short proboscis of the bee. It is obvious that specialization enhances the flower-constancy of the pollinator. As a result, the plant is more certain of pollination, especially cross-pollination, with less expenditure of pollen, and the animal can more economically find and gather up the food. Specialization for controlled pollination by a few insects also increases the speed of evolution, because it results in the biological isolation not only of species, but also of populations. This isolation of populations precedes the evolution of new species. The bright colors of the summer meadow and the fascinating diversity of the flowers are directly related to specialization and to the barriers it has erected. Indeed, the differences among the flowers of the different species are especially large in the families distinctive for their highly specialized pollination by a few particular insects.[9]

Gregor Mendel and Charles Darwin

Darwin, who was familiar with and appreciated Sprengel's work, knew nothing about the genetic bases of evolution. He was not aware of the ingenious work published by his contemporary, the Augustine monk Gregor Johann Mendel. Mendel's concept of genetic variation fit very well with Darwin's idea of random changes in hereditary factors. The scientific world at the time did not realize its value; Mendel himself, a teacher of biology, physics, and mathematics at a school in what was then Austria, probably underestimated its real significance. He had read Darwin's writings without realizing the revolutionary relevance of his own findings to Darwin's theory. In any case, in 1868—only two years after the publication of his work *Experiments on Plant Hybrids*—Mendel was promoted to abbot and had to forsake his experiments for other things. When Darwin died in 1882, two years before Mendel, a great deal was still unclear, and presumably he still felt obliged to confess the apparent absurdity, as he says, of the notion that organs of extreme perfection and complexity such as the human eye could be formed by natural selection. But the forcefulness, clarity, and uncompromising nature of his thinking are revealed in a formulation that appears only a few pages after this comment in the same chapter on "Difficulties of the Theory" in his monumental work *The Origin of Species* (1859). He writes: "If it could be demonstrated that any complex organ existed, which could not possibly have been formed by numerous, successive, slight modifications, my theory would absolutely break down. But I can find out no such case." Nothing influenced and molded biology so greatly as the storm released by Darwin's theory. It changed our whole concept of the world. Since then, research has caught up with Darwin; results from laboratories engaged in the most varied kinds of research again and again have confirmed his ideas. Today his theory is as secure as, for example, the atomic theory of physics. It continues to fascinate us as it did its creator, who closes his book on the origin of species with the words: "There is grandeur in this view of life, with its several powers, having been originally breathed by the Creator into a few forms or one; and that, whilst this planet has gone cycling on according to the fixed law of gravity, from so simple a beginning endless forms most beautiful and most wonderful have been, and are being evolved."

Addendum

Research never comes to an end. I am therefore grateful for the opportunity to add a few remarks on some new findings which appear particularly relevant to some of the topics outlined in the original version of "Insects and Flowers."

Chapter 5
Wind pollination

Aren't we all inclined to consider wind-pollination as wasteful and primitive as compared to animal pollination? The stories highlighted in this book indeed testify the efficiency of the partnership between the pollinating insects and their flowers.

Botanists have long known a number of mechanisms to trap pollen in wind-pollinated plants. Although off the mainstream of our general context I would in particular like the insect biased reader to know about one newly discovered stratagem which takes out much of the chance involved in wind pollination (Niklas and Kyaw Tha Paw U 1982, Niklas and Buchmann 1985, Niklas 1987).

It is true that most of the pollen released by a pine tree go astray. Recent aerodynamic studies in the wind tunnel, however, have demonstrated that the apparent chaos of pollen movement is under the rather tight control of well engineered airflow in the immediate vicinity of the female cone. The cone not only deflects the pollen-carrying wind towards its ovule-carrying zone; when passing over the individual scales the wind drops towards the scale base and the opening of the ovule. In addition the cone as a whole induces turbulences along its leeward side thus also ensuring pollination in this area. The leaves (needles) surrounding many a small species of pine cone slow down the air stream and cause the airborne pollen to settle on the cone. Aerodynamically predetermined airflow patterns differ among the different plant species (such as pine) in ways which favor species-specific pollination and there seems to be a reciprocity between the aerodynamic properties of pollen and the detailed morphology of the cone scales which largely determine the local airflow. The same or similar findings apply to a wide variety of wind pollinated plants including grasses.

Chapter 6
Beetles as pollinators

To do better justice to the beetles and their role as legitimate pollinators we should not only mention the European cases but also have a look into the tropics. Predominant or exclusive pollination by beetles, cantharophily, is known of quite a few plant families such as the Magnoliaceae, Annonaceae, Eupomatiaceae, and Calycanthaceae. These are all phylogenetically old families which corroborates the classic idea that beetle pollination is an archaic type of pollination. However, this is certainly not always so. Instead there are cases in which cantharophily appears to be highly specialized. In such instances specialization for cantharophily goes along with an enlargement of the size of the individual flower and of the number of stamens and carpels. It is also accompanied by the formation of a pollination chamber by the petals in which the beetles may find themselves trapped for a long period of time. There are also well documented cases of flowers which are highly specialized with regard to their beetle customers in having developed ways to heat up enormously in the evening hours which intensifies the cloud of odor surrounding them and sometimes attracts masses of beetles (Thien 1980, Gottsberger 1988, 1989 a,b).

Chapter 7
Kin recognition

From a sociobiological point of view kin and social-group recognition is a major factor in social behavior. Such an ability would allow behavior to be adjusted to the degree of relatedness and thus facilitate kin selection. Such a recognition ability is indeed highly developed in bees and other animals (Fletcher and Michener 1987).

Odors are particularly important cues and may be self-produced by the individual animal or acquired from the environment, for instance through the food. In honeybees it is the comb wax which mediates the acquisition of cues used to recognize a nest-mate and distinguish it from a non-colony member (Breed et al. 1988). In addition and more surprisingly, bees like other animals can also discriminate degrees of relatedness of genetic subgroups within a colony (Breed et al. 1985, Noonan and Kolmes 1989, Page et al. 1989).

Such subgroups are for instance sisters which share a queen mother and drone father. Since the mating system of the honeybee involves the sperm of several males there are offspring of several drones in one colony which form sort of subfamilies and are the basis of a kind of nepotism.

In 1985 a very nice book by Thomas Seeley appeared in Princeton University Press. It deals with the ecology of the honeybee and its manifold adaptations to its elaborate social life. All those not so much interested in physiological processes but in the ecological factors, the evolutionary framework and the forces of selection which underly the social behavior of the honeybee and its striking adaptations find an excellent treatment of the subject here.

Chapter 9
Micropterygids and pollen feeding

A micropterygid moth from New Caledonia has recently been found to be part of a complex relationship between two archaic, relictual groups of insects and plants (Thien et al. 1985). *Zygogynum* (Winteraceae), the moth pollinated plant, is a phylogenetically primitive and vesselless small tree of the tropics which like the micropterygids has a long fossil record dating back to the Early Cretaceous. Its pollinator, *Sabatinca*, uses the nectarless flowers of *Zygogynum* both as feeding and as mating station. Strong odors function as assembling scent and attract 30 and more male and female moths to an opening flower bud which if in its male phase offers pollen and pollenkitt as food. Mating behavior starts with one moth crawling rapidly in circles. The other moths follow its example until most of them move about in the same pattern and finally mate.

Attracting a large number of insects for a long period of time seems to be characteristic for many a magnolioid flowery plant such as *Zygogynum*. The insects feed, mate, and pollinate at the flowers. This pattern of pollination may well be representative of early angiosperms (see also chapter 30, reference 10, T. Thien 1974).

There is another example of a pollen feeding lepidopteran. The ca. 45 species of the neotropical genus *Heliconius* are the only known group of adult butterflies exhibiting this habit. They feed on the nectar and pollen of a number of plant species but are particularly closely related to the cucurbit vines, *Anguria*, and a few of its relatives, *Gurania*. These plants are rather inconspicuous but, once detected, unusually long lasting and reliable food sources with continuous pollen and nectar production for a year and more. For a *Heliconius* this means a life-long feeding station. Gilbert (1975) quotes a specimen of a male *Anguria umbrosa* which produced 10,000 flowers in one year under greenhouse conditions which equals 145g of dry sucrose and 20g of pollen. Interestingly, *Heliconius* is an unusually long-lived butterfly with a life expectancy as an adult of up to half a year. And it disperses pollen to distances larger than those typical of hummingbirds (Murawski 1987).

Heliconius has no biting mouth-parts and is neither able to chew nor to ingest pollen. What it does is as follows: First it scrapes its proboscis tip over the anthers and accumulates a pollen load which is formed into a dry mass on the ventral side of the proboscis near the head. Then the pollen is doused in nectar exuded from the tip of the proboscis and the wet mass agitated several hours through coiling and uncoiling of the proboscis. The butterfly does not add its own gut enzymes to the pollen. Instead proteins and free amino acids are readily released from the pollen upon incubation in nectar. They can be shown to be incorporated into the eggs later produced by the butterfly (Gilbert 1972).

Chapter 10
Floral nectar composition

Extensive analyses of the floral nectar of hundreds of plant species suggest a correlation between nectar composition and pollinator type. It looks as if certain pollinators would prefer certain nectar types. The flowers pollinated by lepidopterans are usually rich in sucrose, whereas the nectar of flowers typically visited by flies and bees with short tongues are usually rich in hexose. Similarly, flowers typically visited by hummingbirds differ in nectar composition from those visited by perching birds. The phenomenon is particularly striking when it occurs in closely related plant species. It may even occur in a single plant. There is a tree (*Inga vera*) in Costa Rica, which changes the quality of its nectar during the course of a day. In the late afternoon it attracts hummingbirds, bees, wasps, and moths with a sucrose-dominated nectar. Only four hours later the nectar increases its hexose content and takes on a sourly odiferous smell which is preferred by bats.

Nectar is not just sugar-water. Amino acids, proteins, lipids and other chemicals are contained in quantities implying a nutritive function. As a rule the concentration of these valuable ingredients (in particular the amino acids) and its consistency increase from phylogenetically primitive to advanced plants with increasingly specialized relationships between the flower and its visitors. Not surprisingly then, typical butterfly flowers show particularly high nectar amino acid contents. Flowers with openly displayed nectar and visited by more or less unspecialized flies have a clearly lower score. Another general tendency is that nectars strong in sugars are usually those also strong in amino acids. A high concentration of amino acids in turn often goes along with detectable amounts of lipids and antioxidants. Proteins are only rather rarely found in nectar and their enzymatic significance seems more likely than their nutritious value. The reader interested in more details on nectar constituents and their relation to pollinator plant coevolution among a very wide range of plants should consult the extensive work of H. G. Baker and I. Baker (1975, 1982, 1983, 1986). There are also still some doubts about the justification to generalize these findings. At least in a number of species amino acids and sugars show considerable intraspecific variation and are believed to be secreted independently from each other (Gottsberger et al. 1989 a,b).

Chapter 12
Honeybees

In this and other chapters the honeybees are the main actors. Since writing my book *Apis* has not only remained the subject of intensive studies, but bee research seems to grow in ever wider circles. Those who want to learn about a wide range of topics related to the "Neurobiology and Behavior of Honeybees" should know of a book recently edited by Menzel and Mercer (1987). A more popular and more easy to read treatment of honeybee biology including many aspects of its foraging behavior is given by J. L. Gould and C. G. Gould (1988). Attention should be given to a book by Thomas D. Seeley (1985) entitled "Honeybee Ecology" by all those mainly interested in the ecological factors that have shaped the honeybee's social behavior. Finally, those readers interested in the ecology and natural history of tropical bees are referred to a book by David W. Roubik (1989), and those interested in the biogeography and taxonomy of honeybees to Ruttner's book (1987).

Chapter 15
Nectar guides

The results of behavioral studies such as those described in chapter 15 are consistent with the classical idea that nectar guides are sort of signposts directing the insect visitor to a concealed reward. Studies by Nickols Waser and Mary Price of the University of California at Riverside over the past decade have gone an important step further quantitatively demonstrating that nectar guides indeed influence pollinator preferences by increasing their foraging efficiency. Using the montane larkspur *Delphinium nelsonii* they identified a case of natural selection by rigorous field and laboratory studies.

Delphinium flowers are usually blue with a contrasting color pattern at their center. There are also white-flowered forms. These produce fewer seeds because they are partially discriminated against by their pollinators, bumblebees and hummingbirds. The implicit selective disadvantage could be shown to result from a quantitatively inferior nectar guide of the white morphs and an increase of the flower-to-flower movement time. Interestingly, the disadvantage is not due to differences in nectar concentration or nectar flow rate, nor to flower shape, or to flower spacing. Enhancing the nectar guide of the white flowers by painting them reduced or even eliminated the discriminative behavior of the pollinators. It reduced the handling times and energetic cost to values typical of the blue flowers.

Natural selection against the white morph is not a consequence of the overall color or rarity of these flowers but a result of the less conspicuously contrasting color pattern. The studies of Waser and Price have beautifully shown its adaptive value (Waser and Price 1983, 1985).

See also below, chapter 17, petal microstructure.

Chapter 17
Pictorial memory

The question of how an insect sees, learns, and remembers has remained a complicated one and it will certainly need more than just one unified answer. One of the basic subquestions still is whether bees are able to learn to distinguish between flower shapes not only by remembering individual features such as those already discussed but also—at least under certain conditions—by remembering something like a complete photographic picture. The bee's capability to recognize the inclination of a stripe pattern (Wehner 1981; see references chapter 17) already points into the direction of such a capability. In the meanwhile J. L. Gould of Princeton University (1985) has designed experiments which strongly indicate that honeybees can store photograph-like pictures of flower shapes, that they have a pictorial memory remembering the exact spatial relationships of all contiguous and non-contiguous elements making up the patterns presented.

Distance estimation

Another exciting news is that an older speculation on distance estimation has turned out to be true: Flying honeybees estimate the distance of an object of unknown size such as a flower by evaluating a size-independent cue, i.e., the apparent speed at which its image moves across its eyes. The consequence is rather practical. Take a high and a low flower. For geometrical reasons the contours of the more distant low flower will always move slower than the nearer high flower, whatever its absolute size (Kirchner and Srinivasan 1989; Srinivasan et al. 1989).

Petal microtexture

We now have to assume that once landed on the flower the bee also can use the surface microstructure (in the size range of micrometers) of the petals to learn and to discriminate between species. In the investigated cases the pattern of microsculpturing is oriented towards the food source and may well serve as yet another nectar guide. Interestingly, this surface microsculpturing is also used in plant taxonomy. The bees may now have shown the way to its functional interpretation and to an understanding of its contribution to species isolation (Kevan and Lane 1985).

Chapters 23 and 24
Orchid fragrances

The question of what exactly the euglossine bees do with the orchid perfume still is a matter of speculation. Usage of the floral perfumes as precursor compounds of the male bee's own sex pheromones is an often quoted hypothesis (Williams and Whitten 1983). To the best of my knowledge, however, direct proof for this is still not available. An overdue experiment would be to label the floral fragrances radioactively and then to see whether and how they appear in the mandibular or other glands of the bee.

In *Ophrys* new details on the chemistry of the flower scents and that of the cephalic secretions of the corresponding pollinators are now available. Clearly, chemical mimetism plays a crucial role in the attraction of the insects to their specific flowers and in the pseudo-copulation with them (Borg-Karlson and Groth 1986; Borg-Karlson and Tengö 1986). Extensive observations in the field have impressively confirmed the high specificity of this insect-plant relationship. As a rule a certain species of *Ophrys* is effectively pollinated by only one insect species. This implies, among other things, that the pollinator not only transports the pollinia but also provides for species isolation (Paulus and Gack 1986; Paulus 1988).

Chapter 25

The last decade has seen remarkable advances in our understanding of the molecular processes underlying simple forms of learning.

They mainly relate to *Aplysia*. This is a marine snail which has attained fame and recognition in neurophysiology for providing excellent model cases of neuronal networks unusually accessible to experimentation. In insects, including the honeybees, we are still far from understanding the cellular or even molecular basis of learning and memory in any detail. It is doubtful whether we will ever come as close as in *Aplysia*. At the single neuron level most insects are simply so much harder to handle experimentally.

The experiments to be shortly reported here all refer to the behavioral level of honeybee biology. We mainly owe them to James L. Gould and his coworkers at Princeton University (Gould 1985, 1988). Some salient features of their outcome are the following.

Bees are capable to recognize and remember flowers pictorially, as opposed to resorting to a number of individual parameters. To demonstrate this honeybees were trained to search for food at the center of vertically oriented pairs of "flower" patterns. These patterns differed with regard to the left-right relationships of their components. With regard to the individual parameters known to be particularly influential (spatial frequency, color area, line angles) they were identical, however. It took the bees only a few training trials to discriminate between the rewarded and the unrewarded pattern. Of course, the evidence for the capability of pictorial learning and memory does not exclude the possibility that bees do use single parameters and part figures under appropriate conditions as well.

A second finding of particular interest is that landmark memory has pictorial properties, too. Its resolution, however, is considerably higher than that for flower shape memory. This difference seems to make sense biologically. The bee can fly closer to a flower to see whether it is the proper food source and thus easily compensate for the "graininess" of the picture. Obviously, it would be rather uneconomical if possible at all to do this with landmarks used for triangulation.

The difference between the learning of flower shapes and landmarks, respectively, is underlined by the difference in the time when "the picture is taken" by the bee. Landmarks are learned during the circling flight *after* having fed on a flower whereas in flower learning the approach pattern (also color and odor) is the essential one as has been known for quite a while.

The question whether bees do establish and use cognitive maps in addition to or instead of just remembering sequences of landmarks when orienting along an individual route during foraging trips is still a matter of debate. Does a bee know the spatial relationships between the landmarks of different routes so well that she can plan a *novel* route to the food source? There are some experiments indicating such an ability (Gould 1988).

Chapter 27
Polarized-light navigation

The honeybee continues to be the subject of intensive research. Among the most remarkable breakthroughs achieved in sensory and orientation biology during the last ten years is the work of Rossel and Wehner on the polarization vision of bees and ants. The fascinating results predicted in chapter 27 are now indeed available (Rossel and Wehner 1984, 1986; Wehner and Rossel 1985; Wehner 1989).

In essence the new data answer two questions. First: How is the e-vector direction (direction of polarization) of the skylight actually determined by the bee? Second: How does the bee "calculate" the position of the sun using its capacity to determine individual e-vector directions in the sky? It turned out that polarization vision is not as exotic a sensory capacity as previously assumed; instead it reduces to rather simple intensity vision. It has also become clear that the bees do no follow such complicated strategies as calculating the position of the sun by using celestial trigonometry but apply a much simpler method instead.

The uppermost dorsal margin of the honeybee eye which comprises only a few rows of ommatidia (Fig. 37) plays a key role in polarization vision. Here the UV-sensitive visual cells are highly polarization sensitive: They run straight through the retina as opposed to the rest of the eye where they twist about their longitudinal axis which reduces or even completely destroys polarization sensitivity. The most fascinating property of the dorsal rim area is that its visual cells in a way contain the bee's celestial map. The polarization direction to which they are maximally sensitive rotates from the back of the eye to its front. Thus the array of the polarization sensitivities of the visual cells forms a template of the polarization pattern in the sky. The spatial layout of the polarization analyzers in the eye roughly matches the e-vector distribution in the sky whenever the bee is aligned with the solar and antisolar meridian (Fig. 78). The bee's map is invariant and hard-wired. It does not follow the dynamics of the celestial polarization pattern going along with the changing position of the sun and thus also the time of day. It is also simplified in that it does not reflect the dependence of the pattern on the elevation in the sky but represents the average values as they occur in the most polarized band of the sky.

The bee uses its map by simply rotating until it is in register with the polarization pattern of the sky. At this instance the visual system generates the largest possible nervous output which tells the bee that it is aligned with the plane of symmetry of the sky's polarization pattern, i.e., with the solar/antisolar meridian. By scanning the sky the bee translates the spatial polarization patterns into temporal modulations of neuronal responses. The result of this process can also be induced experimentally by using unpolarized but intensity modulated UV-light.

The bee's map is not a precise celestial almanac. Under certain experimental conditions when the bee is exposed to only a very small patch of light predictable mistakes in its orientation behavior can be observed. The reason is that a given e-vector of such a small patch is associated with a fixed azimuthal angle relative to the solar and antisolar meridian according to the position of those visual cells in the dorsal eye area which are maximally stimulated. Under natural conditions such difficulties are likely not to be very serious. Usually the bee draws information from large areas of the sky and in accordance with the symmetry of the sky's polarization pattern error angles resulting from analyzers in the right and the left eye cancel each other. Finally, several backup systems guarantee successful navigation under difficult circumstances.

Bee dance

Research on problems associated with the bee's dance communication has recently seen some important new discoveries, too. In particular much has been learned about the signals contained in the dance and thus about likely ways of the transmission of information to the recruits. The particular importance of dance "sounds" (Fig. 80) for the communication in the dark of a hive is underlined by the finding that only the cavity-nesters *Apis mellifera* and *Apis cerana* among the four honeybee species produce them in the typical highly structured form during their wagging run (Towne 1985). By the application of sensitive measuring techniques it has now become clear that substrate-borne vibrations are not emitted by the dancing bee. The sounds typically accompanying a dancer's wagging run are transmitted solely through the air (Michelsen et al. 1986). In addition to sound pressure changes going along with the dance sound, however, a bee performing the wagging dance is also surrounded by an acoustic nearfield. Here the dance sound is accompanied by strong local air currents which are due to the movements of the wings and reach considerable velocities of up to 1m/s. Interestingly the bees attending the dance preferably place their antennae within a few millimeters of the dancer in the region of the maximum air velocity. They were also shown to be able to detect air-particle oscillations in a training experiment (Towne and Kirchner 1989).

It is still not perfectly clear, however, which of the diverse signals contained in the dance are necessary and sufficient in conveying the information from the dancer to the follower bees and how exactly they are perceived. With the knowledge now at hand it seems safe to predict that this will change in the very near future. A strong source for this optimism is a computer driven dancing robot honeybee which has talked to its fellow bees on a comb in a dark hive and successfully directed them to a source of food (Michelsen et al. 1989). The up and down vibration of a magnet driven thin metal plate imitating the bee's wings turned out to be crucial for the success, as did the waggle. Carefully controlled synthetic dances and maybe strange combinations of the various physical properties of a natural bee dance will tell us much more about how the bees communicate.

The above findings all point to a likely significance of the acoustic nearfield around a dancing bee in providing information on the dancer's spatial orientation to the follower bee. And it may well be that for the same reason round dances have to be drastically re-interpreted. Contradicting the classical view the sounds and the air currents around a bee are rather similar in a waggle and a round dance. In both types of dances the direction to the food source is indicated by the mean running direction relative to the vertical whereas the distance to a food source correlates with the duration of the dance sound in both cases (Kirchner et al. 1988). This is exciting news indicating that the bees may be much better oriented towards food sources at close distances than previously thought. Since round and waggle dances turn out to be basically very similar the follower bees may as well perceive the necessary information in the same way in both cases. As it turns out the most obvious and possibly the only significant change in the quality of the messages with food distance is their scatter which becomes smaller the further away the hive is from the food (Kirchner et al. 1988). This scatter may have to be regarded as adaptive instead of just indicating sloppiness of the system (Gould 1985). It may have evolved to spread out the recruits. Natural food sources are not pointlike but patchy. It is likely to be an advantage to scatter the recruits to a certain extent. Given a constant patch size the angle under which it is seen from the hive decreases with distance. So, if there is an optimal angular scatter we would expect it to become smaller with distance which in fact it does. Support of this idea comes from the finding that the scatter is considerably smaller in all three tropical bee species. These commonly use flowering trees as food sources, that is massive, highly localized resources as compared to the more diffuse patches of flowers visited by *Apis mellifera* (Towne 1984, quoted by Gould 1985). To explain the scatter found in the distance information still remains a problem, however.

Individual bee and colony behavior

The topic addressed in the last paragraph, by some considered one of the heart pieces of what a zoologist wants to understand about social insects, has regained attention by the beautiful work of Thomas D. Seeley. The reader is referred to his recent review chapter co-authored by Royce A. Levien in Menzel and Mercer (1987) and to a somewhat older review in Hölldobler and Lindauer (1985).

The question is, how a colony tracks rich sources of nectar and how the bees manage to bridge the gaps between their individual behavior and the behavior of the whole colony. One part of the simplified answer is given by the forager bees. They grade their behavior which ranges from abandoning a patch of flowers to advertising it with vigorous dances in the hive, depending on the quality of the food source. Individual qualities such as availability and sweetness of nectar and distance from the hive are evaluated as one integrated quality.

Another part of the answer is given by the bees receiving the food from the foragers in the hive. These receiver bees change their behavior according to the colony's rate of nectar intake and the empty space available, thereby in turn influencing the foragers' response to the food source quality. In this way the labor force of the many thousands of foragers is coordinated even though they collect at different sites and do not communicate with each other directly. Increasingly, it is ensured that a colony can redirect its efforts within a short time if the quality of one source of food has declined and the recruits have to be sent to patches of high quality instead. Such readjustments of the forager distributions are a common necessity. Only few different patches are visited by the bees simultaneously and each of them only for a few days.

Chapter 28
Bee dance evolution

The inspiring concept originally developed by Martin Lindauer (rev. 1975) on the evolution of the bee dance has recently been revived and expanded mainly by unraveling hitherto unknown capabilities of the two Asian species, *Apis dorsata* and *Apis florea*, under conditions of obscured celestial cues. It may be that these two species no longer have to be considered as bees performing merely simple forms of dance communication on a scale culminating in the behavior of *Apis mellifera* (Dyer 1987).

Thus *Apis dorsata* was found to forage and dance on moonlit nights and to use the unseen sun as the celestial reference (not the moon!) when performing well-oriented dances (Dyer 1985a). *Apis florea*, on the other hand, not only could be made to continue dancing with no visible celestial cues (Königer et al. 1982) but was also shown to orient her dances to landmarks near the nest and not with reference to gravity like the other three species. *Apis florea* can effectively recruit on overcast days; in other words, it is able to determine the position of the sun relative to landmarks visible from the nest.

Lindauer's (1956) observation that *Apis florea* is unable to translate the flight angle into a dance direction using gravity as a reference when made to dance on a slope has recently been confirmed (Dyer 1985b). *Apis florea* is not disoriented in such a situation, however, but does instead complicated things. Its dance orientation is not as restricted as previously assumed. It is now thought to have diverged from the system of the three other species and to show fundamental differences in the processing of celestial and gravitational information. The dances of *Apis florea* remain oriented to its horizontal frame of reference even when performed on the vertical and without vision of the sky, that is under conditions in which the bees can use celestial cues only by reference to landmarks (Dyer 1987). As is well known, the frame of reference is shifted to the plane on which the dances are performed in the three other species.

In summary, it still seems to be quite possible that the dances of bees were originally performed in the horizontal plane and in the open. This is what *Apis florea* normally does and what all other species can be induced to do. Hence gravity based systems are likely to be indeed the derived ones. Contemporary *Apis florea*, however, is not simply exhibiting a primitive way of dance communication but is endowed with its own communication system fundamentally differing from gravity-based systems.

Chapter 30
Evolution and ecology

The reader interested in a mostly evolutionary and ecological in-depth treatment in pollination biology is referred to a highly recommendable book entitled "Pollination Biology" and edited by Leslie Real (1983). He or she will also be interested in the pertinent chapters of "Coevolution of Animals and Plants" edited by Lawrence E. Gilbert and Peter H. Raven (1975). A very useful progress report on floral ecology was written by Gerhard Gottsberger (1989b).

Addendum Bibliography

Baker, H. G., Baker, I. Studies of nectar-constitution and pollinator-plant coevolution. In *Coevolution of Animals and Plants*, eds. Gilbert, L. E., Raven P. H., 100-140. University of Texas Press, Austin and London (1975).

Baker, H. G., Baker, I. Chemical constituents of nectar in relation to pollination mechanisms and phylogeny. In *Biochemical Aspects of Evolutionary Biology*, ed. Nitecki, M. H., 131-172. University of Chicago Press, Chicago, Illinois (1982).

Baker, H. G., Baker, I. Floral nectar sugar constituents in relation to pollinator type. In *Handbook of Experimental Pollination Biology*, eds. Jones C. E., Little, R. J., 117-141. Van Nostrand-Reinhold, Princeton, New Jersey (1983).

Baker, H. G., Baker, I. The occurrence and significance of amino acids in floral nectar. *Plant Syst. Evol. 151*, 175-186 (1986).

Borg-Karlson, A. K., Groth, I. Volatiles from the flowers of four species in the sections Arachnitiformes and Araneiferae of the genus *Ophrys* as insect mimetic attractants. *Phytochemistry 25, 6*, 1297–1299 (1986).

Borg-Karlson, A. K., Tengö, J. Odor mimetism? Key substances in *Ophrys lutea Andrena* pollination relationship (Orchidaceae: Andrenidae). *J. Chem. Ecol. 12, 9*, 1927–1941 (1986).

Breed, M. D., Butler, L., Stiller, T. M. Kin discrimination by worker honey bees in genetically mixed groups. *Proc.Natl.Acad.Sci.USA* 82, 3058–3061 (1985).

Breed, M. D., Williams, K. D., Fewell, J. H. Comb wax mediates the acquisition of nest-mate recognition cues in honey bees. *Proc.Natl.Acad. Sci.USA 85*, 8766-8769 (1988).

Dyer, F. C. Nocturnal orientation of the Asian honey bee, *Apis dorsata*. *Anim. Behav. 33*, 767-774 (1985a).

Dyer, F. C. Mechanisms of dance orientation in the Asian honey bee, *Apis florea*. *J.Comp.Physiol.A 157*, 183-198 (1985b).

Dyer, F. C. New perspectives on the dance orientation of the Asian honeybees. In *Neurobiology and Behavior of Honeybees*, eds. Menzel, R., Mercer, A., 54-65. Springer-Verlag, Berlin Heidelberg (1987).

Feinsinger, P. Coevolution and pollination. In *Coevoluton*, eds. Futuyma, D. J., Slatkin, M., 282-310. Sinauer Associates, Sunderland, Massachusetts (1983).

Fletcher, D.J.C., Michener, C. D. *Kin Recognition in Animals*. Wiley, Chichester, U. K. (1987).

Gilbert, L. E. Pollen feeding and reproductive biology of *Heliconius* butterflies. *Proc.Nat.Acad.Sci.USA 69, 6*, 1403-1407 (1972).

Gilbert, L. E. Ecological consequences of a coevolved mutualism between butterflies and plants. In *Coevolution of Animals and Plants*, eds. Gilbert, L. E., Raven, P. H., 210-240. University of Texas Press, Austin and London (1975).

Gilbert, L. E., Raven, P. H., eds. *Coevolution of Animals and Plants*. University of Texas Press, Austin and London (1975).

Gottsberger, G. The reproductive biology of primitive angiosperms. *Taxon 37(3)*, 630-643 (1988).

Gottsberger, G. Comments on flower evolution and beetle pollination in the genera *Annona* and *Rollinia* (Annonaceae). *Plant Syst. Evol. 167*, 189-194 (1989 a).

Gottsberger, G. Floral ecology. Report on the years 1985 (1984) to 1988. *Progress in Botany, 50*, 352-379 (1989 b).

Gottsberger, G., Arnold, T., Linskens, H. F. Intraspecific variation in the amino acid content of floral nectar. *Botanica Acta 102*, 141-144 (1989 a).

Gottsberger, G., Arnold, T., Linskens, H. F. Are amino acid and sugar concentration correlated in florál nectar? *Acta Bot. Nederl. 92, 4*, 461-464 (1989 b).

Gould, J. L. How bees remember flower shapes. *Science 227*, 1492-1494 (1985).

Gould, J. L., Dyer, F. C., Towne, W. F. Recent progress in the study of the dance language. *Fortschr. Zoologie 31*, 141-161 (1985).

Gould, J. L., Gould C. G. *The Honey Bee*. W. H. Freeman and Co., New York (1988).

Hölldobler, B., Lindauer, M., eds. *Experimental Behavioral Ecology and Sociobiology*. Sinauer Associates, Sunderland, Massachusetts (1985).

Kevan, P. G., Lane, M. A. Flower petal microtexture is a tactile cue for bees. *Proc.Natl.Acad.Sci.USA 82*, 4750-4752 (1985).

Kirchner, W. H., Srinivasan, M. V. Freely flying honey-bees use image motion to estimate object distance. *Naturwissenschaften 76*, 281-282 (1989).

Kirchner, W. H., Lindauer, M., Michelsen, A. Honeybee dance communication. *Naturwissenschaften 75*, 629-630 (1988).

Koeniger, N., Koeniger, G., Punchihewa, R.K.W., Fabritius, Mo., Fabritius, Mi. Observations and experiments on dance communication of *Apis florea* in Sri Lanka. *J.Apic.Res. 21*, 45-52 (1982).

Lindauer, M. *Verständigung im Bienenstaat.* G. Fischer Verlag, Stuttgart (1975).

Menzel, R., Mercer, A. *Neurobiology and Behavior of Honeybees.* Springer-Verlag. Berlin, Heidelberg, New York (1987).

Michelsen, A., Kirchner, W. H., Lindauer, M. Sound and vibrational signals in the dance language of the honeybee, *Apis mellifera. Behav.Eco.Sociobiol. 18*, 207-212 (1986).

Michelsen, A., Towne, W. F., Kirchner, W. H., Kryger, P. The acoustic nearfield of a dancing honeybee. *J.Comp.Physiol.A 161*, 633-643 (1987).

Michelsen, A., Andersen, A. A., Kirchner, W. H., Lindauer, M. Honeybees can be recruited by a mechanical model of a dancing bee. *Naturwissenschaften 76*, 277-280 (1989).

Murawski, D. A. Floral resource variation, pollinator response and potential pollen flow in *Psiguria warscewiczii. Ecology 68*, 1273-1282 (1987).

Niklas, K. J., Kyaw Tha Paw U. Pollination and airflow patterns around conifer ovulate cones. *Science 217*, 442-444 (1982).

Niklas, K. J. Aerodynamics of wind pollination. *Scientific American 255, 7*, 90-95 (1987).

Niklas, K. J., Buchmann, S. L. Aerodynamics of wind pollination in *Simmondsia chinesis* (Link) Schneider. *Amer. J. Bot.* 72 (4), 530–539 (1985).

Noonan, K. C., Kolmes, A. Kin recognition of worker brood by worker honey bees. *Apis mellifera L. J.Insect Behav.* 2, 4, 473-485 (1989).

Page, R. E., Robinson, G. E., Fondrk, M. K. Genetic specialists, kin recognition and nepotism in honey-bee colonies. *Nature 338, 6216*, 576-579 (1989).

Paulus, H. F. Coevolution and unilateral adaptations in flower-pollinator-systems: pollinators as pacemakers in the evolution of flowers. *Verh.Dtsch.Zool.Ges. 81*, 2546 (1988).

Paulus, H. F., Gack, C. Neue Befunde zur Pseudokopulation und Bestäuberspezifität in der Orchideengattung *Ophrys.* Untersuchungen in Kreta, Süditalien und Israel. *Die Orchidee (Sonderheft 1986)*, 4886 (1986).

Real, L. (ed.) *Pollination Biology.* Academic Press, Inc. Orlando, Florida (1983).

Rossel, S., Wehner, R. How bees analyze the polarization patterns in the sky. Experiments and model. *J. Comp. Physiol.A* 154, 607–615 (1984).

Rossel, S., Wehner, R. Polarization vision in bees. *Nature 323, 6084*, 128-131 (1986).

Roubik, D. W. *Ecology and Natural History of Tropical Bees.* Cambridge Univ. Press, Cambridge (1989).

Ruttner, I. Biogeography and Taxonomy of Honeybees. Springer Verlag, Berlin, Heidelberg, New York (1987).

Seeley, T. D. *Honeybee Ecology*. A Study of Adaptation in Social Life. Princeton University Press, Princeton, New Jersey (1985).

Srinivasan, M. V., Lehrer, M., Zhang, S. W., Horridge, G. A. How honeybees measure their distance from objects of unknown size. *J.Comp.Physiol.A 165*, 605-613 (1989).

Thien, L. B. Patterns of pollination in primitive angiosperms. *Biotropica 12*, 1-13 (1980).

Thien, L. B., Bernhardt, P., Gibbs, G. W., Pillmyr, O., Bergström, G., Groth, I., McPherson, G. The Pollination of *Zygogynum* (Winteraceae) by a moth, *Sabatinca* (Micropterigidae): an ancient association? *Science 227*, 540-543 (1985).

Thien, T. Floral biology of *Magnolia*. *Amer. J. Bot.* 61, 1037–1045 (1974).

Towne, W. F. Acoustic and visual cues in the dances of four honey bee species. *Behav. Evol. Sociobiol. 16*, 185-187 (1985).

Towne, W. F., Kirchner, W. H. Hearing in honey bees: detection of air-particle oscillations. *Science 244*, 686-688 (1989).

Waser, N. M., Price, M. V. Pollinator behaviour and natural selection for flower colour in *Delphinium nelsonii*. *Nature 302, 5907*, 422-424 (1983).

Waser, N. M., Price, M. V. The effect of nectar guides on pollinator preference: experimental studies with a montane herb. *Oecologia 67*, 121-126 (1985).

Wehner, R. Neurobiology of polarization vision. *TINS 12, 9*, 353-359 (1989).

Wehner, R., Rossel, S. The bee's celestial compass—A case study in behavioral neurobiology. In *Experimental Behavioral Ecology and Sociobiology*, eds. Hölldobler, B., Lindauer, M. Sinauer Associates, Sunderland, Massachusetts, pp. 11–53 (1985).

Williams, N. H., Whitten, W. M. Orchid floral fragrances and male euglossine bees: methods and advances in the last sesquidecade. *Biol.Bull. 164*, 355-395 (1983).

References

Chapter 1

1. Galil, J. Sycamore wasps from ancient Egyptian tombs. *Israel J. Entomol.* II, 1-10 (1967).
2. Galil, J. Fig biology. *Endeavour 1*, 2, 52-56 (1977).
3. Galil, J., Eisikovitch, D. Further studies on pollination ecology in *Ficus sycomorus*. II. Pocket filling and emptying by *Ceratosolen arabicus* Magr. *New Phytol. 73*, 515-528 (1974).
4. Galil, J., Zeroni, M. and Bar-Shalom (Bogoslavsky), D. Carbon dioxide and ethylene effects in the coordination between the pollinator *Blastophaga quadraticeps* and the syconium in *Ficus religiosa*. *New Phytol. 72*, 1113-1127 (1973).
5. Hennig, W. *Die Stammesgeschichte der Insekten*. Kramer, Frankfurt a.M., 1969.
6. Pliny. *Natural History*, Book XV. Translated by H. Rackham. Harvard University Press, Cambridge, Mass., 1945.
7. Ramirez, W. Fig wasps: Mechanism of pollen transfer. *Science 163*, 580-581 (1969).
8. Ramirez, W. Coevolution of *Ficus* and *Agaonidae*. *Ann Miss. Bot. Gard. 61*, 770-780 (1974).

Chapter 2

1. Nultsch, W. *Allgemeine Botanik*. G. Thieme Verlag, Stuttgart, 1977.
2. Strasburger, E. *Lehrbuch der Botanik*. G. Fischer Verlag, Stuttgart-New York, 1978.

Chapter 3

Books on Pollination Ecology
1. Bertsch, A. *Blüten-lockende Signale*. Otto Maier Verlag, Ravensburg, 1975.
2. Faegri, K., van der Pijl, L. *The principles of pollination ecology*. Pergamon Press, Oxford-New York-Toronto-Sydney-Braunschweig, 1979.
3. Kugler, H. *Blütenökologie*. G. Fischer Verlag, Stuttgart, 1970.
4. Meeuse, B.J.D. *The story of pollination*. The Ronald Press Comp., New York, 1961.
5. Proctor, M., Yeo, P. *The pollination of flowers*. William Collins Sons & Co. Ltd., London-Glasgow-Sydney-Auckland-Toronto-Johannesburg, 1975.

Chapter 4

1. East, E. M. Distribution of self sterility in flowering plants. *Proc. Amer. Philos. Soc. 82* (1940).
2. James, W. O., Clapham, A. R. *The Biology of Flowers*. Clarendon Press, Oxford, 1935.
3. Linskens, H. F. Biochemistry of incompatibility. S. J. Geerts, ed., *Genetics Today 3*, 629-635 (1965).
4. Stocker, O. *Grundriss der Botanik*. Springer Verlag, Berlin-Göttingen-Heidelberg, 1952.
5. Strasburger, E. See Chapter 2.
6. Wells, H. Self-fertilization: advantageous or deleterious? *Evolution 33* (1), 252-255 (1979).

Chapter 5

1. Darwin, Ch. *The origin of species by means of natural selection or the preservation of favoured races in the struggle for life*. John Murray, London, 1859.
2. Sprengel, Ch. K. *Das entdeckte Geheimnis der Natur im Bau und in der Befruchtung der Blumen*. F. Vieweg, Berlin, 1793; Nachdruck Verlag J. Cramer, Lehre, 1972.

Chapter 6

1. Faegri, K., van der Pijl, L. See Chapter 3.
2. Frisch, K. von. *Aus dem Leben der Bienen*. Verst. Wiss. Bd. 1, Springer Verlag, Berlin-Heidelberg-New York, 1969.
3. Knoll, F. *Die Biologie der Blüte*. Verst. Wiss. Bd. 57, Springer Verlag, Berlin-Göttingen-Heidelberg, 1956.
4. Knuth, P. *Handbuch der Blütenbiologie*. Vol. 1: *Einleitung und Literatur*. Verlag W. Engelmann, Leipzig, 1898.
5. Kugler, H. See Chapter 3.

6. Leuenberger, F. *Die Biene*. H. R. Sauerländer & Co., Aarau-Frankfurt a.M., 1954.
7. Lindauer, M. Ein Beitrag zur Frage der Arbeitsteilung im Bienenstaat. *Z. vergl. Physiol. 34*, 299-345 (1952).
8. Lindauer, M. *Verständigung im Bienenstaat*. G. Fischer Verlag, Stuttgart, 1975.
9. Rüdiger, W. *Ihr Name ist Apis*. Ehrenwirth, München, 1977.
10. Schremmer, F. Morphologische Anpassungen von Tieren—insbesondere Insekten—an die Gewinnung von Blumennahrung. *Verh. Dtsch. Zool. Ges. 55*, 375-401 (1961).

Chapter 7

1. Hamilton, W. D. The genetical theory of social behaviour. *J. Theor. Biol. 7*, I. 1-16, II. 17-52 (1964).
2. Wickler, W., Seibt, U. *Das Prinzip Eigennutz*. Hoffmann und Campe, Hamburg, 1977.
3. Wilson, E. O. *Sociobiology: The New Synthesis*. The Belknap Press of Harvard University Press, Cambridge, Mass., 1971.
4. Wilson, E. O. *The Insect Societies*. The Belknap Press of Harvard University Press, Cambridge, Mass., 1972.
5. Wilson, E. O. *On Human Nature*. Harvard University Press, Cambridge, Mass., 1978.

Chapter 8

1. Buchmann, St. L. Buzz pollination of *Cassia quiedondilla* (Leguminosae) by bees of the genera *Centris* and *Melipona*. *Bull. South. Calif. Acad. Sci. 73*, 3, 171-173 (1974).
2. Echlin, P. Pollen, *Sci. Am. 218*, 4, 80-90 (1968).
3. Erdtman, G. *Pollen morphology and plant taxonomy*. Vol. 1: *Angiosperms*. Chronica Botanica Co., Waltham, Mass., 1952.
4. Faegri, K., van der Pijl, L. See Chapter 3.
5. Kugler, H. See Chapter 3.
6. Ledbetter, M. C., Porter, K. R. *Introduction to the fine structure of plant cells*. Springer Verlag, Berlin-Heidelberg-New York, 1970.
7. Pohl, F. Die Pollenerzeugung der Windblütler. *Beih. bot. Centralbl.* Abt. A, 56 (1937).

Chapter 9

1. Buchmann, St. L. See Chapter 8.
2. Buchmann, St. L., Hurley, J. P. A biophysical model for buzz pollination in angiosperms. *J. theor. Biol. 72*, 639-657 (1978).
3. Frisch, K. von. See Chapter 6.
4. Kugler, H. See Chapter 3.
5. Matthes, D. Die "Pollenkehrmaschine" Blütenstaub fressender Käfer. *Umschau 21*, 660-661 (1968).

6. Michener, C. D. An interesting method of pollen collecting by bees from flowers with tubular anthers. *Rev. Biol. Trop.*, *10*, 2, 167-175 (1962).
7. Michener, C. D., Winston, M. L., Jander, R. Pollen manipulation and selected activities and structures in bees of the family Apidae. *Univ. Kans. Sci. Bull. 51*, 19, 575-601 (1978).
8. Schremmer, F. See Chapter 6.
9. Schremmer, F. "Geborgte Beweglichkeit" bei der Bestäubung von Blütenpflanzen. *Umschau 8*, 228-234 (1969).
10. Vogel, St. Ölblumen und ölsammelnde Bienen. Akad. Wiss. Lit., 1-267, F. Steiner, Wiesbaden, 1974.

Chapter 10

1. Faegri, K., van der Pijl, L. See Chapter 3.
2. Kugler, H. See Chapter 3.
3. Schremmer, F. See Chapter 9.
4. Vogel, St. Nektarien und ihre ökologische Bedeutung. *Apidologie 8*, 4, 321-335 (1977).

Chapter 11

1. Andersen, S. O., Weis-Fogh, T. Resilin: A rubberlike protein in arthropod cuticle. *Adv. Insect Physiol. 2*, 1-65 (1964).
2. Eastham, L.E.S., Eassa, Y.E.E. The feeding mechanism of the butterfly *Pieris brassicae* L. *Phil. Trans. Roy. Soc.* (London) ser. B. 659, vol. *239*, 1-43 (1955).
3. Hepburn, H. R. Proboscis extension and recoil in Lepidoptera. *J. Ins. Physiol. 17*, 637-656 (1971).
4. Jacobs, W., Renner, M. *Taschenlexikon zur Biologie de Insekten.* G. Fischer Verlag, Stuttgart, 1974.
5. James, W. O., Clapham, A. R. *The Biology of Flowers*. Clarendon Press, Oxford, 1935.
6. Kugler, H. See Chapter 3.
7. Meeuse, B.J.D. See Chapter 3.
8. Schmitt, J. B. The feeding mechanism of adult Lepidoptera. *Smith Misc. Coll. 97*, 4, 1-28 (1938/39).
9. Schremmer, F. See Chapter 6.
10. Schremmer, F. See Chapter 9.
11. Vogel, St. Kesselfallen-Blumen. *Umschau in Wiss. u. Techn.* 65, 12-16 (1965).
12. Weber, H. *Grundriss der Insektenkunde*. G. Fischer Verlag. Stuttgart, 1966.

Chapter 12

1. Autrum, H., Kolb, G. Spektrale Empfindlichkeit einzelner Sehzellen der Aeschniden. *Z. vergl. Physiol. 60*, 450-477 (1968).

2. Beier, W., Menzel, R. Untersuchungen über den Farbensinn der deutschen Wespe (*Paravespula germanica* F., Hymenoptera, Vespidae): Verhaltenphysiologischer Nachweis des Farbensehens. *Zool. Jb. Physiol. 76*, 441-454 (1972).

3. Bernard, G. D. Red-absorbing visual pigment of butterflies. *Science 203*, 1125-1127 (1979).

4. Darwin, Ch. See Chapter 5.

5. Exner, F., Exner, S. Die physikalischen Grundlagen der Blütenfarbungen. *Sitz.ber. Akad. Wiss. Wien, math.-naturw. Kl. 119*, Abt. 1, 1-55 (1910).

6. Frisch, K. von. Demonstration von Versuchen zum Nachweis des Farbensinnes bei angeblich total farbenblinden Tieren. *Verh. Dtsch. Zool. Ges. Freiburg*, 50-58 (1914).

7. Frisch, K. von. Zur Streitfrage nach dem Farbensinn der Bienen. *Biol. Zentralbl. 39*, 122-139 (1919).

8. Frisch, K. von. *Erinnerungen eines Biologen.* Springer Verlag, Berlin-Göttingen-Heidelberg, 1962. Translation: *A Biologist Remembers.* Pergamon Press, Oxford, 1967.

9. Knoll, F. Insekten und Blumen. *Abh. Zool. Bot. Ges. Wien 12*, 1-645 (1921-1926).

10. Kugler, H. Blütenökologische Untersuchungen mit Hummeln. *Planta 10* (1930).

11. Kugler, H. Blütenökologische Untersuchungen mit Hummeln. *Planta 25* (1936).

12. Kühn, A., Pohl, R. Dressurfahigkeit der Bienen auf Spektrallinien. *Naturwiss. 9*, 738-740 (1921).

13. Kühn, A. Über den Farbensinn der Bienen. *Z. vergl. Physiol. 5*, 762-800 (1927).

14. Menzel, R. Über den Farbensinn der deutschen Wespe (*Paravespula germanica* F., Hymenoptera): ERG und selektive Adaptation. *Z. vergl. Physiol. 75*, 86-104 (1971).

15. Schremmer, F. Versuche zum Nachweis der Rotblindheit von *Vespa rufa* L. *Z. vergl. Physiol. 28*, 457-466 (1941).

16. Sprengel, Ch. K. See Chapter 5.

17. Swihart, S. L. The neural basis of colour vision in the butterfly, *Papilio troilus. J. Insect Physiol. 16*, 1623-1636 (1970).

18. Swihart, S. L. Colour discrimination by the butterfly *Heliconius charitonius. Anim. Behav. 19*, 156-164 (1971).

19. Swihart, S. L. The neural basis of colour vision in the butterfly, *Heliconius erato. J. Insect Physiol. 18*, 1015-1025 (1972).

20. Swihart, S. L., Gorden, W. C. Red photoreceptor in butterflies. *Nature, 231*, No. 5298, 126-127 (1971).

Chapter 13

1. Autrum, H. Die biologischen Grundlagen des Farbensehens. *Naturwissenschaft und Medizin (n + m) 1*, 4, 3-15 (1964).

2. Autrum, H., v. Zwehl, V. Die spektrale Empfindlichkeit einzelner Sehzellen des Bienenauges. *Z. vergl. Physiol.* *48*, 357-384 (1964).
3. Burkhardt, D. Colour discrimination in insects. *Adv. Ins. Physiol.* *2*, 131-173 (1964).
4. Daumer, K. Reizmetrische Untersuchungen des Farbensehens der Bienen. *Z. vergl. Physiol.* *38*, 413-478 (1956).
5. Helversen, O. von. Zur spektralen Unterschiedsempfindlichkeit der Honigbiene. *J. comp. Physiol.* *80*, 439-472 (1972).
6. Hering, E. *Zur Lehre vom Lichtsinn*. Karl Gerolds Sohn, Wien, 1878.
7. Hertel, H. Chromatic properties of identified interneurons in the optic lobes of the bee. *J. comp. Physiol.* *137*, 215-231 (1980).
8. Kühn, A. Zum Nachweis des Farbenunterscheidungsvermögens der Bienen. *Naturwiss.* *12*, 116-118 (1924).
9. Kühn, A. Über den Farbensinn der Bienen. *Z. vergl. Physiol.* *5*, 762-800 (1927).
10. Menzel, R., Blakers, M. Colour receptors in the bee eye—morphology and spectral sensitivity. *J. comp. Physiol.* *180*, 11-33 (1976).
11. Menzel, R. Farbensehen bei Insekten—ein rezeptorphysiologischer und neurophysiologischer Problemkreis. *Verh. Dtsch. Zool. Ges.* 26-40 (1977).
12. Menzel, R. Spectral sensitivity and color vision in invertebrates. In *Handbook of Sensory Physiology* (ed. Autrum et al.). *7*, 504-580 (1979).
13. Snyder, A. W., Pask, C. Spectral sensitivity of dipteran retinula cells. *J. comp. Physiol.* *84*, 59-76 (1973).

Chapter 14

1. Autrum, H. See Chapter 13.
2. Daumer, K. Reizmetrische Untersuchungen des Farbensehens der Bienen. *Z. vergl. Physiol.* *38*, 413-478 (1956).
3. Daumer, K. Blumenfarben, wie sie die Bienen sehen. *Z. vergl. Physiol.* *41*, 49-110 (1958).
4. Grant, K. A., Grant, V. *Hummingbirds and their flowers*. Columbia University Press, New York-London, 1968.
5. Ilse, D. Über den Farbensinn der Tagfalter. *Z. vergl. Physiol.* *8*, 658-692 (1928).
6. Kay, Q.O.N. Preferential pollination of yellow-flowered morphs of *Raphanus raphanistrum* by *Pieris* and *Eristalis* spp. *Nature 261*, 5557, 230-232 (1976).
7. Kugler, H. Die Ausnutzung der Saftmalsumfarbung bei den Rosskastanienblüten durch Bienen und Hummeln. *Ber Dtsch. Bot. Ges. 54*, 394-400 (1936).
8. Kugler, H. Der Blütenbesuch der Schlammfliege (*Eristamyia tenax*). *Z. vergl. Physiol. 32*, 328-347 (1950).
9. Kugler, H. Blütenökologische Untersuchungen mit Goldfliegen (Lucilien). *Ber. Dtsch. Bot. Ges. 64*, 327-341 (1951).
10. Lex, Th. Duftmale an Blüten. *Z. vergl. Physiol. 36*, 212-234 (1954).

11. Porsch, O. Grellrot als Vogelblumenfarbe. *Biologia Generalis 7*, 647-674 (1931).
12. Vogel, St. Farbwechsel und Zeichnungsmuster bei Blüten. *Österr. bot. Z. 97*, 44-100 (1950).

Chapter 15

1. Daumer, K. See Chapter 14, No. 3.
2. Free, J. B. Effect of flower shapes and nectar guides on the behavior of foraging honeybees. *Behaviour 37*, 269-285 (1970).
3. Frisch, K. von. Der Farbensinn und Formensinn der Biene. *Zool. Jahrb. Abt. allg. Physiol. Tiere 35*, 1-182 (1914).
4. Knoll, F. See Chapter 12.
5. Kugler, H. UV-Male auf Blüten. *Ber. Dtsch. Bot. Ges. 79*, 2, 57-70 (1966).
6. Kugler, H. Hummeln als Blütenbesucher. *Ergebn. d. Biologie 19*, 143-323 (1943).
7. Lutz, F. E. The colour of flowers and the vision of insects, with special reference to ultraviolet. *Ann. of the New York Acad. Sci. 29*, 181 (1924).
8. Manning, A. Some aspects of the foraging behaviour of bumblebees. *Behaviour 9*, 2/3, 164-201 (1956).
9. Manning, A. The effect of honey-guides. *Behaviour 9*, 114-139 (1956).
10. Scora, R. W. Dependency of pollination on patterns in *Monarda* (Labiatae). *Nature 204*, 1011-1012 (1964).
11. Sprengel, Ch. K. See Chapter 5.

Chapter 16

1. Beck, G., Ritter von Mannagetta und Lerchenau. Die Pollennachahmung in den Blüten der Orchideengattung *Eria. Sitz/ber. Acad. Wiss. Wien, Math.-naturwiss. Kl. 123*, 1033-1046 (1914).
2. Osche, G. Zur Evolution optischer Signale bei Blütenpflanzen. *Biol. i. uns. Zeit 9*, 6, 161-170 (1979).
3. van der Pijl, L., Dodson, Ch. *Orchid Flowers, Their Pollination and Evolution*. Univ. of Miami Press, Coral Gables, 1969.
4. Vogel, St. Mutualismus and Parasitismus in der Nutzung von Pollenträgern. In *Verh. Dtsch. Zool. Ges. 1975*, 102-110, G. Fischer Verlag, Stuttgart, 1975.
5. Vogel, St. Evolutionary shifts from reward to deception in pollen flowers. In *The pollination of flowers by insects*, ed. A. Richards, *Linn. Soc. Symp. Ser. Nr. 6*, 89-96, Academic Press, London and New York (1978).

Chapter 17

1. Anderson, A. M. Shape perception in the honey bee. *Anim. Behav. 25*, 62-79 (1977).

2. Anderson, A. M. Parameters determining the attractiveness of stripe patterns in the honey bee. *Anim. Behav. 25*, 80-87 (1977).
3. Anderson, A. M. Visual scanning in the honey bee. *J. comp. Physiol. 130*, 173-182 (1979).
4. Autrum, H. Über zeitliches Auflösungsvermögen und Primärvorgänge im Insektenauge. *Naturwiss. 39*, 290-297 (1952).
5. Frisch, K. von. See Chapter 15.
6. Hertz, M. Die Organisation des optischen Feldes bei der Biene II. *Z. vergl. Physiol. 11*, 107-145 (1930).
7. Hertz, M. Über figurale Intensitäten und Qualitäten in der optischen Wahrnehmung der Biene. *Biol. Zbl. 53*, 10-40 (1933).
8. Horridge, G. A., ed. *The compound eye and vision of insects.* Clarendon Press, Oxford, 1975.
9. Jacobs-Jessen, U. F. Zur Orientierung der Hummeln und einiger anderer Hymenopteren. *Z. vergl. Physiol. 41*, 597-641 (1959).
10. Jander, R., Volk-Heinrichs, I. Das strauchspezifische visuelle Perceptor-System der Stabheuschrecke (*Carausius morosus*). *Z. vergl. Physiol. 70*, 425-447 (1970).
11. Jander, R. Visual pattern recognition and directional orientation in insects. *Ann. New York Acad. Sci. 188*, 5-11, 1971.
12. Jander, R., Schweder, M. Über das Formunterscheidungsvermögen der Schmeissfliege *Calliphora erythrocephala*. *Z. vergl. Physiol. 72*, 186-196 (1971).
13. Jander, R., Fabritius, M., Fabritius, M. Die Bedeutung von Gliederung und Kantenrichtung für die visuelle Formunterscheidung der Wespe *Dolichovespula saxonica* am Flugloch. *Z. f. Tierpsychol. 27*, 881-893 (1970).
14. Schnetter, B. Visuelle Formunterscheidung der Honigbiene im Bereich von Vier- und Sechsstrahlsternen. *Z. vergl. Physiol. 59*, 90-109 (1968).
15. Seidl, R. Die Sehfelder und Ommatidien-Divergenwinkel der drei Kasten der Honigbiene. *Verh. Dtsch. Zool. Ges. 1980*, 367 (1980).
16. Voss, Ch. Über das Formensehen der roten Waldameise (*Formica rufa*-Gruppe). *Z. vergl. Physiol. 55*, 225-254 (1967).
17. Wehner, R., Lindauer, M. Die optische Orientierung der Honigbiene (*Apis mellifica*) nach der Winkelrichtung frontal gebotener Streifenmuster. *Verh. Dtsch. Zool. Ges. Göttingen 1966, 30*, 239-246 (1967).
18. Wehner, R. The generalization of direction stimuli in the honey bee, *Apis mellifera*. *J. Insect Physiol. 17*, 1579-1591 (1971).
19. Wehner, R., ed. *Information processing in the visual systems of arthropods.* Springer Verlag, Berlin-Heidelberg-New York, 1972.
20. Wehner, R. Pattern recognition. In *The compound eye and vision of insects*, ed. G. Horridge, 75-113, Oxford University Press, London, 1975.
21. Wehner, R., Flatt, J. Visual fixation in freely flying bees. *Z. Naturforsch. 32*, 469-471 (1977).
22. Wehner, R. Spatial vision in arthropods. In *Handbook of Sensory Physiology* VII/6c, 288-661, Springer Verlag, 1981.

23. Zettler, F. Die Abhängigkeit des Übertragungsverhaltens von Frequenz-und Adaptationszustand, gemessen am einzelnen Lichtreceptor von *Calliphora erythrocephala*. *Z. vergl. Physiol. 64*, 432-449 (1969).

Chapter 18

1. Aufsess, A. von. Geruchliche Nahorientierung der Biene bei entomophilen und ornithophilen Blüten. *Z. vergl. Physiol. 43*, 469-498 (1960).
2. Fischer, W. Untersuchungen über die Riechschärfe der Honigbiene. *Z. vergl. Physiol. 39*, 634-659 (1957).
3. Frisch, K. von. Über den Geruchssinn der Bienen und seine blütenbiologische Bedeutung. *Zool. Jb. Physiol. 37*, 1-238 (1919).
4. Gubin, W. A. Über die Geruchsempfindlichkeit bei Honigbienen. *Pschelovodstvo 7*, 17-19 (1957).
5. Kaissling, K. E., Priesner, E. Die Riechschwelle des Seidenspinners. *Naturwiss. 57*, 1, 23-28 (1970).
6. Lex, Th. Duftmale an Blüten. *Z. vergl. Physiol. 36*, 212-234 (1954).
7. Neuhaus, W. Über die Riechschärfe des Hundes für Fettsäuren. *Z. vergl. Physiol. 35*, 527-552 (1953).
8. Porsch, O. Vogelblumen. *Umschau 29*, 70-75 (1925).
9. Ribbands, C. R. The scent perception of the honey bee. *Proc. Roy. Soc. B 143*, 367-379 (1955).
10. Schwarz, R. Über die Riechschärfe der Honigbiene. *Z. vergl. Physiol. 37*, 180-210 (1955).
11. Teichmann, H. Über die Leistung des Geruchssinnes beim Aal (*Anguilla anguilla* L.). *Z. vergl. Physiol. 42*, 206-254 (1959).
12. Vareschi, E. Duftunterscheidung bei der Honigbiene—Einzelzell-Ableitungen und Verhaltensreaktionen. *Z. vergl. Physiol. 75*, 143-173 (1971).

Chapter 19

1. Dostal, B. Riechfähigkeit und Zahl der Riech-Sinneselemente bei der Honigbiene. *Z. vergl. Physiol. 41*, 179-203 (1958).
2. Forel, A. *The Sense of Insects*. Methuen, n.p., 1908.
3. Kaissling, K. E. Insect olfaction. In *Handbook of Sensory Physiology* Vol. *VI*, 351-431, ed. L. M. Beidler, Springer Verlag, Berlin-Heidelberg-New York, 1971.
4. Kramer, E. The orientation of walking honey bees in odour fields with small concentration gradients. *Physiol. Entomol. 1*, 27-37 (1976).
5. Krause, B. Elektronmikroskopische Untersuchungen an den Plattensensillen des Insektenfühlers. *Zool. Beitr. 6*, 161-205 (1960).
6. Lacher, V., Schneider, D. Elektrophysiologischer Nachweis der Reichfunktion von Porenplatten (Sensilla placodea) auf den Antennen der Drohne und der Arbeitsbiene (*Apis mellifica* L.). *Z. vergl. Physiol. 47*, 274-278 (1963).
7. Lacher, V. Elektrophysiologische Untersuchungen an einzelnen Re-

zeptoren für Geruch, Kohlendioxyd, Luftfeuchtigkeit und Temperatur auf den Antennen der Arbeitsbiene und der Drohne (*Apis mellifica* L.) *Z. vergl. Physiol.* 48, 587-623 (1964).

8. Lindauer, M., Martin, H. Über die Orientierung der Biene im Duftfeld. *Naturwiss.* 50, 509-514 (1963).

9. Martin, H. Zur Nahorientierung der Biene im Duftfeld. Zugleich ein Nachweis für die Osmotropotaxis bei Insekten. *Z. vergl. Physiol.* 48, 481-533 (1964).

10. Martin, H. Leistungen des topochemischen Sinnes bei der Honigbiene. *Z. vergl. Physiol.* 50, 254-292 (1965).

11. Neuhaus, W. Zur Frage der Osmotropotaxis, besonders bei der Honigbiene. *Z. vergl. Physiol.* 49, 475-484 (1965).

12. Schneider, D., Steinbrecht, R. A. Checklist of insect olfactory sensilla. *Symp. zool. Soc. London* 23, 279-297 (1968).

13. Slifer, E. H., Sekhon, S. S. The fine structure of the plate organs on the antenna of the honey bee, *Apis mellifera* L. *Expl. Cell. Res.* 19, 410-414 (1960).

14. Slifer, E. H., Sekhon, S. S. Fine structure of the sense organs on the antennal flagellum of the honey bee, *Apis mellifera* Linnaeus. *J. Morph.* 109, 351-381 (1961).

15. Vareschi, E. See Chapter 18.

Chapter 20

1. Behrend, K. Reichen in Wasser und in Luft bei *Dytiscus marginalis* L. *Z. vergl. Physiol.* 75, 108-122 (1971).

2. Ilse, D. See Chapter 14.

3. Kaib, M. Die Fleisch- und Blumenduftreceptoren auf der Antenne der Schmeissfliege *Calliphora vicina*. *J. comp. Physiol.* 95, 105-121 (1974).

4. Kaissling, K. E. See Chapter 19.

5. Knoll, F. Lichtsinn und Blumenbesuch des Falters von *Macroglossum stellatarum* (Insekten und Blumen III). *Abh. Zool.-Bot. Ges. Wien 12*, 121-378 (1922).

6. Kugler, H. See Chapter 14, No. 9.

7. Kugler, H. Über die optische Wirkung von Fliegenblumen auf Fliegen. *Ber. Deutsch. Bot. Ges.* 69, 387-398 (1956).

8. Lederer, G. Biologie der Nahrungsaufnahme der Imagines von *Apatura* und *Limenitis*, sowie Versuche zur Feststellung der Gustoreception durch die Mittel- und Hinterfusstarsen dieser Lepidopteren. *Z. Tierpsychol.* 8, 41-59 (1951).

9. Liermann, A. Correlation zwischen den antennalen Geruchsorganen und der Biologie der Musciden. *Z. Morph. Ökol. Tiere 5*, 1-97 (1925).

10. Meinecke, C.-C. Reichsensillen und Systematik der Lamellicornia (Insecta Coleopera). *Zoomorph.* 82, 1-42 (1975).

11. Myers, J. H. The structure of the antenna of the Florida queen butterfly, *Danaus gilippus berenice (Cramer)*. *J. Morph.* 125, 315-328 (1968).

12. Myers, J. H., Walter, M. Olfaction in the Florida queen butterfly: Honey odour receptors. *J. Insect Physiol.* 16, 573-578 (1970).

13. Schaller, A. Sinnesphysiologische und psychologische Untersuchungen an Wassekäfern und Fischen. *Z. vergl. Physiol. 4*, 370-464 (1926).
14. Schneider, D., Steinbrecht, R. A. See Chapter 19.
15. Schneider, D., Lacher, V., Kaissling, K. E. Die Reaktionsweise und das Reaktionsspektrum von Riechzellen bei *Antheraea pernyi* (Lepidoptera, Saturniidae). *Z. vergl. Physiol. 48*, 632-662 (1964).
16. Schremmer, F. Sinnesphysiologie und Blumenbesuch des Falters von *Plusia gamma* L. *Zool. Jb. Abt. System. 74*, 373-434 (1941).
17. Slifer, E. H., Lees, A. D. The sense organs of the antennal flagellum of aphids (Homoptera), with special reference to the plate organs. *Quart. J. micr. Sci. 105*, 21-29 (1964).
18. Slifer, E. H., Sekhon, S. S. Fine structure of the sense organs on the antennal flagellum of a flesh fly, *Sarcophaga argyrostoma* R.-D. (Diptera, Sarcophagidae). *J. Morph. 114*, 185-208 (1964).
19. Yamada, M. The dendritic action potentials in an olfactory hair of the fruit-piercing moth, *Oraesia excavata. J. Insect Physiol. 17*, 169-179 (1971).

Chapter 21

1. Davis, H. A. Model for transducer action in the cochlea. *Cold Spring Harb. Symp. quant. Biol. 30*, 181-190 (1965).
2. Dumpert, K. Alarmstoffrezeptoren auf der Antenne von *Lasius fuliginosus* (Latr.) (Hymenoptera, Formicidae). *Z. vergl. Physiol. 76*, 403-425 (1972).
3. Hansen, K., Kühner, J. Properties of a possible acceptor protein. *Int. Symp. Olf. and Taste IV*, ed. D. Schneider, 350-356. Wissenschaftl. Verlagsges. Stuttgart, 1972.
4. Kafka, W. A., Ohloff, G., Schneider, D., Vareschi, E. Olfactory discrimination of the two enantiomers of 4-methyl-hexanoic acid by the migratory locust and the honeybee. *J. comp. Physiol. 87*, 227-284 (1973).
5. Kaissling, K. E. See Chapter 19.
6. Kaissling, K. E. Sensory transduction in insect olfactory receptors. 25. *Colloqu. Ges. Biol. Chemie, Mosbach*, ed. L. Jaenicke, 243-273. Springer Verlag Berlin-Heidelberg-New York, 1974.
7. Kaissling, K. E., Priesner, E. Die Riechschwelle des Seidenspinners. *Naturwiss. 57*, 23-28 (1970).
8. Kaissling, K. E., Kasang, G., Bestmann, H. J., Stransky, W., Vostrowsky, O. A new pheromone of the silkworm moth *Bombyx mori*. Sensory pathway and behavioral effect. *Naturwiss. 65*, 382-384 (1978).
9. Kasang, G., Kaissling, K. E. Specificity of primary and secondary olfactory process in *Bombyx* antennae. *Int. Symp. Olf. and Taste IV*, ed. D. Schneider, 200-206. Wiss. Verlagsges. Stuttgart, 1972.
10. Kasang, G., Schneider, D., Schäfer, W. The silkworm moth *Bombyx*

mori. Presence of the (E,E) stereoisomer of bombykol in the female pheromone gland. *Naturwiss.* 65, 337 (1978).

11. Schneider, D., Block, B. C., Boeck, J., Priesner, E. Die Reaktion der männlichen Seidenspinner auf Bombykol und seine Isomeren: Elektroantennogramm und Verhalten. *Z. vergl. Physiol.* 54, 192-209 (1967).

12. Steinbrecht, R. A. Zur Morphometrie der Antenne des Seidenspinners, *Bombyx mori* L.: Zahl und Verteilung der Riechschwellen (Insecta, Lepidoptera). *Z. Morph. Tiere* 68, 93-126 (1970).

13. Steinbrecht, R. A. Der Feinbau olfaktorischer Sensillen des Seidenspinners (Insecta, Lepidoptera). Rezeptorfortsätze und reizlietender Apparat. *Z. Zellforsch.* 139, 533-565 (1973).

14. Steinbrecht, R. A., Müller, B. On the stimulus conducting structures in insect olfactory receptors. *Z. Zellforsch.* 117, 570-575 (1971).

15. Stieve, H. Photorezeption und ihre molekularen Grundlagen. In *Biophysik*, ed. W. Hoppe et al. Springer Verlag, Berlin-Heidelberg-New York, 1977.

16. Thurm, U. Grundzüge der Transduktionsmechanismen in Sinneszellen. In *Biophysik*, ed. W. Hoppe et al. Springer Verlag, Berlin-Heidelberg-New York, 1977.

Chapter 22

1. Dethier, V. G. A surfeit of stimuli: a paucity of receptors. *Am. Sci.* 59, 6, 706-715 (1971).

2. Dethier, V. G. *The Hungry Fly*. Harvard University Press, Cambridge, Mass.-London, 1976.

3. Fredman, St. M. Peripheral and central interactions between sugar, water and salt receptors of the blowfly, *Phormia regina*. *J. Ins. Physiol.* 21, 265-280 (1975).

4. Gelperin, A. Stretch receptors in the foregut of the blowfly. *Science* 157, 208-210 (1967).

5. Gelperin, A. Abdominal sensory neurons providing negative feedback to the feeding behavior of the blowfly. *Z. vergl. Physiol.* 72, 17-31 (1971).

6. Getting, P. A. The sensory control of motor output in fly proboscis extension. *Z. vergl. Physiol.* 74, 103-120 (1971).

7. Pollack, G. Labellar lobe spreading in the blowfly: regulation by taste and satiety. *J. comp. Physiol.* 121, 115-134 (1977).

8. Wilczek, M. The distribution and neuroanatomy of the labellar sense organs of the blowfly *Phormia regina* Meigen. *J. Morph.* 122, 175-202 (1967).

Chapter 23

1. Allen, P. A. Pollination in *Coryanthes speciosa*. *American Orch. Soc. Bull.* 19, 528 (1951).

2. Allen, P. A. Pollination in *Gongora maculata*. *Ceiba* 4, 121-124 (1954).
3. Arditti, J. Orchids. *Sci. Am. 214*, 1, 70-78 (1966).
4. Bringer, B. Territorial flight of bumble-bee males in coniferous forest on the northernmost part of the island of Öland. *Zoon Suppl. 1*, 15-22 (1973).
5. Daumann, E. Zur Bestäubongsökologie von *Cypripedium calceolus* L. *Österr. Bot. Z. 115*, 434-446 (1968).
6. Dodson, C. H. The importance of pollination in the evolution of the orchids of tropical America. *Bull. Am. Orch. Soc. 31*, 525-534, 641-649, 731-735 (1962).
7. Dodson, C. H. Studies in orchid pollination: The genus *Coryanthes*. *American Orch. Soc. Bull. 34*, 680-687 (1965).
8. Dodson, C. H. The role of chemical attractants in orchid pollination. In *Biochemical coevolution*, 83-107. Oregon State University Press, Eugene (1970).
9. Dodson, C. H. Coevolution of orchids and bees. In *Coevolution of animals and plants*, ed. L.E.G. Gilbert and P. H. Raven, 91-99. University of Texas Press, Austin-London, 1975.
10. Dodson, C. H., Dressler, R. L., Hills, G. H., Adams, R. M., Williams, N. H. Biologically active compounds in orchid fragrances, *Science 164*, 1243-1249 (1969).
11. Dressler, R. L. Biology of the orchid bees (Euglossini). *Ann. Rev. Ecol. Syst. 13*, 373-394 (1982).
12. Evoy, W. H., Jones, B. P. Motor patterns of male euglossine bees evoked by floral fragrances. *Anim. Behav. 19*, 583-588 (1971).
13. Haas, A. Die Mandibeldrüse als Duftorgan bei einigen Hymenopteren. *Z. Naturf. 39*, 484 (1952).
14. Haas, A. Vergleichende Verhaltensstudien zum Paarungsschwarm solitärer Apiden. *Zeitschr. Tierpsychol. 17*, 402-416 (1960).
15. Krüger, E. Über den Bahnflug der Männchen der Gattung *Bombus* und *Psithyrus*. *Zeitschr. Tierpsychol. 8*, 61-75 (1951).
16. Kullenberg, B., Bergström, G., Bringer, B., Carlberg, B., Cederberg, B. Observations on scent marking by *Bombus* Latr. and *Psithyrus* Lep. males (Hym., Apidae) and localization of site of production of the secretion. *Zoon Suppl. 1*, 23-32 (1973).
17. van der Pijl, L., Dodson, C. H. See Chapter 16.
18. Sakagami, S. F. Über den Bau der männlichen Hinterschiene von *Eulaema nigrita* Lepeltier (Hymenoptera, Apidae). *Zool. Anzeiger 175*, 347-354 (1965).
19. Vogel, St. Duftdrüsen im Dienste der Bestäubung. Über Bau und Funktion der Osmophoren. *Akad. Wiss. u. Lit. Mainz, Mth.-naturwiss. Kl. 10*, 601-673 (1962).
20. Vogel, St. Parfümsammelnde Bienen als Bestäuber von Orchidaceen und *Gloxinia*. *Österr. Bot. Z. 113*, 302-361 (1966).
21. Vogel, St. "Parfümblumen" und parfümsammelnde Biene. *Umschau 10*, 327 (1967).

22. Williams, N. H., Dodson, C. H. Selective attraction of male euglos-
    sine bees to orchid floral fragrances and its importance in long-dis-
    tance pollen flow. *Evol. 26*, 84-95 (1972).
23. Zucchi, R., Sakagami, S. F., Camargo, de J. Biological observations
    on a neotropical bee, *Eulaema nigrita*, with a review on the biology of
    Euglossine (Hymenoptera, Apidae). A comparative study. *Journ. Fac.
    Sci.* Hokkaido Univ. ser. VI. *17*, 271-380 (1969).

Chapter 24

1. Bergström, G. Role of volatile chemicals in *Ophrys*-pollinator interactions. In *Biochemical Aspects of Plant and Animal Coevolution*, ed. J. B.
   Harborne, 207-231. Academic Press, London, 1978.
2. Coleman, E. Further observations on the pseudocopulation of the
   male *Lissopimpla semipunctata* Kirby (Hymenoptera Parasitica) with
   the Australian orchid, *Cryptostylis leptochila*. *F. v. M. Proc. R. Entomol.
   Soc. Lond. (A), 13*, 82-83 (1938).
3. Correvon, H., Pouyanne, A. Un curieux cas de mimétisme chez les
   Ophrydées. *J. Soc. nat. d'Horticult. France 17*, 29-31 (1916).
4. Dodson, C. H. The importance of pollination in the evolution of the
   orchids of tropical America. *Amer. Orch. Soc. Bull. 31*, 525-534, 641-
   649, 731-735 (1962).
5. Godfrey, M. J. The fertilization of *Ophrys speculum, O. lutea* and *O.
   fusca. J. Bot.* (Lond.) *63*, 33-40 (1925).
6. Kerr, W. E., Lopez, C. R. Biologia da reproducão de *Trigona (Plebeia)
   droryana* F. Smith. *Rev. Brasil. Biol. 22*, 335-341 (1963).
7. Kullenberg, B. Investigations on the pollinations of *Ophrys* species.
   Oikos 2, 1-19 (1950).
8. Kullenberg, B. Studies on *Ophrys* L. pollination. *Zool. Bidr. Uppsala 34*,
   1-340 (1961).
9. Kullenberg, B. New observations on the pollination of *Ophrys* L. (Orchidaceae). *Zoon Suppl. 1*, 9-14 (1793a).
10. Kullenberg, B. Field experiments with chemical sexual attractants on
    aculeate Hymenoptera males. II. *Zoon Suppl. 1*, 31-42 (1973b).
11. Kullenberg. B., Bergström, G. Chemical communication between liv-
    ing organisms. *Endeavour 34*, 59-66 (1975).
12. Linné, C. von. Öländska och Gothländska resa. Stockholm-Uppsala,
    1745.
13. Pouyanne, A. La fécondation des *Ophrys* par les insectes. *Bull. Soc.
    Hist. Nat. Afr. N. 8* (1917).
14. Priesner, E. Reaktionen von Riechrezeptoren männlicher Solitärbi-
    enen (Hymenoptera, Apoidea) auf Inhaltsstoffe von *Ophrys*-Blüten.
    Zoon. Suppl. 1, 43-54 (1973).
15. Proctor, M., Yeo, P. *The pollination of flowers*. W. Collins Sons & Co.,
    Glasgow, 1975.
16. Stoutamire, W. P. Australian terrestrial orchids, thynnid wasps, and
    pseudocopulation. *Am. Orch. Soc. Bull. 1974*, 13-18 (1974).

17. Vogel, St. See Chapter 23, No. 18.
18. Wolff, T. Pollination and fertilization of the fly Ophrys, *Ophrys insectifera* L. in Allindelille fredskov, Denmark. *Oikos 2*, 20-59 (1950).

Chapter 25

1. Autrum, H., v. Zwehl, V. See Chapter 13.
2. Bogdany, R. J. Linking of learning signals in honey bee orientation. *Behav. Ecol. Sociobiol. 3*, 323-336 (1978).
3. Daumer, K. See Chapter 14, No. 3.
4. Edrich, W. Honey bees: Photoreceptors participating in orientation behaviour to light and gravity. *J. comp. Physiol. 133*, 111-116 (1979).
5. Eickwort, G. C. Biology of the European mason bee, *Hoplitis anthocopoides* (Hymenoptera: Megachilidae), in New York State. *Search* (Cornell Univ. Agric. Stat.) *9*, 1-29 (1973).
6. Free, J. The flower constancy of honey bees. *J. anim. Ecol. 32*, 119-131 (1963).
7. Frisch, K. von. See Chapter 15.
8. Frisch, K. von. Über den Geruchssinn der Biene und seine blütenbiologische Bedeutung. *Zool. Jb. Abt. Allg. Physiol. 37*, 1-225 (1920).
9. Frisch, K. von. Die Psychologie der Bienen. *Z. Tierpsychol. 1*, 9-21 (1937).
10. Frisch, K. von. *Dance Language and Orientation of Bees*. The Belknap Press of Harvard University Press, Cambridge, Mass., 1967.
11. Grant, V. The flower constancy of bees. *Bot. Rev. 16*, 379-398 (1950).
12. Heinrich, B. Foraging specializations of individual bumblebees. *Ecol. Monogr. 46*, 105-128 (1976).
13. Kaiser, W. The spectral sensitivity of the honey bee's optomotor walking response. *J. comp. Physiol. 90*, 405-408 (1974).
14. Kaiser, W. The relationship between visual movement detection and colour vision in insects. In *The compound eye and vision in insects*, ed. G. A. Horridge. Clarendon Press, Oxford, 1975.
15. Kaiser, W., Liske, E. Optomotor reactions of stationary flying bees during stimulation with spectral light. *J. comp. Physiol. 89*, 391-408 (1974).
16. Kaiser, W., Seidl, R., Vollmar, J. Spectral sensitivities of behavioural patterns in honey bees. *J. comp. Physiol. 122*, 27-44 (1977).
17. Koltermann, R. Lern- und Vergessensprozesse bei der Honigbiene—aufgezeigt anhand von Duftdressuren. *Z. vergl. Physiol. 63*, 310-334 (1969).
18. Kriston, I. Zum Problem des Lernverhaltens von *Apis mellifica* L. gegenüber verschiedenen Duftstoffen. *Z. vergl. Physiol. 74*, 169-189 (1971).
19. Kugler, H. See Chapter 3.
20. Lauer, J., Lindauer, M. Genetisch fixierte Lerndispositionen bei der Honigbiene. *Akad. d. Wiss. u. Lit., Math.-naturwiss. Kl., Inf. Org. 1*, 5-87.

21. Lindauer, M. Allgemeine Sinnesphysiologie: Oientierung im Raum. *Fortschr. Zool. 16*, 58-140 (1963).
22. Linsley, E. G., Mac Swain, J. W., Raven, P. H. Comparative behavior of bees and Onagraceae. *Univ. Calif. Publ. Ent. 33*, 1-58 (1963).
23. Masuhr, T., Menzel, R. Learning experiments on the use of side-specific information in the olfactory and visual system in the honey bee (*Apis mellifica*). In *Information processing in the visual systems of arthropods*, ed. R. Wehner, 315-322. Springer Verlag, Berlin-Heidelberg-New York, 1972.
24. Menzel, R. Untersuchungen zum Erlernen von Spektralfarben durch die Honigbiene (*Apis mellifica*). *Z. vergl. Physiol. 56*, 22-62 (1967).
25. Menzel, R. Das Gedächtnis der Honigbiene für Spektralfarben. I. Kurzzeitiges und langzeitiges Behalten. *Z. vergl. Physiol. 60*, 82-102 (1968).
26. Menzel, R. Das Gedächtnis der Honigbiene für Spektralfarben. II. Umlernen und Mehrfachlernen. *Z. vergl. Physiol. 63*, 290-309 (1969).
27. Menzel, R., Erber, I., Masuhr, T. Learning and memory in the honeybee. In *Experimental analysis of insect behaviour*, 195-217. Springer Verlag, Berlin-Heidelberg-New York, 1974.
28. Menzel, R., Erber, I. Learning and memory in bees. *Sci. Am. 239, 1*, 102-110 (1978).
29. Nelson, M. C. Classical conditioning in the blowfly (*Phormia regina*). *J. comp. Physiol. 77*, 353-368 (1971).
30. Opfinger, E. Über die Orientierung der Biene an der Futterquelle. *Z. vergl. Physiol. 15*, 431-487 (1931).
31. Quinn, W. G., Harris, W. A., Benzer, S. Conditioned behaviour in *Drosophila melanogaster* (Learning, memory, odor discrimination, colour vision). *Proc. Natl. Acad. Sci. USA 71*, 708-712 (1974).
32. Schnetter, B. Experiments on pattern discrimination in honey bees. In *Information processing in the visual system of arthropods*, ed. R. Wehner, 95-201. Springer Verlag, Berlin-Heidelberg-New York, 1972.
33. Wehner, R. Zur Physiologie des Formensehens bei der Honigbiene. *Z. vergl. Physiol. 55*, 145-166 (1967).

Chapter 26

1. Beier, W. Beeinflussung der inneren Uhr der Bienen durch Phasenverschiebung des Licht-Dunkel-Zeitgebers. *Z. Bienenforsch. 9*, 356-378 (1968).
2. Beier, W., Lindauer, M. Der Sonnenstand als Zeitgeber für die Biene. *Apidologie 1*, 5-28 (1970).
3. Beling, J. Über das Zeitgedächtnis der Bienen. *Z. vergl. Physiol. 9*, 259-338 (1929).
4. Beutler, R. Biologisch-chemische Untersuchungen am Nektar von Immenblumen *Z. vergl. Physiol. 12*, 72-176 (1930).
5. Heinrich, B. Bumblebee foraging and the economics of sociality. *Am. Scientist 64*, 384-395 (1976).

6. Huber, H. Die Abhängigkeit der Nektarsekretion von Temperatur, Luft- und Bodenfeuchtigkeit. *Planta 48*, 47-98 (1956).
7. Kerner, A. von Marilaun. *Pflanzenleben*. II. Die Fortpflanzung und ihre Organe. Bibl. Inst. Meyer, Leipzig-Wien, 1913.
8. Kleber, E. Hat das Zeitgedächtnis der Bienen biologische Bedeutung? *Z. vergl. Physiol. 22*, 221-262 (1935).
9. Koltermann, R. 24-Std.-Periodik in der Langzeiterinnerung an Duft- und Farbsignale bei der Honigbiene. *Z. vergl. Physiol. 75*, 49-68 (1971).
10. Koltermann, R. Periodicity in the activity and learning performance of the honeybee. In *Insect Behaviour*, ed. L. Barton Browne, 218-227. Springer Verlag, Berlin-Heidelberg-New York, 1974.
11. Körner, J. Zeitgedächtnis und Alarmierung bei den Bienen. *Z. vergl. Physiol. 27*, 445-459 (1940).
12. Medugorac, J. Die Orientierung der Bienen in Raum und Zeit nach Dauernarkose. *Z. Bienenforsch. 9*, 105-119 (1967).
13. Medugorac, J., Lindauer, M. Das Zeitgedächtnis der Bienen unter dem Einfluss von Narkose und sozialen Zeitgebern. *Z. vergl. Physiol. 55*, 450-474 (1967).
14. Renner, M. Ein Transozeanversuch zum Zeitsinn der Honigbiene. *Naturwiss. 42*, 540 (1955).
15. Renner, M. Der Zeitsinn der Arthropoden. *Ergebn. Biol. 20*, 127-158 (1958).
16. Renner, M. Über ein weiteres Versetzungsexperiment zur Analyse des Zeitsinnes und der Sonnenorientierung der Honigbiene. *Z. vergl. Physiol. 42*, 449-483 (1959).
17. Renner, M. The contribution of the honey bee to the study of time-sense and astronomical orientation. *Cold Spr. Harb. Symp. Quant. Biol. XXV*, 361-367 (1960).
18. Von Stein-Beling, J. Über das Zeitgedächtnis der Bienen. *Steirischer Imkerbote 18*, 11, 238-242 (1966).
19. Wahl, O. Beitrag zur Frage der biologischen Bedeutung des Zeitgedächtnisses der Bienen. *Z. vergl. Physiol. 18*, 709-717 (1933).
20. Wasser, M. M., Real, L. A. Effective mutualism between sequentially flowering plant species. *Nature 281*, 670-672 (1979).

Chapter 27

1. Bisetzky, A. R. Die Tänze der Bienen nach einem Fussweg zum Futerplatz. *Z. vergl. Physiol. 40*, 264-288 (1957).
2. Boch, R. Die Tänze der Bienen bei nahen und fernen Trachtquellen. *Z. vergl. Physiol. 38*, 136-167 (1956).
3. Edrich, W. Honey bees: photoreceptors participating in orientation behaviour to light and gravity. *J. comp. Physiol. 133*, 111-116 (1979).
4. Esch, H. Über die Schallerzeugung beim Werbetanz der Honigbiene. *Z. vergl. Physiol. 45*, 1-11 (1961).

5. Esch, H. Beiträge zum Problem der Entfernungsweisung in den Schwänzeltänzen der Honigbienen. *Z. vergl. Physiol. 48*, 534-546 (1964).

6. Esch, H., Bastian, J. A. How do newly recruited honeybees approach a food site? *Z. vergl. Physiol. 68*, 175-181 (1970).

7. Frisch, K. von. See Chapter 25, No. 10.

8. Frisch, K. von, Lindauer, M. Himmel und Erde in Konkurrenz bei der Orientierung der Bienen. *Naturwiss. 41*, 245-253 (1954).

9. Frisch, K. von, Lindauer, M., Schmeidler, F. Wie erkennt die Biene den Sonnenstand bei geschlossener Wolkendecke? *Rundschau 10*, 1-7 (1960).

10. Gould, J. L. Honey bee recruitment: the dance language controversy. *Science 189*, 685-693 (1975).

11. Gould, J. L. The dance-language controversy. *Quart. Rev. Biol. 51*, 2, 211-244 (1976).

12. Lindauer, M. Über die Einwirkung von Duft- und Geschmackstoffen sowie anderen Faktoren auf die Tänze der Bienen. *Z. vergl. Physiol. 31*, 348-412 (1948).

13. Lindauer, M. Schwarmbienen auf Wohnungssuche. *Z. vergl. Physiol. 37*, 263-324 (1955).

14. Lindauer, M. Sonnenorientierung der Bienen unter der Äquatorsonne und zur Nachtzeit. *Naturwiss. 44*, 1-6 (1957).

15. Lindauer, M. Angeborene und erlernte Komponenten in der Sonnenorientierung der Bienen. *Z. vergl. Physiol. 42*, 43-62 (1959).

16. Lindauer, M. *Verständigung im Bienenstaat.* G. Fischer Verlag, Stuttgart, 1975. *See also* Lindauer, M. *Communication among Social Bees.* Harvard University Press, Cambridge, Mass., 1961.

17. Lindauer, M., Martin, H. Die Schwereorientierung der Bienen unter dem Einfluss des Erdmagnetfelds. *Z. vergl. Physiol. 60*, 219-243 (1968).

18. Menzel, R., Snyder, A. Polarized light detection in the bee, *Apis mellifera, J. comp. Physiol. 88*, 247-270 (1974).

19. Ramskou, Th. *Solstenen* Rhodes international Forlag. Kobenhavn (1969).

20. Rossel, S., Wehner, R., Lindauer, M. E-vector orientation in bees. *J. comp. Physiol. 125*, 1-12 (1978).

21. Schifferer, G. Über die Entfernungsangabe bei den Tänzen der Bienen. Staatsexamensarbeit Univ. München 1952.

22. Scholze, E., Pichler, H., Heran, H. Zur Entfernungsschätzung der Bienen nach dem Kraftaufwand. *Naturwiss. 51*, 69-70 (1964).

23. Wehner, R. Polarized-light navigation by insects. *Sci. Amer. 235*, 1, 106-114 (1976).

24. Wehner, R. Spectral cues in skylight navigation of insects. *Experientia 34*, 904 (1978).

25. Wenner, A. M. Sound production during the waggle dance of the honey bee. *Anim. Behav. 10*, 79-95 (1962).

Chapter 28

1. Blest, A. D. The evolution, ontogeny and quantitative control of the settling movements of some New World Saturniid moths, with some comments on distance communication by honey-bees. *Behaviour 16*, 188-253 (1960).
2. CruzLandim, C. da, Ferreira, A. Mandibular gland development and communication in field bees of *Trigona* (Scaptotrigona) *postica. J. Kansas Entomol. Soc. 41*, 474-481 (1968).
3. Dethier, V. G. Communication by insects: physiology of dancing. *Science 125*, 331-336 (1957).
4. Esch, H. See Chapter 27, No. 4.
5. Esch, H. Die Bedeutung der Lauterzeugung für die Verständigung der stachellosen Bienen. *Z. vergl. Physiol. 56*, 199-220 (1967a).
6. Esch, H. The evolution of bee language. *Sci. Am. 216*, 4, 96-104 (1967b).
7. Free, J. B. The flower constancy of bumble-bees. *J. Anim. Ecol. 39*, 395-402 (1970).
8. Frisch, K. von. See Chapter 27, No. 7.
9. Frisch, K. von. Dialects in the language of the bees. *Sci. Am. 207*, 2, 79-87 (1962).
10. Jacobs-Jessen, U. F. Zur Orientierung der Hummeln und einiger anderer Hymenopteren. *Z. vergl. Physiol. 41*, 597-641 (1959).
11. Kerr, W. E., Ferreira, A., de Mattos, N. S. Communication among stingless bees—additional data. *J. New York Entomol. Soc. 71*, 80-90 (1963).
12. Kerr, W. E., Esch, H. Communicacão entre as abelhas sociais brasilieras e sua contribuicão pāra o entendimento da sua evolução *Ciencia e Cult* (Sao Paulo) *17*, 529-538 (1965).
13. Koeniger, N. Neue Aspekte der Phylogenie innerhalb der Gattung *Apis. Apid. 7*, 357-366 (1976).
14. Lindauer, M. Uber die Verständigung bei indischen Bienen. *Z. vergl. Physiol. 38*, 521-557 (1956).
15. Lindauer, M., Kerr, W. E. Die gegenseitige Verständigung bei den stachellosen Bienen. *Z. vergl. Physiol. 41*, 405-434 (1958).
16. Lindauer, M., Kerr, W. E. Communication between the workers of stingless bees. *Bee World 41*, 29-41, 65-71 (1960).
17. Lindauer, M. See Chapter 27, No. 16.
18. Michener, Ch. D. *The social behavior of the bees*. The Belknap Press of Harvard University Press, Cambridge, Mass., 1974.
19. Unhoch, N. *Anleitung zur wahren Kenntnis und zweckmässigsten Behandlung der Bienen*. München, 1823.
20. Wilson, E. O. See Chapter 7, No. 4.

Chapter 29

1. Allen, J., Cameron, S., McGinley, R., Heinrich, B. The role of workers and new queens in the ergonomics of a bumblebee colony (Hymenoptera: Apoidea). *J. Kans. Entomol. Soc. 51* (3), 329-342 (1978).

2. Eickwort, G. C., Ginsberg, H. S. Foraging and mating behaviour in Apoidea. *Ann. Rev. Entomol. 25*, 421-446 (1980).

3. Hasselroth, T. B. Studies on Swedish bumblebees (Genus *Bombus* Latr.): their domestication and biology. *Opusc. Entomol. Suppl. 17*, 1-192 (1960).

4. Heinrich, B. Thermoregulation in bumblebees. I. Brood incubation by *Bombus vosnesenskii* queens. *J. comp. Physiol. 88*, 129-140 (1974).

5. Heinrich, B. Thermoregulation in bumblebees. II. Energetics of warm-up and free flight. *J. comp. Physiol. 96*, 155-166 (1975).

6. Heinrich, B. Mechanisms of heat exchange between thorax and abdomen in bumblebees. *J. exp. Biol. 64*, 561-585 (1976).

7. Heinrich, B. The physiology of exercise in the bumblebee. *Am. Sci. 65*, 455-465 (1977).

8. Heinrich, B. *Bumblebee Economics*. Harvard University Press, Cambridge, Mass.-London, 1979a.

9. Heinrich, B. Keeping a cool head: honeybee thermoregulation. *Science 205*, 1269-1271 (1979b).

10. Inouye, D. W. Resource partitioning in bumblebee: experimental studies of foraging behavior. *Ecology 59*, 4, 672-678 (1978).

11. Johnson, L. K., Hubbell, St. P. Aggression and competition among stingless bees: field studies. *Ecology 55*, 127-129 (1974).

12. Michener, Ch. D. See Chapter 28.

13. Morse, D. H. Resource partitioning in bumblebees: the role of behavioral factors. *Science 197*, 678-680 (1977).

14. Pyke, G. H. Optimal foraging in bumblebees and coevolution with their plants. *Oecologia* (Berl.) *36*, 281-293 (1978).

15. Pyke, G. H. Optimal foraging in bumblebees: rule of movement between flowers within inflorescences. *Anim. Behav. 27*, 1167-1181 (1979).

16. Richards, K. W. Biology of *Bombus polaris* Curtis and *B. hyperboreus* Schönherr at Lake Hazen, North West Territories (Hymenoptera Bombini). *Quaest. Entomol. 9*, 115-157 (1973).

Chapter 30

1. Baker, H. G., Hurd, P. H. Intrafloral ecology. *Ann. rev. entomol. 13*, 385-414 (1969).

2. Faegri, K., van der Pijl, L. See Chapter 3.

3. Grant, V., Grant, K. A. *Flower pollination in the Phlox family*. Columbia Univ. Press, New York-London, 1965.

4. Hennig, W. *Die Stammesgeschichte der Insekten*. Kramer, Frankfurt a.M., 1969.

5. Leppik, E. E. Origin and evolution of bilateral symmetry in flowers. *Evol. Biol. 5*, 49-85 (1971).

6. Mayr, E. Selektion und gerichtete Evolution. *Naturwiss. 52*, 8, 173-180 (1965).

7. Mayr, E. Grundlagen der Evolutionsbiologie. *Naturwiss. 56*, 392-397 (1969).

8. Stebbins, L. G. Adaptations of cross-pollination. In *Flowering plants-evolution above the species level*, ed. L. G. Stebbins. The Belknap Press of Harvard Univ. Press, Cambridge, Mass., 1974.
9. Takhtajan, A. *Evolution und Ausbreitung der Blütenpflanzen*. G. Fischer Verlag, Stuttgart, 1973.
10. Thein, L. B. Floral biology of Magnolia. *Amer. J. Bot. 61*, 10, 1037-1045 (1974).

Sources of the Illustrations

The line drawings were prepared by the author or taken from other authors, as follows:

Figs. 1-3: Galil, 1977
Fig. 4: various authors
Fig. 5: (in part) Echlin, 1968
Fig. 6: Strasburger, 1978
Fig. 10: Renner; Suchantke, 1965
Fig. 14: Hegi, 1906
Fig. 16: Schremmer, 1959
Fig. 17: (top) Schremmer, 1961
Fig. 18: Matthes, 1968
Fig. 19: (a) Schremmer, 1961; (b and c) Vogel, 1974
Fig. 20: Buchmann and Hurley, 1978
Fig. 21: Knoll, 1956
Fig. 23: Heinrich, 1973
Fig. 24: Kükenthal-Renner, 1980
Fig. 25: Jacobs-Renner, 1974 and Kükenthal-Renner, 1980
Figs. 26-28: Estham and Eassa, 1955
Fig. 29: Smith, 1930
Fig. 30: Schremmer, 1969
Fig. 31: Meeuse, 1961
Fig. 32: (in part) Heinrich, 1979
Figs. 34-35: Knoll, 1926
Fig. 36: v. Helversen, 1972
Fig. 37: Wehner, 1975
Fig. 39: Kugler, 1966
Fig. 40: Knoll, 1956
Fig. 41: Free, 1970
Fig. 45: Hertz, 1933
Fig. 46: Vareschi, 1971

Fig. 47: v. Frisch, 1965 and Kaissling, 1971
Figs. 48-50: Martin, 1964
Fig. 51: Martin, 1965
Fig. 52: Kaissling, 1971 and other authors
Fig. 53: Umschau 29, 1925
Fig. 57: Steinbrecht, 1973 and Kaissling, 1979
Fig. 59: Stieve, 1977
Fig. 60: Hansen and Heumann, 1971 and Shiraishi and Tanabe, 1974
Fig. 61: Getting, 1971 and Fredman, 1975
Fig. 62: (top) Heinrich, 1979; (bottom) Vogel, 1966
Fig. 63: Vogel, 1966
Figs. 64-66: Arditti, 1966
Fig. 68: various authors
Figs. 69, 71-72: Kullenberg, 1961
Fig. 70: Priesner, 1973
Figs. 73, 75: Menzel and Erber, 1979
Fig. 74: Schnetter, 1972
Figs. 76-77: v. Frisch, 1965
Fig. 78: Wehner, 1975
Fig. 81: v. Frisch, 1962
Figs. 82-83: Dethier, 1957
Figs. 84-86: Lindauer and Kerr, 1958
Fig. 87: Esch, 1967

Figs. 88-89: Heinrich, 1979
Fig. 90: Heinrich, 1977
Figs. 91-92: Heinrich, 1979
Fig. 93: Morse, 1977
Fig. 94: Leppik, 1971
Fig. 95: Grant and Grant, 1965
Fig. 96: Barrington, 1979

Permission to reproduce previously published drawings was kindly granted by the following publishers and institutions:

Fig. 8: from Ch. K. Sprengel, *Das entdeckte Geheimnis der Natur im Bau und in der Befruchtung der Blumen*, Senckenbergische Bibliothek, Frankfurt, Berlin, 1793.

Fig. 9: from H. Pager, *Bee World 54*, 2, 61 (1973). International Bee Research Association, Gerrards Cross, GB.

Fig. 11: from E. O. Wilson, *The Insect Societies*, The Belknap Press of Harvard University Press, Cambridge, Mass., 1972.

Fig. 12: from W. Jacobs, M. Renner, *Taschenlexikon zur Biologie der Insekten*, G. Fischer Verlag, Stuttgart, 1974.

Fig. 15: from St. L. Buchmann, Buzz pollination of *Cassia quiedondilla* (Leguminosae) by bees of the genera *Centris* and *Melipona*, Southern California Academy of Sciences, Los Angeles, 1974.

Fig. 43: from E. Hadorn, R. Wehner, *Allgemeine Zoologie*, G. Thieme Verlag, Stuttgart, 1978.

Fig. 44: from K. von Frisch, *Tanzsprache und Orientierung der Bienen*, Springer Verlag, Heidelberg, 1965.

Fig. 54: from C.-C. Meinecke, *Riechsensillen und Systematik der Lamellicornia*, Springer Verlag, Heidelberg, 1975.

Fig. 55: from K.-E. Kaissling, E. Priesner, *Die Riechschwelle des Seidenspinners*, Springer Verlag, Heidelberg, 1970.

Fig. 67: from St. Vogel, *Duftdrüsen im Dienste der Bestäubung: Über Bau und Funktion der Osmophoren*, F. Steiner Verlag, Wiesbaden, 1962.

Fig. 80: from H. Esch, *Beiträge zum Problem der Entfernungsweisung in den Schwänzeltänzen der Honigbienen*, Springer Verlag, Heidelberg, 1964.

Fig. 97: from W. Henning, *Die Stammesgeschichte der Insekten*, W. Kramer Verlag, Frankfurt, 1969.

Pls. 3 bottom, 5 top, 6 top, 12, 19 (p. 134), 20, 29 top, 38, 39, 40: Dr. R. Loftus.

Pls. 10, 11 top left: Institut für Film und Bild.

Pl. 11 bottom right and left: Prof. Dr. U. Maschwitz.

Pl. 11 middle right: Prof. Dr. M. Mühlenberg.

Pl. 31: Prof. Dr. K.-E. Kaissling.

All other plates are those of the author.

Index

generator potential, 210–11, 214
genes, 346
genetic diversity, 345–46
genetic survival, 33
gentian, 88, 149, 150, 168; marsh,
150; spring, 22; stemless, 22, 44,
89, 142, 236
Gentiana: acaulis, 89, 168; *clusii*, 22,
44, 142; *germanica*, 149; *pneumonanthe*, 150
Gentianaceae, 88
Geometridae, 58
Geranium: sylvaticum, 336; *triste*, 275
germination, 14–15, 18
Gesneriaceae, 232
giant honeybee, 302, 303
gland cells, 97
globeflower, 86, 142
glossa, 92, 93, 137
Gloxinia, 232
goatsbeard, 275
Godfery, M. J., 239
Goethe, Johann Wolfgang von, 24,
91, 316
golden cinquefoil, 149
goldenrod, 88–89, 332, 333
Gongora maculata, 233, 234
Gorytes, 246, 248; *campestris*, 239; *mystaceus*, 239, 240, 246
grape hyacinth, 114, 115
grasshopper, 199
Grassi, Ernesto, 29
grass of Parnassus, 27, 85, 90, 135
guide marks: olfactory, 171–73; visual, 147–60, 168–69
gustation, 219–24
Gymnadenia odoratissima, 88
gynostemium, 233–34, 241

Haeckel, Ernst, 335
hairs: of bees, 72–73, 128, 129; of
flies, 102; gustatory, 220–22, 263;
olfactory, 197, 212; tactile, 263
Halictus, 104
Hamilton, William D., 62
hawkmoths, 50, 58, 86, 104, 105,
106. *See also* hummingbird hawkmoth

head flower, 46–47
head-proboscis reaction, 155–56, 219,
223
hearing, sense of, 296
heather, 22
Hedera helix, 85, 88, 201
Heinrich, Bernd, 317, 320, 321–22,
323
Helianthemum nummularium, 21, 42–
43, 142
Helianthus rigidus, 155
Heliconius, 117, 354–55
hellebore, 86–87
helleborine: broad, 88; marsh, 142
Helleborus, 86–87
Helmholtz, Hermann von, 119
Helversen, Otto von, 122–23
Hemimetabola, 59
Hepburn, H. Randall, 98
herb Paris, 266–67
Hering, Ewald, 126
hermaphrodite flowers, 18
Hes, Carl von, 110
Heterocera, 57–58. *See also* moths
heterostyly, 27
hindlegs, of bee, 72–74, 225, 226,
228, 260–61
Hodgkin, Alan Lloyd, 210
Hofmeister, Wilhelm, 16
Holometabola, 59
honey: feeding of, 35; leaf, 108; production of, 107–8
honeybees (*Apis mellifera*): and ancient
humans, 38–40; antennae of, 191;
brain of, 273; brood care in, 37,
63–64; color learning by, 253; color
vision of, 122; drones, 63; dwarf,
302; eggs of, 35–36; eyes of, 125,
162; flower constancy in, 250–51;
forager, 35, 365; genetic relationships among, 63–64; giant, 302,
303; idleness in, 36; larva of, 35;
mouthparts of, 94–95; pattern recognition by, 165–66, 167–68, 268–
69; pollen-collecting apparatus of,
49, 72–74, 128–31; predation on,
50–51; proboscis of, 104; productivity of, 318, 320; sex determina-